THE
DESIGNER'S
HANDBOOK

THE
DESIGNER'S
HANDBOOK

Alastair Campbell

MACDONALD & CO
LONDON & SYDNEY

A QED BOOK

First published in Great Britain in 1983 by
Macdonald & Co (Publishers) Ltd
London & Sydney

Maxwell House
74 Worship Street, London EC2A 2EN

ISBN 0-356-09389-1

This book was designed and produced by
QED Publishing Limited,
32 Kingly Court, London W1

Production director Edward Kinsey
Editorial director Jeremy Harwood
Senior editor Nicola Thompson
Art editor Caroline Courtney
Assistant editor Sabina Goodchild
Assistant designers Alex Arthur, Hilary Krag
Editorial Judy Martin
Photographs by Michael Freeman, Jon Wyand,
Clive Boden, Malcolm Hoare
Illustrations by John Woodcock, Edwina Keene,
Abdul Aziz Khan, Martin Woodford, Elaine Keenan

Filmset in Great Britain by QV Typesetting Limited, London
Colour origination by Hong Kong Graphic Arts Service
Centre, Hong Kong, and by Starf Photolitho, Rome.
Printed in Hong Kong by Leefung Asco Printers Limited

The author would like to thank the many people who have helped in the
preparation of this book, especially the following: Clive Crook; Roger
Pring; Michael Freeman; Geoffrey Lee of Diagraphic Typesetters; Tony
Blann, Martin Elgie and David Wilden of Rodney Howe Ltd; Dick
Boddy; Nicholas Dawe of Folio; Bernard Thornton of Linden Artists;
Fabian Russell-Cobb; and in particular the entire staff of QED.

Contents

INTRODUCTION

Laser scanners, digital cathode ray tubes, microprocessors — current design technology is sometimes as daunting for contemporary designers as a printing press might have been to a medieval scribe. Whatever the technology, however, the basic task of design has not varied over the centuries; the chief aim of any design — and, hence, of any designer — should be to communicate its intentions with clarity, flair and aesthetic appeal.

Of course, the design task is now far more complex than it was for the scribe, working away in his cell. All that concerned him were his pens or brushes, paints or inks and the parchments on which his designs were directly created. Today's designers have a far more complex and daunting task. Though their aim remains the same, the technology involved in achieving it has multiplied to the point where it seems almost bewildering in its complexity. At no time in design history have designers been required to know and understand as much as they are today. To work effectively, it is often essential to break down or transcend the barriers that have been created, paradoxically enough, by technological progress. This can be achieved only by a thorough grounding in these self-same technologies insofar as their workings apply to the business of design. These facts have given rise to the profession of 'graphic designer'; the traditional role of the craftsman has now been swamped by technological advances.

Take typesetting, for instance. In the typesetting industry of today, old-style craftsmen are being replaced by, or transformed into, a new generation of technicians, whose prime allegiance is more to the micro-chip than to design traditions and aesthetics. This places an even greater responsibility on the designer. Not only must he or she respond to such innovations positively — after all, they are excellent design tools, if used correctly — but, at the same time, police them, so that aesthetic standards are preserved. Much the same has happened in reproduction and printing and much the same knowledge and interest is required. As opposed to the medieval scribe, no modern designer can now design in isolation, but some designers, when faced with digital CRT machines, may have the same feelings as the scribe confronted with the first movable type.

To fulfil their responsibilities to the job, therefore, today's designers must accumulate a wealth of knowledge from a variety of previously unrelated sources. It is virtually impossible to gather this knowledge from any one source, so one of the aims of this book is to fill this gap. It aims to provide an essential reference guide to the technology of design by giving the designer access to information previously available only in lengthy and highly-specialized technical tomes. However, the approach is also realistic; the only area not covered in detail is that of computer graphics, for the simple reason that the hardware capable of producing an image of acceptable resolution for general design purposes is still prohibitively expensive. Indeed, it is common for designers — for reasons of budget schedule, or just plain fear of the technology — to commission illustrators to simulate computer-produced images. However, the day is rapidly approaching when computer standards — can be determined for the future.

What else does the book offer? In planning it, I decided it should fulfil three basic functions. The text, in general, serves as an introduction to the design process, primarily for the novice designer or, indeed, user of design, though I hope that some of the information in it will serve as a reminder to seasoned professionals that a refresher course in basics can sometimes be useful. At the same time, it is designed to provide instant reference — in the form of tint charts, cast-off tables and so on — for the experienced designer. Finally, I believe it can provide an insight into various technical aspects of the design process which readers may not previously have experienced.

First and foremost, remember that a designer's task must always be viewed from its aesthetic and artistic aspects. The more readily information is available at the designer's fingertips, the easier it is for him or her to get on with the work in hand. Never drown in the sea of technology. And, in case this all sounds too daunting, remember that, as yet, there is no substitute for the imagination, personality and individuality of a live designer — no robot, or computer, has yet been programmed — or ever will be — to take over the job.

Alastair Campbell

1
THE DESIGN BRIEF
The client/Briefing checklist/Fees/
Schedules/Contracts/Budgets/
Roughs

Whatever its end purpose, all design starts from the same basis. This is that the task of the designer is to fulfil two fundamental considerations — one to the client, the other to the client's market. In every undertaking, these considerations are most important and upon them rest the design's success or failure.

The client It is extremely rare for a designer to work without a commission of some kind and, even if an original concept comes from him or her, someone else — the client — will eventually pay for the work. Although, in purest terms, the client is ultimately the person who pays the bills and who takes final decisions, he or she may not necessarily be the one who is most informed about how the market is to be reached. This is why advertising agencies, design groups, publishers and art directors frequently act as marketing advisors and intermediaries.

Briefing This, the first stage in virtually any job, is the moment when its parameters must be established. Certain vital factors such as budgets and schedules will be discussed, but the first consideration for the designer to decide is whether he or she is suitable for the job. Under no circumstances must the designer overestimate his or her capabilities, and for this reason it is essential to establish the scope and complexity of any commission during the initial stages of the first briefing.

Briefings differ according to whether the designer is freelance or works as a staff designer. The former is often given a greater degree of freedom than the latter, who may find that the job specifications have to fit within a predetermined house style. This is particularly so in the case of corporate programmes and in publishing. Since freelance designers are often also given a greater degree of financial responsibility than staff designers, it is very important that they are able to inspire the client with confidence at a briefing.

The language the designer uses must always be tailored to the understanding of everybody present. For instance, if the briefing is with an art director language can be more specialized than if non-technical people are present. It is a great mistake to try to impress an audience by using technical terms, as this can often be intimidating. Nearly all designers have their own ideas but although these can be useful in forming a basis for discussion, it is unwise to stick to them rigidly. A dogmatic approach may well cost the designer the commission — he or she must expect everything and anything to be raised from all sides until some kind of composite picture evolves.

Even if the designer's work is known to the client, it is always a good idea to take examples of previous work to a briefing in order to assist discussion of ideas that may be difficult to explain verbally. This makes it much easier for the designer to put forward his or her point of view. It is also essential to take a pad of paper for making notes. Sometimes a calculator and a cassette recorder can be useful when complex technical details need to be worked out or noted for future reference. It is of paramount importance that the designer remembers to ask all the necessary questions about the job before going on to the next stage of the commission. To make sure that nothing is forgotten, a checklist of questions covering all eventualities should be prepared in advance, even though some questions may be irrelevant once the exact nature of the job has been established. Areas of doubt may lead to problems later; it could be embarrassing to have to contact the client after the initial briefing with questions the meeting was arranged to answer.

After all the basic facts are established, the designer then has to decide whether or not to accept the commission. Some people will make this decision at the first briefing. However, as every aspect of a job, such as the costing and schedule, should be given careful thought before work is undertaken, it may not be possible to give an immediate answer. It is always better to take time considering whether a job is possible before agreeing to take on a commission, rather than risk letting the client down later.

Briefing checklist for the designer
A list of general questions thought of in advance will provide a basic structure for discussion at the briefing.

Client Make sure you know exactly who this is — and get the spelling of their name right!

Date and time Make a note of when the first meeting takes place — if you are dealing with related products at separate meetings this will reduce the chance of confusion later.

People present Write down the names of all the people present at the meeting and do not be afraid to ask how any unfamiliar ones are spelt. Just as important, find out what their role is and why they are at the meeting. It may well be that someone present who did not contribute much could be the person with whom you will mostly be working.

Job description Agree on a name for the project or at least give it a working title.

Market It is essential that you understand who the job is aimed at — to some extent the market will dictate the level of design. Establish, for instance, whether the job is to be aimed at a more sophisticated audience ('up-market'), or a less sophisticated one ('down-market'), and find out what the age group of the intended readership will be as this can influence design. Clients usually have a fairly clear picture of the type of people — their age-group, tastes and lifestyle — who comprise their market. It is up to you to ask for relevant information so the design can be tailored accordingly: sophisticated diagrams, for example, will not be appropriate for a readership of young children. No matter how well executed, a design should be produced with a particular audience in mind.

Budget considerations Establish whether a budget has been set — usually it will have been, but sometimes clients are out of touch with current prices. Always agree to give the client a detailed breakdown of all costs, including your own time. It is a good idea to overestimate slightly when working out the budget so that the client is not presented with an unexpectedly inflated bill when the work is finished. In cases where the budget has already been determined, it is your responsibility to decide how the money should be apportioned within the job, although everybody working on the same project should be consulted. Broadly speaking, budgets should make provision for the following:

Design fee This is what you charge the client and the figure should be adhered to, provided the job specification does not change in any way.

Copywriting/text The cost of this can be difficult to work out but it becomes easier with experience. You should make a rough estimate of how many words will have to be commissioned — writers generally charge per 1000 words (in the UK) or per word (in the USA).

Illustration/photography To an extent the intended readership will dictate the degree of sophistication of imagery and therefore expenditure. If pictures have to be bought in from an agency or library, a picture researcher will probably have to be hired and copyright fees may have to be paid.

Printing Designers handling a high volume of work usually have a constant, sometimes unwelcome, stream of printers knocking at the door offering print quotations — three is generally considered adequate. When choosing a printer cost must be balanced against quality. Not surprisingly, the aim of most designers is to achieve the highest possible standard — and maintain it overall — at the lowest possible price. Sometimes it is more expedient to ask a printer to quote for all related services such as typesetting and colour separations, but today these are usually handled by specialists and you should obtain independent quotations. Typesetters usually charge per 1000 ens or by the number of keystrokes required to complete the job. There will be extra charges for complicated setting — for instance where words have to be set or run around an irregular shape.

Originators of black-and-white and colour images will want to know not only the quantity, but also the size of each individual image and whether there will be any cut-outs or other peculiarities. If

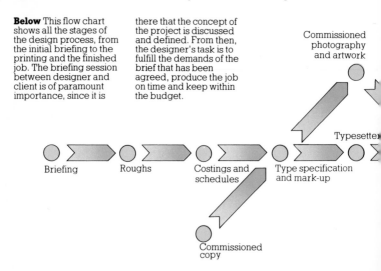

Below This flow chart shows all the stages of the design process, from the initial briefing to the printing and the finished job. The briefing session between designer and client is of paramount importance, since it is there that the concept of the project is discussed and defined. From then, the designer's task is to fulfill the demands of the brief that has been agreed, produce the job on time and keep within the budget.

Briefing

Roughs

Costings and schedules

Commissioned copy

Type specification and mark-up

Typesetter

Commissioned photography and artwork

a job involves a large quantity of separations, as in an illustrated book, some origination houses can be persuaded to estimate on a flat rate basis — that is, they will give a single price for each separation regardless of size.

Although final details may depend on the design solution, the printer will need to be given the following information before a price can be quoted: the run, extent, format, printings, paper quality, approximate number of halftones and the type of binding. The printer will also need to know whether final film or flat artwork will be supplied, or whether the job will require complete page make-up. If the latter is the case, the printer will need much more specific information, such as sample layouts showing the proportion of type to halftone illustrations, ruled lines and so on. It is usually necessary to obtain confirmation quotations from the printer once a design has been approved by the client.

When obtaining quotations it is important to remember that the fields in which printers work are as varied as those of designers. A large, traditional book printer, for instance, may not be able to turn a rush job around quickly, while a trade printer who does general work of all kinds, though extremely quick, may be very expensive. Also, a small printer (sometimes called a 'jobbing printer') might not be able to bind a booklet and would therefore send the job outside, thus increasing the cost.

Schedules In virtually all cases the client will tell the designer when the job should be completed and the designer should then give an immediate indication as to whether it can be done in the time. If it seems completely outside the bounds of possibility, the designer should say so straight away. How much time a job will take to do varies according to its complexity and the experience of the designer. Another important factor is how fast the designer and everyone else involved with the project normally works. Some people enjoy working under pressure but others do not and this can affect the quality of the work produced. Of all the elements involved in scheduling, only the more technical ones, such as printing, can be forecast with any degree of accuracy, and even these will be prone to a certain degree of flexibility.

Contracts During the early stages of a design commission, some kind of written agreement should be drawn up between the client

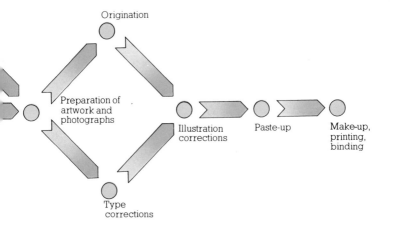

Origination

Preparation of artwork and photographs

Illustration corrections

Paste-up

Make-up, printing, binding

Type corrections

and the designer. In many cases the commission may not occur until after the presentation of an initial concept of a design idea, since the designer may be tendering for the job (competing with other designers). The extent of an agreement or contract will normally reflect the complexity of the work commissioned. Small jobs, such as a letterhead or a poster, may only require a letter, whereas jobs such as a complete corporate programme will require a proper contract, or memorandum of agreement. Even before a contract is drawn up, a few guidelines should be observed:

Put everything in writing No matter how seemingly insignificant, all points raised at a meeting — whether resolved or not — should be put in writing. This will reduce the chance of any misunderstanding arising in the future.

Agree the fee before starting work It is sometimes difficult, if not impossible, to know exactly how much a job will cost at the outset, but a minimum and maximum limit should be given to the client before any work is undertaken. In any event, once a final presentation has been made, the fee must be agreed with the client. If possible, try to agree some sort of rejection or cancellation fee at this stage as well. A client may not accept a design solution for any number of reasons, but a job is much less likely to be rejected on a whim if a fee has already been agreed should it prove unacceptable. On the other hand, you cannot force a client to accept unsatisfactory work, so before the rejection fee is paid expect the client to ask for further solutions. If these are still not accepted, make sure you are paid for the work you have done.

Costing design time
Costing out the time involved in any commission accurately is vitally important. As a rule of thumb, a designer working alone should cost an appropriate hourly rate, based on a notional annual salary, and multiply by 2. If studio space is shared, the minimum multiplier should be 2½ and, if other people are employed, 3 to 4, since the extra overheads must be taken into account.

Agree schedule of payments The method by which payments are made largely depends on how you conduct your business. If you are working on your own you will have a very clear view of your finances and know when you need to be paid. The larger your company or group is, the more the terms of payment need to be controlled.

The complexities and timespan of the job will also affect the schedule of payments. The simplest and most common method is to give the client an invoice once the work has been completed. Other methods of payment are merely variations on this. Sometimes the designer may ask for advance payment of anything between 10 and 50 percent of the designer's fee; generally speaking, the larger the job, the larger the advance that can be expected. Sometimes when fairly substantial sums of money are involved, payments are spread over a longer period of time. The criteria for spreading the payments depends to a large extent on the amount of money the designer will have to pay out during the course of a job for typesetting, photography and so on. The client will also have to make sure that paying out advances will not cause serious problems with his or her cash flow. The simplest way to do this is for the designer to be paid a fixed sum of money at regular intervals, say monthly, over the timespan of the job. Most clients, however, prefer payments to be related to specific, tangible moments in the job schedule. For example, the total fee may be split into three equal instalments with one-third payable at the beginning of the job or on signature of a contract (as a gesture of faith), one-third on approval of the design, and the final instalment once the job is completed.

Roughs Once briefed, the next stage is for the designer to show the client a preliminary drawing which is known variously as a rough, visual, scamp or tissue. This can take a variety of forms — from an outline rough, giving an indication of a basic idea, to a detailed, realistic facsimile of the final thing. Again, the level required varies according to the demands of the client or whoever is being given the presentation. A rough for an art director, say, need not necessarily be rendered as fully as one being prepared for a sales-person.

Although the medium in which the rough is executed must be sympathetic to the style of the design, pencil and felt-tipped pen are usual choices. The former is better for more detailed work, particularly if typography plays an important part in the design, whereas the latter is ideal for rendering rapid impressions of photographs or artwork

One of the purposes of the preliminary rough is to create a talking point — it should never be inflexible. For instance, if the design incorporates pictures, at this stage you do not have to supply the actual transparencies that are going to be used. What is important is to establish what type of images are envisaged. Similarly, in a typographical design, there is no need to choose the exact fount to be used, but the rough should certainly show headings, subheadings and the projected area the text type is to occupy.

The designer may wish or may be asked to present two or three alternative versions of these first thoughts, and because this can be extremely time-consuming, the problems of time and cost-effectiveness should be considered yet again. Even if you are not completely satisfied with a piece of work, there is always a point at which you should stop making further changes to it. This is particularly the case when making a preliminary rough, which may well have to be altered several times. It is usually a good idea at the initial briefing to tell the client how many and what standard of roughs you plan to submit.

A 'finished' rough, on the other hand, must be an accurate facsimile of the final product. Although any images still need not be exact or final, they must give a very good impression of the final artwork or photographs; rough images should therefore be quite elaborate renderings, coloured if applicable. It is also sound practice to bring examples of the illustrator's or photographer's work to the approval meeting, so that the client has a clear idea of what style and standard the end product will eventually be. In some cases, more especially in advertising, the actual, final artwork or photographs form part of the presentation, even at the risk of rejection by the client.

What is finally presented should obviously be as attractive and professional as possible. In most cases the finished rough should be mounted on black card, protected with an acetate covering and given a black or coloured surround. Remember that the client may well wish to use it for display purposes and may even want to photograph it. Sometimes, all typesetting — headlines, text, captions and so on — must be 'live', or real, otherwise 'dummy', or false type and dry-transferred headings can be used. If live copy is required the designer must establish an effective liaison with the writer, so that the illustrative treatment reflects the text and is ready when required. However, even if dummy type is being used, the headings should be live if possible.

2
COMMISSIONING
Words/Photography/Illustration/
Artist's agents/Copyright

There are few design jobs which can be completed entirely by the designer's skills alone, and most involve the added expertise of specialists such as illustrators, photographers, writers, editors and so on. In many cases, such people may have already been comissioned for a particular job, but more often it is up to the designer to enlist the services of any extra necessary professional services that are required.

Words Commissioning words is normally the responsibility of an editor rather than the designer, but sometimes the designer will be called upon to commission as well. In ideal circumstances, the designer should specify the total number of words required and, if the design is sufficiently advanced, the number of lines and the measure (number of characters per line) to which they should be typed. This is by far the most efficient method, as it means that problems which arise if the copy has to be cut and reset can be avoided. However, a degree of rigidity may also be imposed on the design at a relatively early stage.

Sometimes, particularly in book publishing, the text supplied may be 'final': in other words, it cannot be changed or cut and so it is the crucial determining factor in the design. More frequently, the designer asks the person responsible for the words to cut, fill, add and even rewrite if the need arises.

If a designer is totally responsible for the text, and possibly required to commission a technical specialist, it is a good idea to involve a copy editor to ensure that the final text is of an acceptable standard. Whatever the job, the designer and editor or copywriter must collaborate; neither process can be carried out in isolation. This is especially important if captioning is involved, though this is normally done, particularly in book publishing, at a later stage.

The procedure involved in preparing and editing text varies, depending on how many people are required to read it and what form it takes. The 'raw', or first, copy will be read and then submitted for the client's approval. It will then be amended and sent for typesetting. The typeset text should be read initially for literal errors (spelling mistakes) by the typesetter's own readers and then returned to the editor or designer, who will each check it in turn.

Photography Photographs used by designers either exist already and are held by picture libraries and museums or must be specially commissioned. If a photograph is commissioned, the brief given to the photographer must be as full as possible which may well necessitate the client being present. The photographer should be selected specifically for the job in hand since most photographers specialize in a particular subject area such as fashion, food, still life, travel, reportage and so on. They may also specialize in a format, though this will be determined mainly by their chosen subject area. Fashion photographers, for instance, tend to use small formats which are easy to manipulate.

The immediate decisions concern format — large, medium, or small — and whether the photographs are to be colour, black-and-white, or a selection of both. The type of picture needed should be described as clearly as possible, particularly in terms of atmosphere and style, though familiarity with the photographer's work will pre-empt lengthy discussion.

Economic constraints must also be taken into consideration. Photographers normally charge by the day, and it must be ascertained whether the day rate includes expenses, since this can add considerably to the cost. Expenses normally consist of the cost of film and processing, travel costs, hire of models or props and so on. These ancillary costs may be particularly important if special effects are required. Another important thing to remember is that if a photograph requires a special set to be built in the photographer's studio, a fee will usually be charged — usually at half the day rate — for the time it takes to be built, as it is preventing the photographer from doing other work.

The photographer can supply the designer with either prints or transparencies, so you should specify which of these you require. It is normal for more than one shot of the subject to be presented, unless large formats are involved. This gives the designer a greater degree of choice and the photographer a reasonable margin of error.

Ownership of the copyright and of the photographs must be established in advance. There are many ways in which this works including the following:

1 The designer, on behalf of the client, will búy the copyright and original work in its entirety, including *all* the shots taken on that assignment whether they are used or not. This is particularly the case when large investments in photographic commissions can only be justified by further use of the photographs. In such cases it is important that any assignment of copyright is made in writing with the signatures of both the client and the photographer. Also make sure that the photographer fully understands what is being agreed. This is specially important when the photographer is confronted with such daunting, but quite usual and legitimate, clauses as this:

'In consideration of the total amount to be paid by your company to me on delivery of the work detailed herein, I hereby assign to your company the ownership of the original work and the whole of the copyright and rights in the nature of copyright throughout the world in the said work for the full period of copyright and all renewals and extensions thereof.'

If there is nothing in writing to the contrary, both ownership of the copyright and of the original work automatically belong to the photographer.

2 The client, having bought all rights, may agree to the pictures being placed in a photographic library, with the photographer receiving a percentage of the monies the client receives and the library receiving the other half.

3 The client may only require ownership of rights and pictures of the photographs *actually used*, with the 'overs', or unused pictures being returned to the photographer. In some cases the client will insist on being informed, and sometimes asked for formal permission, before any re-use of photographs. The client may also insist on an acknowledgement being printed alongside the photograph.
4 The client may be granted use of the photographs for one time only with any further use being subject to a further fee. In this case, the photographer will retain all rights and ownership.

Existing pictures are usually obtained from a picture library, agency or museum photography department by a researcher working from a brief prepared by the designer and, if necessary, from the text. The brief should specify the total number of pictures, subject areas and the budget limitations; unless particular pictures are required, the selection should be as wide as possible within the subject area. The time taken to obtain pictures must also be considered, particularly if a selection from an international source is required.

It is essential at the earliest possible stage to specify which reproduction rights are needed so that the costs can be taken into account. This normally means specifying exactly in what form, size and country the photographs will appear, so that reduction fees, usually payable upon publication, can be calculated. Many museums and galleries prefer to charge a hire fee rather than a reproduction fee, so these pictures should be returned as soon as possible. Photographs borrowed from other sources should also be returned as soon as possible after use, otherwise holding fees, as well as reproduction fees, may be charged.

Many sources, particularly museums, sell prints or transparencies as duplicates — prints from existing negatives or specially commissioned photographs — but if they are re-used for another purpose other than that for which they were bought then further permission should be sought.

Whatever the source of the photograph, take care of the original as replacement fees can be extremely high, especially if the picture is a rare one. Transparencies should be carefully checked for any kind of mark as soon as they are received. If there is a mark on a transparency, it is essential to inform the agency or supplier immediately that it was damaged on receipt so that they do not make a charge for it. Picture agencies frequently supply duplicated transparencies which are not usually as sharp as the originals, and these should also be thoroughly examined for acceptability. Finally, designers who frequently handle transparencies should take out an insurance policy to cover themselves against any possible damage or loss.

Illustration The designer must remember that, like photographers, every illustrator specializes either in subject area or through having an individual style. These considerations must be borne in mind at the commissioning stage, since the style of the illustration must be sympathetic with the subject it is illustrating. Again, familiarity with the artist's work is desirable. Designers should be wary of asking an illustrator to produce work in a style with which he or she is unfamiliar — the result may not be terribly successful and may also be costly.

Fees must be established in advance, and the designer should give the illustrator the fullest possible brief. The illustrator should be told whether the illustration is to be reproduced in full-colour, specially mixed colours or black-and-white, the size to which the artwork is to be drawn, whether any overlays are required for mechanical tints, and so on. As cost is always such an important factor — illustration can be far more expensive than photography — this must be balanced against quality. Any substandard work which cannot be improved should be rejected, in which case a rejection fee (established in advance) is usually paid. It is also vital to establish very clear deadlines for delivery of the material, preferably well in advance of the date at which the work is actually required to allow time for approval and possible alterations. Many designers and art directors will threaten cancellation or a reduction of the fee if work is not delivered on time.

The actual artwork is frequently drawn at a larger size than the one at which it will finally print. Half-up (actually, one and a half up, or x 1.5) or twice up (x 2) is the most common scale for illustration work. Use of this technique can make the printed version look crisper and tighter; it can also help cut costs at the separation stage because it is cheaper to originate a number of illustrations in proportion. Many illustrators, however, stipulate that their work must be used at the size at which it is drawn, and some prefer their work to be enlarged; this is because the style and character of their work may suffer unless the artwork is reproduced at the same size or larger.

Some illustrators prefer to provide roughs before they quote for a job — it can be difficult to estimate the time a drawing may take to do, and in any case the illustrator may not have the same solution in mind as the designer. An advance pencil rough will also ensure that the brief has been fulfilled and that all the elements required

THE LAW OF COPYRIGHT

For all designers, understanding what copyright means and the regulations covering it is a vital part of the job. The subject is complex and frequently misunderstood; broadly speaking, copyright is designed to protect original work and stop it from being used or copied without the agreement of the person who originally created it, unless the copyright has been legally relinquished. This must be agreed formally in writing in what lawyers term an 'assignment' of copyright. This is irrevocable, as opposed to giving permission to reproduce a copyright work. In the latter case, the user of the work is granted the right to reproduce it under certain terms, conditions and circumstances — and in no others. The artist retains so-called residual copyright.

Paintings, sculptures, drawings, engravings, manuscripts and photographs all enjoy natural copyright protection, with the creator of the work owning the copyright in it from the moment of its creation. This ruling seems simple, but, in fact, the legal position is more complex, because of the problem of commissions. Some work is protected by copyright, even if commissioned, and some is not. Commissioned photographs and portraits — whether painted, drawn or engraved — are not the artist's copyright, but all other work is, unless the artist has relinquished copyright protection. Conversely, an artist's employer owns copyright in any work produced during the period of employment, again unless the rules of copyright are formally varied to the contrary. Copyright in artwork lasts for the artist's lifetime and for 50 years after his or her death, during which time the copyright is owned by the artist's heirs. Copyright in photographs lasts for 50 years from first publication. Unpublished photographs are protected indefinitely.

If work is reproduced without express or implied permission, the user is in breach of copyright and can be sued by the artist. If the breach is proved, the artist can obtain an injunction to prevent the publication, or the further distribution and sale of the work, damages, and a share in any profits made from the work's illegal sale.

Copyright exists naturally in all completed work, with the exceptions given here. It also cannot be used to protect an idea, though it does protect rough notes and sketches. Though there is no legal requirement to do so, it is sensible to indicate any claims to copyright with a credit line, including name, the copyright symbol and the year of creation.

are present. For the final artwork the illustrator may prefer working on a particular type of surface. Most surfaces are acceptable, although a flexible one is most desirable since, for reproduction purposes, it can be scanned direct (see p90).

The designer's responsibilities do not end when the accepted illustration is passed for press. It is also necessary to establish who owns the illustration, as opposed to the copyright. It is law that, unless it is clearly stipulated that their client is buying the artwork, the original remains the property of the illustrator after its initial use and he or she retains the copyright. However, as with commissioned photography, there are almost infinite variations on the type of arrangement an illustrator may make with whoever the client is.

Artist's agents Generally speaking, one of the most expedient ways to gain immediate access to a wide variety of illustrative skills is to consult an agent. Agents usually operate in specific fields such as publishing or advertising, or in specialized subject areas such as natural history, but many agents will accept work of any kind. Larger agencies have up to about 40 or 50 artists on their books who they manage to keep supplied with work more or less full-time, with probably another 20 or so that they can call on as a back-up, but whom they may not be able to keep fully occupied. Obviously, it is these larger agencies who will be able to offer the widest range of services, although smaller agencies, operating with as few as 12 artists, but in more specialized or sophisticated markets, offer an equally valuable service. Smaller agencies often only represent more sought-after, well-known names, although most agencies, whatever their size, have a few big names on their books. One immediate advantage of using agents, apart from the sheer volume of choice, is that they are frequently far more flexible than an artist when it comes to negotiating fees. A general fear is that by dealing with an agent a job will inevitably end up costing more than by negotiating directly with the artist. However, the agents claim that this is not the case and that artists are able to devote more time to the job in hand if they do not have to worry about fees and finding future work. As agents charge artists a percentage of their fees as commission, they tend to be helpful and keen to establish financial solutions that satisfy both the artist and the client.

Nevertheless, there are always exceptions, and if the budget is a major factor it is nearly always possible to find an artist who will do a job cheaply, but remember that the standard of work may not be quite so high.

Another aspect that causes concern among art directors and designers is that by using agents it is easy to lose the rapport and creative feedback that is generated by dealing directly with an artist. However, agents are moving towards a less proprietorial attitude, and most will happily allow, and even encourage, a direct working relationship between artist and client.

Agents will pay much greater attention to the territories in which rights are granted. Artists generally accept that they are paid for work done regardless of where it is seen, whereas an agent may want to charge for specific territorial or multiple rights, although this usually only applies to further use of artwork. Agents will clarify these details at the outset but designers should remember that many clients, particularly publishers, will want to purchase outright usage of the work, in any form whatsoever, and will assume that this is the case when the artist is commissioned.

3
THE DESIGN PROCESS

Typography/Preparing
manuscript/Casting-off/Marking
up copy/Copyfitting/Proof
correction/Grids/Layouts/
Picture preparation/Artwork
preparation/Colour correction/
Paste-up/Printing/Book
production/Flat plans/Magazine
production

In many respects, it is curious that the term 'graphic design' is given to a profession in which the time spent on actual *design* represents such a small proportion of the whole job. In practice, the designer acts as a coordinator, his or her knowledge having to incorporate extensive aspects of every ancillary reproduction process from typesetting systems to complete magazine or book printing. This knowledge permits the designer to make aesthetic decisions with the maximum amount of flexibility within each technical parameter, and indeed such aesthetic awareness must be used to police the standards of technological advancement.

It is important, therefore, that the designer is totally familiar with every aspect of the design process in order that he or she may tackle with confidence and assurance the most important part of their involvement — that of design itself.

Typography Among the many basic considerations of typographic design, the two which require greatest understanding are the varying width of alphabetical characters and the spaces between them. This understanding is essential in order to achieve the twin aim of aesthetic appeal and legibility.

The width of alphabetic characters, or the space alloted to them, depends largely on the equipment used to produce them. For instance, a manual typewriter, in order to maintain consistent letterspacing, uses exaggeratedly wide serifs on letters such as 'i' and 'l'. This gives a string of characters (words) an even appearance by reducing the amount of white space. Some electric typewriters are slightly more sophisticated with a system of three character widths, but phototypesetting machines use up to about 11 widths. On more advanced computer-controlled systems the number of character widths can be infinite. This greater flexibility of typesetting machines ensures optically even spacing between characters.

Perhaps the next most important consideration in typographic design is that of word spacing. The problem is made all the more difficult by a convention that was introduced in medieval times. Because they wanted to make facing pages in books symmetrical, scribes insisted that both the left- and righthand edges of text should be vertically aligned. This could only be achieved by abbreviating words which led to the introduction of additional symbols, called contractions, being used to fill the spaces which had been left by abbreviated words or short lines.

Point sizes

For many years, printing was an inexact science. No two printers could agree on a standard system of type measurement, which meant that type cast by one foundry could not be used with type cast by another. It was not until the 18th century that the pioneering French typographer Pierre Fournier successfully proposed a standard typesetting unit called the point. This was developed by another Frenchman, Firmin Didot, into a European standard. Even today, however, the process is not complete, since Britain and the USA base their system on one point measuring 0.01383in, the European equivalent being 0.0148in. The 12 point unit is a pica in the first system and a cicero in the second. The metric system, however, is now becoming the first universal standard. **Right** The unit system used in typesetting for measurement and counting. Usually 18 units make up an em, the size of the unit varying with the type size. In the word Mot, the M is 18 units wide, the o 10 units wide and the t 6 units wide. The system enables spacing to be finely adjusted.

inches

centimetres

picas

ciceros

72pt em divided into 18 units

36pt em divided into 18 units

18 units | 10 units | 6 units

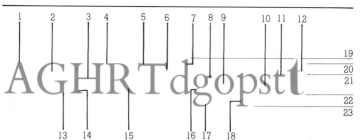

Each character in a line of type has its own individual characteristics. The terminology relating to different parts of a typeset character is extensive and a wide range of words are in common usage. Those illustrated (**above**) are apex (**1**), counter (**2**), bar (**3**), serif (**4**), arm (**5**), beak (**6**), ascender (**7**), ear (**8**), bowl (**9**), spine (**10**), cross-stroke (**11**), hairline (**12**), spur (**13**), bracket (**14**), tail (**15**), link (**16**), loop (**17**), descender (**18**), ascender line (**19**), capital line (**20**), x-height (mean line) (**21**), base line (**22**), descender line (**23**).

A typeface's point or body size is defined as the distance from the top of the ascender to the bottom of the descender. The amount of space varies from typeface to typeface. If there is no extra space between lines, the type can be measured from base line to base line, the distance between the two being referred to as leading, or line feed in phototypesetting.

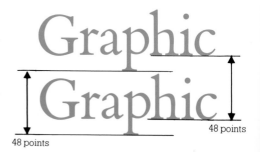

48 points

48 points

This convention was sustained by the introduction of movable type, though more by its mechanical requirements than by aesthetic considerations. In order to make an impression from a group of pieces of type, all the pieces had to be locked together under tension in a metal frame called a forme. This means that all the lines of type, including spaces, must be the same length otherwise all the type falls out of the forme as soon as it is lifted. In other words, the whole area between each edge of the forme must be filled with metal — either with type or spaces. The convention of vertically aligning edges of blocks of text was made possible by distributing approximately equal spaces between each of the words along a line. Today, this technique of ensuring that all the lines on a page are of the same length is known as justified type-setting. Text with even word spacing is usually vertically aligned on the left ('ranged left'), with the right margin set ragged (un-justified).

With modern typesetting methods setting type justified is not necessary, and indeed can be undesirable since much research supports the theory that unjustified text, with even word spacing, as opposed to justified setting with variable wordspacing, is more comfortable to read.

Type measurement Because the earliest type consisted of solid blocks (body) upon which the area to be printed (face) was punch-ed, all measurements related to these three-dimensional objects. However even though most modern typesetting systems still use these measurements, they involve a two-dimensional system.

There are three type measurements with which the designer must be familiar: points, picas and units. These measurements can be confusing in that the Anglo-American is different from the Euro-pean system, although both use the term 'point'. The art of printing spread swiftly through Europe following its initial development in Germany, so swiftly that the many type foundries that sprang up were casting type which was incompatible with that of another foundry. It was not until the early eighteenth century that an at-tempt was made to standardize a system of type measurement. This happened in France, when Pierre Fournier proposed a stan-dard unit of measurement which he called the point. The innova-tions made by Fournier were developed by another Frenchman, Firmin Didot, to produce a European standard, but neither Britain nor America adopted this although their system was based on it.

Anglo-American system This is based on the division of one inch into 72 parts, called points. Each point is 0.013833in, and 12 points make a pica (or pica em) and measure 0.166in. Although in the USA this system is still universal, in the UK it has been complicated by the introduction of metrification.

European system The European point is 0.0148in and 12 of these form a unit measuring 0.1776in. This 12 point unit is called a *cicero* in France and Germany, a *riga tipografica* (riga) in Italy, and an *augustijn* (aug) in the Netherlands.

There is no relationship between the Anglo-American point and the Didot point, and neither of them relate to the metric system. Thus in Europe, including the UK, typographic measurements in points co-exist with metric, which are used in virtually every other allied trade. For this reason, type measurements are gradually being metricated and eventually all type sizes will be in millimetres.

Although many designers refer to a pica em simply as an 'em', technically this is incorrect — an em is the square of the body of a piece of type, regardless of its size (so called because the letter 'M' originally occupied the full unit width of a piece of type). A 36 point em, for instance, measures 36 points, not 12. The most important measurement in controlling line length is that of each character width. This measurement is determined by dividing an em into vertical 'slices'. These are called set points or, more commonly in phototypesetting, units. The number of units in an em varies from one typesetting system to another, but probably the most popular is 18, and the more units there are in an em, the greater the possibility of refinement. Units control not only the width of characters, but also the spaces between them. Although the actual size of the unit varies according to the size of the type, because there are always the same number to the em, regardless of size, the proportions always remain the same.

In the design of typefaces, each character is given a fixed amount of space known as set-width or 'set', which are measured in units, as are the spaces in between each character or word. The set-width of a character controls the amount of space between itself and the next character and can be varied for special purposes — either increased to allow greater space or decreased. The latter is only possible in phototypesetting and electronic typesetting systems and is obviously limited as there comes a point when characters will lose their legibility.

Because different founts vary considerably in their characteristics, the set-widths of characters will also vary from typeface to typeface so that a condensed typeface, for instance, will have a narrow set-width relative to its body size.

Typeface name comparisons

Typeface	Alphatype	Compugraphic	Dymo
Caledonia	Caledo	California	Highland
Century Expanded	Century X	Century Light	Century Expanded
Clarendon	Clarendon	Clarendon	Clarendon
Futura Book	Alpha Futura	Futura Book	Photura Book
Futura Light	Futura Light	Futura Light	Techno Light
Futura Medium	Futura Medium	Futura Medium	Techno Medium
Futura Bold	Futura Bold	Futura Bold	Techno Bold
Garamond	Garamond	Garamond	Garamond
Helvetica	Claro	Helios II	Newton
Melior	Uranus	Mallard	Ballardvale
News Gothic	Alpha Gothic	News Gothic	News Gothic
Optima	Musica	Oracle	Chelmsford
Palatino	Patina	Paladium	Andover
Stymie	Stymie	Stymie	Stymie
Times Roman	English	English Times	Times New Roman
Univers 55	Versatile	Univers Medium II	Univers Medium
Univers 65	Versatile	Univers Bold II	Univers Bold

Typefaces Much to the bewilderment of the designer, there are many thousands of typefaces available today. But this is a relatively recent phenomenon — during the first 400 years of movable type the form it took depended upon the mechanical limitations of the printing processes of the day, and only in the nineteenth century did type design even begin to transcend the barriers of craft into art. Even then, typeface designs had to be translated by craftsmen using individual punches to cut the precise form desired. Only in the last few decades, with the advent of photographically reproduced typefaces, has type design proliferated to its present, seemingly saturated, state.

Typefaces can be classified in six basic groups — Gothic, Old Style, Transitional, Modern, Egyptian, and Sans Serif — and these roughly trace the historical development of type design.

Gothic Movable type was developed in Germany and the design of the type reflected the local handwriting, known as Gothic, Black Letter or Textura. The letterform itself was written in such a way that curved forms were difficult to reproduce and were thus kept to a minimum, which resulted in a distinctive typeface.

Old Style It was the introduction of printing to Italy that led to type design taking on the appearance it has today. Formal documents were handwritten in a style known as Chancery Italic, which is much lighter and more legible than Gothic. These Old Style letterforms are characterized by a robust triangular serif (a small line used to complete the main stroke of a letter) and many forms, of which Bembo is a classic example, have been adapted for modern typesetting processes.

Typeface name comparisons

Harris	Mergenthaler Linotype	Monotype/ Monophoto	Varityper
Laurel	Caledonia	Caledonia	Highland
Century Expanded	Century Expanded	Century Exanded 658	Century Expanded
Clarique	Clarendon	Clarendon	Clarendon
Futura Book	Spartan Book		
Futura Light	Spartan Light		Techno Light
Futura Medium	Spartan Medium		Techno Medium
Futura Bold	Spartan Black		Techno Extra Bold
Garamond	Garamond	Garamond	Garamond
Vega	Helvetica	Helvetica	Megaron
Medallion	Melior	Melior	Hanover
News Gothic	Trade Gothic	News Gothic	News Gothic
Zenith	Optima	Optima	Chelmsford
Elegante	Palatino		Andover
Cairo	Memphis		Stymie
Times Roman	Times Roman	Times	Times Roman
Galaxy Medium	Univers	Univers 689	Univers Medium
Galaxy Demi	Univers	Univers 693	Univers Bold

Transitional Gradually, type design became more influenced by the refinement of printing processes — and its associated materials such as paper and ink — than by the conventions of handwriting, and printers' type began to assume its own separate identity. Transitional faces are identified by their generally lighter colour than Old Style, the emphasis of the curved strokes tending to be vertical rather than diagonal and the serifs more horizontal. Probably the best known example of a transitional face is that named after its English designer John Baskerville in the mid-eighteenth century.

Modern During the eighteenth century, developments became more rapid and in 1798 another style of type emerged. This was the work of an Italian printer named Giambattista Bodoni and became known as the Modern style. Bodoni, who was clearly influenced by the then current vogue for classical Greek and Roman artistic styles, gave his name to the design which most typified Modern faces, and had maximum contrast between thick and thin strokes, with fine horizontal hairline serifs, while the ascenders (the parts above the body such as in 'b' and 'h') and descenders (the parts below the body as in 'g', 'p' and 'y') are both extended.

Egyptian The Industrial Revolution in the nineteenth century brought the introduction of mechanical typesetting and this combined with market demand — particularly in advertising — to produce yet more type forms. The advertising requirements at the time were for loud, bold designs which would stand out from their surrounds. This desire was fulfilled by a type design which was bold and black, and with serifs carrying as much weight as the rest of the letter. This form became known as Egyptian or Slab Serif. More exaggerated — and in some cases illegible — forms were called Fat Face.

Sans Serif The bolder a typeface becomes, the smaller its counters are, until a point is reached when it becomes illegible. Because of the search for ever more striking designs, it was this factor which led to serifs being abandoned altogether. These were called Sans Serif types and were initially used for posters, but before long they became used for general printing.

Using type The evolution of type design does not rest solely on historical precedent, but also on the continuing development of production methods, with typefaces being designed, or re-designed, for specific technological innovations. With the introduction of Linotype and Monotype at the beginning of the twentieth century — the first mechanical typesetting machines — existing typefaces were remodelled and adapted to the characteristics of the two systems. Linotype produces each complete line as a single piece of metal, whereas Monotype produces individual characters and spaces with which to form a line.

An important factor in type selection is the paper and printing process to be used. Earlier typefaces were designed to be printed by letterpress on handmade, cartridge or other uncoated papers. Thus, when printed on modern, smooth papers, they can often appear fragile and light. It is also the case that Modern faces, such as Bodoni and Walbaum, look more mellow and robust if printed by letterpress on uncoated paper. Similarly, the typesetting equipment can alter the appearance of a typeface — phototypesetting, for example, generally produces a lighter effect than the equivalent metal face.

Reversed type, that is white type on a black or coloured

The examples here are all 36pt. A face with a large x-height is called a large appearing face and one with a small x-height a small appearing face.

abc *Bembo*

abc *Times*

abc *Rockwell*

Loose
The form typography is to take

Normal
The form typography is to take

Tight
The form typography is to take

Very tight
The form typography is to take

Overlapping
The form typography is to take

Letterspacing defines the space between letters, which can be adjusted depending on the designer's requirements. The type of spacing required is normally specified as normal, loose, tight and very tight. In phototypesetting, these instructions are translated into units or half units, depending on the system. The results are extremely flexible up to a fraction of a millimetre.

The x-height of small caps is the same as that of lowercase characters. Designed small caps are of even weight. Photographically reduced small caps tend to look lighter when set with normal type.

Designed SMALL CAPS

Reduced SMALL CAPS

A variation on SMALL CAPS

When two or more characters are joined and set as a single unit, they are termed ligatures. Common examples are ff, fi, fl and ffl. They should not be used when letterspacing is tight, as the result may look gappy.

fi fl ff ffi ffl

fi fl ff ffi ffl

When the spacing between specified characters is deliberately reduced, leaving the rest of the setting the same, the result is called kerning. The technique is frequently used with certain letter combinations, such as Yo, Te, LY and la. When these are set, there is often too much space between them, compared to the rest of the setting. Kerning solves this problem. If used properly, it can greatly improve letter-fit, legibility and the evenness of a line of typesetting — it is particularly useful with large display type.

VAULT VAULT

AT	AY	AV	AW	Ay	Av	Aw
FA	TO	TA	Ta	Te	To	Ti
Tr	Tu	Ty	Tw	Ts	Tc	LT
LY	LV	LW	Ly	PA	VA	Va
Ve	Vo	Vi	Vr	Vu	Vy	RT
RV	RW	RY	Ry	WA	Wa	We
Wo	Wi	Wr	Wu	Wy	YA	Ya
Ye	Yo	Yi	Yp	Yq	Yu	Yv

Numerals exist in two styles — non aligning and aligning. Non aligning numbers are small with ascenders and descenders; aligning numbers are same size, aligning on the base line. A choice is available in many founts, so it is best to specify.

1234567890

1234567890

Most phototypesetting systems can only produce fractions in Roman typefaces, not italic ones, and true fractions only in halves, thirds, quarters and eighths. The alternatives are to set the fractions full size with a slash, or to use piece fractions.

| 1/8 | 1/4 | 3/8 | 1/2 | 5/8 | 3/4 | 7/8 | 1/3 | 2/3 |

| 1/8 | 1/4 | 3/8 | 1/2 | 5/8 | 3/4 | 7/8 | 1/3 | 2/3 |

| $\frac{1}{8}$ | $\frac{1}{4}$ | $\frac{3}{8}$ | $\frac{1}{2}$ | $\frac{5}{8}$ | $\frac{3}{4}$ | $\frac{7}{8}$ | $\frac{1}{3}$ | $\frac{2}{3}$ |

The solid round dots often used to emphasize items in lists are called bullets. These are normally available in small, medium and large. Specify where they are to be centred.

• SMALL BULLET CENTRE ON CAP HEIGHT

● MEDIUM BULLET CENTRED ON CAP HEIGHT

● LARGE BULLET CENTRED ON CAP HEIGHT

Rules are a very useful compositional device. They can be used to help visual organization by providing form and structure; they can also provide a sense of character for what would otherwise be straight type. In common with linespacing, rules are defined in points or fractions of a point. Some also have names — a ¼-point rule is usually referred to as a hairline rule, while a ½-point rule is a fine rule. Lengths are normally specified in picas. When using rules, there are two important points to remember. Firstly, specify the spacing required below and above them. Secondly, check proofs carefully when continuous rules have been specified for breaks and jaggedness.

12pt	11.75pt	11.5pt	11.25pt	11pt	10.75pt
10.5pt	10.25pt	10pt	9.75pt	9.5pt	9.25pt
9pt	8.75pt	8.5pt	8.25pt	8pt	7.75pt
7.5pt	7.25pt	7pt	6.75pt	6.5pt	6.25pt
6pt	5.75pt	5.5pt	5.25pt	5pt	4.75pt
4.5pt	4.25pt	4pt	3.75pt	3.5pt	3.25pt
3pt	2.75pt	2.5pt	2.25pt	2pt	1.75pt
1.5pt	1.25pt	1pt	0.75pt	0.5pt	0.25pt

Broken

3 point shaded or total

Dots placed in a regularly spaced series to guide the reader's eye are known as leaders. The specified spacing between the dots will naturally vary but, whatever the spacing, the dots should be set in a regular pattern. The two most frequently used are aligning leaders, in which the dots are aligned vertically downwards, and diamond leaders, in which they are staggered.

Dot every 6 points . . . .

Dot every 12 points . . . .

Dot every 24 points . . . .

Vertically aligned leaders

Staggered leaders

background, usually demands a heavier typeface, since faces with fine lines as an integral part of the design such as a Modern face or a light weight of type, are susceptible to the erosion of the image by surplus ink, and parts may well disappear as a result. Gravure printing can have the same detrimental effect upon the same range of typefaces.

Besides such practical considerations, type selection will be influenced by aesthetic demands. For example, Sans Serif faces, being simple, uncluttered and unpretentious, are sometimes more suitable for technical literature. They are also used extensively for children's books, the design of the letterforms such as the 'a' and 'g' more closely resembling today's handwriting. Serifed faces are more suitable for text matter in books, particularly novels, and are also used by the majority of newspapers.

Tables, indexes and bibliographies requiring complex typography, are best suited to a typeface with a wide range of weights and italic, such as Garamond or Bembo, while Times offers a particularly comprehensive range of symbols for setting mathematical formulae. Colour and leading are the two other most important considerations when selecting typefaces. When set as text, each typeface produces its own tonal value, which is referred to by typographers as colour. This colour is influenced by the amount of space between each line, called leading — a name which derives from the days of handsetting, when fillets of metal, known as leads, were used to space the lines further apart. The equivalent term in photo- and computer composition is line feed, although leading is still in common usage, particularly among designers.

Some typefaces are what are known as 'large appearing', that is, when the overall height of the body of the lower case letterform (the x-height) is large in comparison with its ascenders and descenders. Conversely, typefaces with small x-heights and large ascenders and descenders are known as small appearing.

Procedure
Preparing manuscript All copy, whatever typeface or typesetting system is chosen, first has to be prepared before the typesetter starts work. It is difficult, if not impossible, to establish a clear typographic structure if the text is not typewritten and it usually helps if it is typed to the approximate line length as the final, typeset form. The copy should be typed with double line spacing and ample margins at left and right for editorial comments, corrections and typesetting instructions. This can save considerable amounts of time and money, the latter being especially the case when the copy is to be filmset, since corrections with this process can be very costly. However, the tendency today is for copy to be entered directly on to a word-processing system — many of which are compatible with electronic typesetters and which typesetters themselves can use, which enables final corrections to be made even before the copy emerges as typeset text in any form. Retyping to the line length can also serve to confirm the typographic structure of a layout, and will allow the designer to make an accurate estimate of the number of lines, and thus pages, a manuscript will take up. At some stage, whether at the same time or after the text face has been determined, stylistic decisions must be taken on such things as size and position of headings, subheadings, crossheadings, references, footnotes and so on, even though additional sub-editing may be required later. This normally

means that the designer must read the text before such decisions can be taken. Ideally, however, the designer should predetermine the typographic structure so that text can be written accordingly, especially where visual impact may be just as important as the content of the words themselves.

Casting-off Estimating the number of characters and lines which a piece of typed copy will occupy in its typeset form is called 'casting-off'. This is an important process for the design of a book or any printed matter.

The methods by which the length of a manuscript can be calculated are at best only approximations. It is advisable when casting-off to round up any calculations and even to allow for a margin of error — about 5 or 10 percent — to the calculations. This allowance should take into account the complexity of the manuscript and the number of words per line once it is set in type, although short lines, hyphenated words or exaggerated white spaces due to words being carried over to the next line will further complicate the estimate.

If typed on a fixed-spacing typewriter, casting-off the manuscript is made much easier because there are always the same number of characters per line, which can be measured with a ruler or typescale. If the manuscript is typed on a machine with a variable character width, the count must then be made manually. Manuscript paper is also extremely useful as it is printed with pica measures on it, and this makes casting off much easier.

First, an approximation must be made of an average line, each word space counting as a single character, and this is achieved by counting the number of characters in, say, five lines and then dividing the number of characters by five (the number of lines counted). This will give a fairly accurate average line count, which is then multiplied by the total number of lines of manuscript. Again, this can be measured by using a depth scale rather than by counting each individual line to give the total number of characters involved. This figure can also be useful when estimating the cost of typesetting.

The next thing to establish is the amount of space the typeset manuscript will fill, and this will vary according to the typeface chosen. Normally, this is where cost considerations must be made; it is only very rarely that a designer is asked to increase the amount of space text may occupy, particularly in book work. More usually, the problem is to balance readability with fitting the text into a predetermined number of pages.

The way this is calculated is by referring to a sample alphabet, in the appropriate type size, provided by either the typesetter or the manufacturer of the equipment being used. Particular care should be taken to refer to a sample produced by the exact equipment which will be used for the job — as well as the correct unit set (see p20) — since the line length of the same typeface produced by different foundries may vary.

Many manufacturers produce a special set of tables covering their complete range of typefaces which make it easier to calculate text lengths. These can be presented in different forms; some will give the number of lower case letters per line for each face and size over a given length, while others may be given reference numbers which, when used in conjunction with a special copyfitting table, will give the number of characters per line. Others may give the number of characters per pica for every size of every typeface. Because many type samples are not accompanied by copyfitting tables, a table can be used which gives the numbers of characters per pica for a variety of alphabet lengths.

Some type specimen sheets include a sample text set in a variety of different leadings, as well as a complete type synopsis. These sheets are worth collecting since it is through them that a designer can assess the appearance of what, on the surface, may seem to be insignificant minor amendments to a specification.

Marking up copy Once a manuscript has left the editor's hands, the designer marks on it a set of instructions so that the compositor or operator can typeset it. These instructions specify the founts required and the general style of the typography. They should always be attached to the manuscript for permanent reference. On the manuscript itself, the exact words, lines, headings or paragraphs to be capitalized, italicized, set in a bold face, small capitals or a different size must be clearly indicated. There may come a point when these instructions become too dense to follow clearly, and in such cases it is better to use a coding system based on numerals or letters and keyed to a master style sheet. One reason for this is that typesetting can be extremely costly and a seemingly minor instructional error may involve massive resetting — so it pays to get it right first time.

It must be remembered that there may be more than one operator keying-in the copy and that a completely separate team — either within the typesetting company or completely outside — will be responsible for the page make-up. For this reason, it is wise to confine the type mark-up to the manuscript itself, and the layout instructions, such as the position of the text on the page, to the layouts themselves.

Proofs The first proof (or piece of typeset copy) provided by the typesetter is known as a galley proof. This is usually the last chance to get everything right, so it should be scrutinized with meticulous care. In the first instance this is generally done by the typesetter's own reader who will check it against the manuscript and mark any errors in red. All other corrections or alterations should be marked in a different colour — this ensures that typesetters do not charge for their own errors.

Next, the author or editor, or both, will be required to read the galley proof even though, in principle, all editorial alterations and corrections should have already been incorporated into the manuscript because of the cost of resetting type. In addition, the editor will need to check the text for such things as line lengths, 'widows' (single words set on a line at the end of a paragraph) and make adjustments accordingly. The designer should also check it for more aesthetic inconsistencies or anomalies such as wrong founts, erratic word spacing or 'rivers', which are white lines running down a column of text caused by the coincidence of word spaces on different lines falling adjacent to each other.

It should be possible at this stage, with straightforward text, to return the corrected galleys to the typesetter for final galleys — for 'paste-up' or for making into page film. However, it is quite usual for typesetters to supply second — and sometimes third and even fourth — proofs before final approval is given. The number of galleys supplied depends, of course, on the complexity of the job, and with very complicated setting such as timetables or mathematical formulae, it may be necessary to go to many proofs.

How many times proofs can be returned is usually determined by schedule limitations, rather than the need to achieve perfection.

Copyfitting tables

Many type specimen sheets or books include special tables to help estimate the amount of space copy will fill. The tables usually give the number of characters per pica for each size of every typeface, or the number of characters for each size of a variety of given measures. The table shown here has been devised to cover any typeface at any size on any typesetting system; however, it can work accurately only if the length of the lowercase alphabet of the face to be used is known. To use the table, first measure the length of the lowercase alphabet in points. The alphabet must be in the desired size and unit spacing, and the type produced on the typesetting system that will eventually be used for the actual job. Look at the lefthand column of the chart and select the number nearest to the alphabet length of the typeface to be used. The figure immediately to the right of this gives the number of characters per pica for the typeface that has been selected — at the correct size and on the correct system — and the number of characters in any measure can be calculated simply by multiplying the characters per pica figure by the length of line to be set (in picas). In other words, an alphabet length of 113 points gives a reading of 3.05 characters per pica (when read off against 114). A line measure of 26 picas will have 79 characters per line (3.05 x 26 = 79). To save having to make this calculation, the table gives the number of characters for a range of measures up to 40 picas.

Length of lower case alphabet (in points)

Number of characters per pica

Length of line to be set (in picas)

	1	7	8	9	10	11	12	13
60	5.80	41	46	52	58	64	70	75
62	5.61	39	45	51	56	62	67	73
64	5.44	38	44	49	54	60	65	71
66	5.27	37	42	47	53	58	63	69
68	5.12	36	41	46	51	56	61	67
70	4.97	35	40	45	50	55	60	65
72	4.83	34	39	43	48	53	58	63
74	4.70	33	38	42	47	52	56	61
76	4.58	32	37	41	46	50	55	60
78	4.46	31	36	40	45	49	54	58
80	4.35	30	35	39	44	48	52	57
82	4.24	30	34	38	42	47	51	55
84	4.14	29	33	37	41	46	50	54
86	4.05	28	32	36	40	45	49	53
88	3.95	28	32	36	40	43	47	51
90	3.87	27	31	35	39	43	46	50
92	3.78	26	30	34	38	42	45	49
94	3.70	26	30	33	37	41	44	48
96	3.63	25	29	33	36	40	44	47
98	3.55	25	28	32	36	39	43	46
100	3.48	24	28	31	35	38	42	45
102	3.41	24	27	31	34	38	41	44
104	3.35	23	27	30	33	37	40	43
106	3.28	23	26	30	33	36	39	43
108	3.22	23	26	29	32	35	39	42
110	3.16	22	25	28	32	35	38	41
112	3.11	22	25	28	31	34	37	40
114	3.05	21	24	27	31	34	37	40
116	3.00	21	24	27	30	33	36	39
118	2.95	21	24	27	29	32	35	38
120	2.90	20	23	26	29	32	35	38
122	2.85	20	23	26	29	31	34	37
124	2.81	20	22	25	28	31	34	36
126	2.76	19	22	25	28	30	33	36
128	2.72	19	22	24	27	30	33	35
130	2.68	19	21	24	27	29	32	35
135	2.58	18	21	23	26	28	31	34
140	2.49	17	20	22	25	27	30	32
145	2.40	17	19	22	24	26	29	31
150	2.32	16	19	21	23	26	28	30
155	2.25	16	18	20	22	25	27	29
160	2.18	15	17	20	22	24	26	28
165	2.11	15	17	19	21	23	25	27
170	2.05	14	16	18	20	23	25	27
175	1.99	14	16	18	20	22	24	26
180	1.93	14	15	17	19	21	23	25
185	1.88	13	15	17	19	21	23	24
190	1.83	13	15	16	18	20	22	24
195	1.78	12	14	16	18	20	21	23
200	1.74	12	14	16	17	19	21	23

14	15	16	17	18	19	20	22	24	26	28	30	32	34	36	38	40
81	87	93	99	104	110	116	128	139	151	162	174	186	197	209	220	232
79	84	90	95	101	107	112	123	135	146	157	168	180	191	202	213	224
76	82	87	92	98	103	109	120	131	141	152	163	174	185	196	207	218
74	79	84	90	95	100	105	116	126	137	148	158	169	179	190	200	211
72	77	82	87	92	97	102	113	123	133	143	154	164	174	184	195	205
70	75	80	84	89	94	99	109	119	129	139	149	159	169	179	189	199
68	72	77	82	87	92	96	106	116	126	135	145	155	164	174	184	193
66	70	75	80	85	89	94	103	113	122	132	141	150	160	169	179	188
64	69	73	78	82	87	92	101	110	119	128	137	147	156	165	174	183
62	67	71	76	80	85	89	98	107	116	125	134	143	152	161	170	178
61	65	70	74	78	83	87	96	104	113	122	131	139	148	157	165	174
59	64	68	72	76	81	85	93	102	110	119	127	136	144	153	161	170
58	62	66	70	75	79	83	91	99	108	116	124	133	141	149	157	166
57	61	65	69	73	77	81	89	97	105	113	121	129	138	146	154	162
55	59	63	67	71	75	79	87	95	103	111	119	127	134	142	150	158
54	58	62	66	70	73	77	85	93	101	108	116	124	131	139	147	155
53	57	61	64	68	72	76	83	91	98	106	113	121	129	136	144	151
52	56	59	63	67	70	74	81	89	96	104	111	118	126	133	141	148
51	54	58	62	65	69	73	80	87	94	102	109	116	123	131	138	145
50	53	57	60	64	67	71	78	85	92	99	107	114	121	128	135	142
49	52	56	59	63	66	70	77	84	90	97	104	111	118	125	132	139
48	51	55	58	61	65	68	75	82	89	96	102	109	116	123	130	136
47	50	54	57	60	64	67	74	80	87	94	100	107	114	120	127	134
46	49	53	56	59	62	66	72	79	85	92	98	105	112	118	125	131
45	48	52	55	58	61	64	71	77	84	90	97	103	110	116	122	129
44	47	51	54	57	60	63	70	76	82	89	95	101	108	114	120	127
43	47	50	53	56	59	62	68	75	81	87	93	99	106	112	118	124
43	46	49	52	55	58	61	67	73	79	85	92	98	104	110	116	122
42	45	48	51	54	57	60	66	72	78	84	90	96	102	108	114	120
41	44	47	50	53	56	59	65	71	77	83	88	94	100	106	112	118
41	44	46	49	52	55	58	64	70	75	81	87	93	99	104	110	116
40	43	46	48	51	54	57	63	68	74	80	86	91	97	103	108	114
39	42	45	48	51	53	56	62	67	73	79	84	90	95	101	107	112
39	41	44	47	50	52	55	61	66	72	77	83	88	94	99	105	110
38	41	44	46	49	52	54	60	65	71	76	82	87	92	98	103	109
37	40	43	46	48	51	54	59	64	70	75	80	86	91	96	102	107
36	39	41	44	46	49	52	57	62	67	72	77	82	88	93	98	103
35	37	40	42	45	47	50	55	60	65	70	75	80	85	89	94	99
34	36	38	41	43	46	48	53	58	62	67	72	77	82	86	91	96
32	35	37	39	42	44	46	51	56	60	65	70	74	79	84	88	93
31	34	36	38	40	43	45	49	54	58	63	67	72	76	81	85	90
30	33	35	37	40	41	44	48	52	57	61	65	70	74	78	83	87
30	32	34	36	38	40	42	46	51	55	59	63	67	72	76	80	84
29	31	33	35	37	39	41	45	49	53	57	61	66	70	74	78	82
29	30	32	34	36	38	40	44	48	52	56	60	64	68	72	76	80
27	29	31	33	35	37	39	43	46	50	54	58	62	66	70	73	77
26	28	30	32	34	36	38	41	45	49	53	56	60	64	68	71	75
26	27	29	31	33	35	37	40	44	48	51	55	59	62	66	70	73
25	27	29	30	32	34	36	39	43	46	50	54	57	61	64	68	71
24	26	28	30	31	33	35	38	42	45	49	52	56	59	63	66	70

Design The style, or design, of a surface is a process of constant decision-making which evolves from an initial concept. While the finished, printed, item may represent what appears to be a single and whole solution, it can only materialize as the result of making a constant string of decisions, usually spread over a protracted period of time. Even the most fastidious and accurate roughs will be subject to change during the evolution of a job.

Before any copy is sent for typesetting, the designer must first have determined the context which the job fits — whether the design is purely typographic or whether illustrations are also involved. The designer will need to determine the types of heading involved and to find a satisfactory way of displaying any required emphasis in the text, whether it be single words or complete paragraphs. There are several ways of achieving this; methods include capitalization, a change of size or weight, a change of fount, addition of colour, use of space or indentation, or any combination of these, although, of course, overemphasis may be counter-productive.

Naturally, the layout of text is determined by the number of lines that will fit within a page and this in turn is affected by the combination of type size and leading. The intended size, for instance, may be difficult to read when set solid (without space between lines), so additional line spacing may be added in the form of leading. This will result in reducing the number of lines on each page, which, in turn, will mean that more pages may be required in which to fit the text. It is also important to make allowances both aesthetically and

PROOF CORRECTION MARKS

Proofs that are being corrected should be marked up in the margin as well as in the text. This is because the printer always looks down the margin to see where the corrections occur. Proof correction marks are standard, but those shown (**below**) were only recently introduced. These are now being adopted although many people still use the old systems.

Instruction to printer	Textual mark	Marginal mark
Correction is concluded	None	/
Leave unchanged	typeface groups	✓
Remove unwanted marks	typeface groups	✗
Push down risen spacing material	typeface groups	⊥
Refer to appropriate authority	typeface groups	?
Insert new matter	⋏ groups	typeface ⋏
Insert additional matter	type ⋏ groups	⋏ Ⓐ
Delete	typeface groups	♂
Delete and close up	typeface groups	⊓
Substitute character or part of one or more words	typeface groups	y / groups /
Wrong fount, replace with correct fount	typeface groups	⊗
Correct damaged characters	typeface groups	✗

Instruction to printer	Textual mark	Marginal mark
Set in or change to italics	typeface groups	
Set in or change to capitals	typeface groups	
Set in or change to small capitals	typeface groups	
Capitals for initials small caps for rest of word	typeface groups	
Set in or change to bold type	typeface groups	
Set in or change to bold italic type	typeface groups	
Change capitals to lower case	typeFACE groups	
Change small capitals to lower case	typeFACE groups	
Change italic to roman	typeface groups	
Invert type	typeface groups	
Insert ligature	filmsetter	
Substitute separate letters for ligature	filmsetter	fi
Insert full point	typeface groups	
Insert colon	typeface groups	
Insert semi-colon	typeface groups	;
Insert comma	typeface groups	
Insert quotation marks	typeface groups	
Insert double quotation marks	typeface groups	
Substitute character in superior position	typeface groups	
Substitute character in inferior position	typeface groups	
Insert apostrophe	typeface groups	
Insert ellipsis	typeface groups	. . .
Insert leader dots	typeface groups	
Substitute or insert hyphen	typeface groups	
Insert rule	typeface groups	
Insert oblique	typeface groups	
Start new paragraph	are called set points. The dimension of	
No fresh paragraph, run on	are called set points. The dimension of	

Instruction to printer	Textual mark	Marginal mark
Transpose characters or word	groups typeface	
Transpose characters (2)	tpeyface groups	1 2 3
Transpose lines	The dimensions of / are called set points.	
Transpose lines (2)	2 The dimension of / 1 are called set points.	1 / 2
Centre type	[typeface groups]	[ ]
Indent 1 em	typeface groups	1 EM
Delete indent	typeface groups	
Set line justified	typeface groups	
Set column justified		
Move matter to right	typeface groups	
Move matter to left	typeface groups	
Take over to next line	typeface groups	t.o.
Take back to previous line	typeface groups	t.b.
Raise matter	typeface groups	
Lower matter	typeface groups	
Correct vertical alignment	typeface groups	||
Correct horizontal alignment	typeface groups	
Close up space	type face groups	
Insert space between words	typefacegroups	
Reduce space between words	typeface groups	
Reduce or insert space between letters	typeface groups	
Make space appear equal	typeface groups	
Close up to normal line spacing	(typeface) (groups)	( )
Insert space between paragraphs	are called set points. / The dimension of	7pt
Reduce space between paragraphs	are called set points. / The dimension of	
Insert parentheses or square brackets	typeface groups	(/) /
Figure or abbreviation to be spelt out in full	12 point / twelve pt.	spell out
Move matter to position indicated	are called The set points. / dimensional	

practically for the blank spaces that may appear as the result of editorial or typographical constraints, such as subheadings and paragraphing, since, as well as the possibility of appearing ugly, such spaces will inevitably increase the number of lines.

The number of typeset lines can be counted by using a typescale or better still, a depth scale, or line counter — which gives a much greater number of increments. When using such equipment, always measure from base line to base line of each line of type.

When illustrations are to be included in a design, the problems are multiplied. Illustrations are usually accompanied by a caption, which needs to be as close as possible to it. Conversely, the captions for a group of illustrations on a page may be placed together, in which case the pictures to which they refer must be clearly identified. There are a number of ways of doing this; the most common is to use 'directionals' such as 'above' or 'top left', or alternatively to use numbers. Another method is to use graphic devices, or 'ornaments', but care should be taken when using these because the result can easily look messy or ambiguous. Illustrations should also be placed as near as possible to the relevant passage of main text, whether captions are used or not.

It is also important, when incorporating illustrations, to achieve a degree of consistency in the layout so that illustrations are not only balanced with each other, but with the text.

Grids Almost all jobs which involve the integration of pictures with type should be designed on a purpose-made plan, or grid. The exceptions are those of the 'one-off' variety — those which involve few words or illustrations such as record covers and book jackets.

The purpose of a grid is two-fold; firstly, it ensures consistency, whether the job is a single broadsheet, whether it requires page turns or if it forms the basis of a series design such as product labels of a chain store. Secondly, it serves as a reference for all the various craftsmen involved in production.

The grid should show all the features common to all pages, such as column widths, text and illustration areas, positions of headings and folios (page numbers), trim size, folds, gutters, column depths, margins and so on. It is important that this information is as complete as possible, since designers, illustrators, photographers, editors and printers will all be working from it. The grid, however, should never be regarded as a straight-jacket; if an idea demands it, many of the dimensions can be ignored.

The way a printed grid is produced depends on the number of pages or folds involved and the type of printing process selected. Printed grids are common in large jobs — books for example — and their use helps minimize the amount of time required to prepare layouts; it also helps reduce any errors which might occur if each page was drawn up individually. Otherwise, pencil grids are adequate, but, in either case, accuracy is important.

The master drawing of the grid is best prepared on a transparent sheet, as this can then be used to check that originated proofs are the right size and that each double page spread has been made up correctly. This is done by simply laying the grid over a proof. It is best to draw the grid on a material that is robust, dimensionally stable and which accepts fine lines in ink readily. Polyester draughting film is one of the most suitable.

If the grid is printed, it is advisable to have two versions prepared — one on semi-transparent layout paper and the other on thin board. The first can be used for tracing-off illustrations and for making rough layouts. However, it should not be used for checking the size of illustrations as layout paper is dimensionally unstable. The second is for more accurate paste-up purposes, whether 'camera-ready' (for photographically converting into page film) or otherwise. Grids are best printed in pale blue ink as this is not sensitive to photographic reproduction. Always remember to check the grid itself for accuracy, as soon as it is returned from the printer, since inaccurately printed grids, however slight the error, cannot be used.

Layouts Having progressed through the preparatory stages, the designer can begin the task of assembling all the different elements — the photographs, artwork, text and so on, to be prepared for eventual printing.

This is done by drawing layouts — literally, laying out the various elements together on semi-transparent paper ('layout' or 'detail' paper). This serves two purposes; firstly, the designer can manipulate the images and type until a satisfactory result — both aesthetically and practically — is achieved. Secondly, it enables other people to carry out their part of the job, such as editors or authors who, once they know how much space is allocated and the position relative to the picture, can write captions.

Layouts can also be useful for the various people involved in production such as typesetters — especially if complicated setting is required — and origination houses, who sometimes need them for

Printed grids are an essential part of the design process, particularly in book and leaflet design. Their use helps to minimize the amount of time required to prepare drawings; it also helps to reduce the errors which might otherwise occur if every double page was to be drawn up separately. The basic grid should include all the essential elements around which the designer must work, the column depths and type widths and text and illustration areas to margins and the positions of folios. When all this information is combined in permanent form, it serves as reference both for the designer and the various craftsmen involved in production. Frequently, two forms of grid are printed. The master drawing is often made on to a transparent sheet; the subsequent transparent grids can be used for rough paste-up, for tracing off illustrations and for checking the size and positioning of illustration proofs. Polyester film is frequently used. Cardboard grids are used for final paste-up.

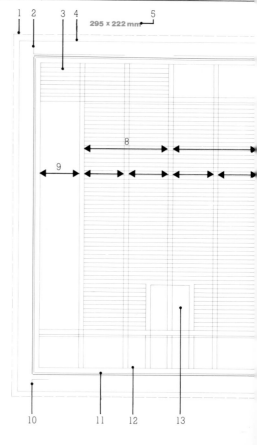

reference when making colour separations. Although layouts take the form of a working 'blue-print', which may contain much technical information, in many cases, particularly small jobs of a one-off nature, the layout may simply be a photocopy or duplicate of a presentation visual. All relevant instructions to artists and craftsmen can be added to the photocopy.

Layouts should contain as much information as possible. Headings should be written in (or drawn as a facsimile of the relevant typeface, so that the length can be assessed); areas of text and captions should be accurately indicated with their exact number of lines; and illustrations drawn in (with a code number which matches that on the artwork, photograph or transparency, whether it is to appear in full-colour, black-and-white or other colours, and to whom the credit is to be given). The page numbers, whether they are four-colour pages or otherwise and so on should also be given. Layouts should always be photocopied before they are sent out, and the originals should remain with the designer.

Layouts are frequently made before illustrations and, although less often, photographs, are commissioned. For this reason, layouts involving artwork should be drawn to a high level of accuracy, since the artist will need to know the *exact* dimensions of an illustration, especially if it is to occupy a free shape (one that has a loosely defined perimeter). If the illustration is to contain specific information, say of a technical nature, as in maps, charts and diagrams, the layout must be fully worked out — even to the extent

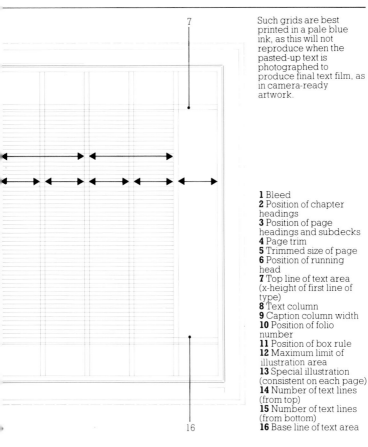

Such grids are best printed in a pale blue ink, as this will not reproduce when the pasted-up text is photographed to produce final text film, as in camera-ready artwork.

1 Bleed
2 Position of chapter headings
3 Position of page headings and subdecks
4 Page trim
5 Trimmed size of page
6 Position of running head
7 Top line of text area (x-height of first line of type)
8 Text column
9 Caption column width
10 Position of folio number
11 Position of box rule
12 Maximum limit of illustration area
13 Special illustration (consistent on each page)
14 Number of text lines (from top)
15 Number of text lines (from bottom)
16 Base line of text area

of writing in any labelling (annotation), so that the artist has a precise visual guide to what is required.

Selecting photographs The use and selection of photographs takes many forms, these being mainly determined by the requirements of the job in hand. For instance, a photograph for an advertisement may have been taken by referring to an accurate layout by the designer, in which case selection will be restricted to mostly technical considerations such as exposure, sharpness and colour. The photographer should always supply more than one alternative. On the other hand, photograph selection for an illustrated book may be from stock material supplied by picture libraries, which may range from the excellent to the barely discernible, and in which case the overall effect of a design will depend as much on aesthetic judgements as on technical ones.

Photographs exist in two forms: either as flat prints — whether colour or black-and-white — or as transparencies, which are always in colour. Although colour prints can be made to a very high quality, these are considered less suitable for reproduction purposes than transparencies. This is because light has to be reflected from a print, thereby losing its strength (it starts to become grey), whereas light is passed directly through a transparency, thus retaining its full strength and consequently, optimum colour saturation (the degree to which white, grey or black is eliminated.)

Photographers, to be on the safe side, usually supply bracketed shots — that is, photographs of the same subject, but shot using a variety of slightly different exposures and camera angles. It is important, therefore, to know which density will reproduce best, though the only real guide to this is experience. Generally, however, the picture that *looks* best invariably reproduces to a better standard, simply because the best looking picture is most likely to be the one at the correct exposure — the exposure which is at right level of density for reproduction. For instance, a red object photographed on a white background will give an exaggeratedly bright (fully saturated) and perhaps desirable red if slightly underexposed, but the background will reproduce as an undesirable grey. On the other hand, a slightly overexposed shot may give a perfect white background but with a slightly washed-out red subject.

Colour transparencies should be viewed on a colour-corrected light box, that is a light box which has had its light source balanced to give the correct type of light (colour temperature) required for viewing colour film.

Many photographers, particularly in situations where colour is of paramount importance, such as in the reproduction of fine art, will include in the transparency some sort of colour scale. This will be outside the area of the transparency to be used. This scale, called colour control patches, gives highly accurate reproductions of each of the three layers of film emulsion — cyan, magenta and yellow. In addition, there are patches of black and combinations of the three emulsion colours. These patches indicate any bias there may be in a transparency, whether as a result of the lighting conditions in which the picture was taken or because of natural fading of the transparency over a period of time. Apart from being useful during the processing of the film, colour control patches are helpful to colour origination houses when making separations.

Sometimes the designer is faced with the problem of having to produce a colourful result, but only having black-and-white photographs to use, particularly when the subject is of an historical nature. The way round this is, from the black-and-white original, to use combinations of colours from the four-colour process to produce duotones, tri-tones, three, two and one-colour tints and so on. This is done by the colour origination house. Use of four colours naturally means that the combinations of colour must fall within the limits of the process, and one of the most popular combinations is black plus one other colour.

Although not immediately apparent, good reproduction of black-and-white photographs can be difficult to achieve, so care must be taken in selecting a suitable original. In reproduction, the image is broken into tiny dots (see p82), so solid blacks lose their density, whereas lighter tones suffer from loss of detail and whites become grey. This means that the ideal black-and-white original is one that has maximum contrast from black to white and yet retains all the detail and subtle shades of the mid-tones — a result that is difficult to achieve.

Photographs and transparencies should be carefully checked with a magnifying glass for sharpness and for blemishes, such as scratches. Damaged pictures frequently need retouching and this is normally done by a specialized studio. If this is decided as necessary, and the picture is from a library or museum, permission must be obtained first, or a duplicate made. Retouching can be taken to greater extremes if portions of the photograph are considered undesirable or if alterations or substitutions are required.

Sizing pictures The first step when marking up pictures for reproduction is to determine which portion of the original, if any, needs to be cropped (excluded from the printed image), although, of course, the designer will already have a rough impression of this from the initial layout. This is done by a procedure known as scaling: first the picture area of the original is traced to square it up on a transparent overlay. Then the tracing is placed on top of the corresponding picture area on the layout, with one corner of each matching. Next, a diagonal line is drawn from this corner to the opposite corner of the picture area on the layout, the line being extended to meet an edge of the area of the original. Where the diagonal lines meets this edge is the corner of the final image, the remainder being cropped. The tracing, with the area to be cropped clearly marked, should be attached to the original picture and the dimensions of the image as it will finally appear should be added as well.

The next step is to calculate the reduction — or enlargement — percentage. This is because the dimension controls of reproduction cameras and scanners are calibrated in percentages, rather than sizes. However, it is still necessary to indicate linear dimensions because the edges of the image at its final size will have to be cleaned up, or masked. Same size reproduction is 100%, while pictures to be reduced in size are less than 100% and those to be enlarged are greater. For instance, a reduction in size from 60mm to 40mm would mean a reduction of 66%, while an enlargement from 40mm to 60mm gives an enlargement of 150%. Only one dimension each of the final size and of the original size, though of the same axis, is necessary to make this calculation. The mathematical formula for calculating the enlargement or reduction percentage is: (size of final image $\div$ size of original) x 100. Knowing the percentage of reduction or enlargement is also useful in that it is possible to group pictures of the same, or very similar, ratio together, thus saving money because they can be

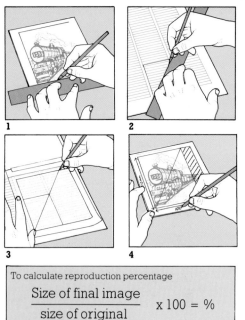

Picture fit must be specified before an illustration can be sent for separation. This involves first squaring up the picture area on a transparent overlay **(1)**. The designer takes the overlay and uses it to draw a diagonal line on the layout across the area the picture is intended to fill **(2)**. This shows how much of the picture area can be fitted into the alloted space **(3)**. The layout dimensions are marked on the overlay, plus, if appropriate, the area to be cropped **(4)**. This is shaded in. If the picture is to be increased or reduced in size, the percentage enlargement or reduction is calculated. Same size is 100 percent. Thus, a reduction in size from 60mm to 40mm square would mean a percentage reduction of 66 percent.

To calculate reproduction percentage

$$\frac{\text{Size of final image}}{\text{size of original}} \times 100 = \%$$

scanned at the same time.

It should also be specified on the overlay whether the image is to be squared up, cut out, or cut into another image. A squared-up image is one that sits on the page with its edges square, while a cut out picture is one that has a free shape, its background having been removed. With transparencies, it is best to select those in which a subject with a fairly simple outline is set against a white or pale background, otherwise the resulting image may have dark or messy edges. With black-and-white originals, unwanted areas should be painted out with process white paint. 'Cut into' means that a picture overlaps, or sits completely within, another. The origination house should be given very clear instructions, specifying which picture is to be cut into which, plus a layout showing their positions with all the dimensions marked.

Other essential information to include on the picture overlay is a code number. Each picture in a job should have its number recorded on the layouts. This is in case the origination house has any queries about a specific picture or needs to be given any special instructions, such as whether it is to appear as a duotone, or if a colour original is to be reproduced as a black-and-white. Origination houses always assume that if a colour original is supplied, then colour separation is required and, similarly, if black-and-white is supplied it is to appear as a black-and-white.

Preparing artwork If artwork to be reproduced is flat (with no additional 'bits' — usually overlays — to be incorporated) and in four-colour, the marking-up procedure is the same as that for transparencies. Complications arise however, if other elements are to be incorporated into the final image. These elements appear on the artwork in the form of overlays of draughting film taped over the base artwork. Registration marks are added to show how each overlay fits together with the base artwork, and type is pasted down and any lines drawn onto the film. Each separate overlay fulfills a different function; a map, for instance, with a base drawn in four-colour may have the following overlays:

1 Type and other line work to appear in black.
2 Type and other line work to reverse out of colour.
3 Type and line work to appear in cyan.
4 Type and line work to appear in magenta.
5 Areas to appear as cyan tint.
6 Areas to appear as magenta tint.

A map is an extreme example in that there could be almost any number of overlays, each one representing a different combination of line printings and almost limitless tint combinations. It is most common to have only one overlay on a four-colour piece of artwork, this being for type.

Black-and-white artwork can be made to appear in four-colour by the use of mechanical tints which are laid by the printer or origination house. These can be selected from a process colour tint chart (see p96-125) or alternatively, they can be specified as combinations of specially-mixed colours.

Areas to print as tints can be prepared in one of two ways. The first is to use one overlay with key lines defining each area to be tinted — in other words, only one overlay is required to show all the various colours. The second is to use a different overlay for each combination of tints, although this can get very cumbersome if many colours are to be used. The former, therefore, is more convenient but can be more expensive since it involves a considerable amount of hand-work (as opposed to photographic) by the lithographic planners — the people who lay tints in an origination house.

Colour correction Proofs can be returned for colour correction from the origination house in one of two forms and the designer should ask for whichever is preferred. Either the illustrations are proofed in the exact position that they will be in when finally printed, or they are proofed — at the correct size — in random

Cutting out an unwanted background is a frequently used design procedure. This is much easier to accomplish with a light background, since the image area can be more clearly defined than with a dark one. In this instance, it is important to shade out the areas that are not to reproduce, to define the outline of the figure. Dimensions should be clearly marked on the overlay.

order. The latter are called scatter proofs — they are much cheaper to produce than proofs in position as more can be included on a proofing plate.

The most crucial task is to check the colour closely against the original. If there is a discrepancy, ask the origination house to correct it. In order to know the extent to which colour can be corrected, it is important to understand how colour separation works (see p86). Any increase or decrease in the amount of colour is achieved not, as might be supposed, by altering the amount of ink on the plate (although further, but minor, corrections can be made by this method at the actual printing stage), but by enlarging or reducing the size of the halftone dots on the separation film. A colour is strengthened by reducing ('etching') the dot size on the *negative* film which, in turn, means that the dots are larger when converted to positive film. To reduce a colour, dots are etched on the *positive* film.

However, sometimes a proof has too much or too little of one colour which can only be accurately corrected by adjusting the proportions of one or two of the other colours. To increase the amount of magenta, say, it may be necessary to decrease the amount of cyan and possibly yellow.

There is a limit to which a dot size can be altered without having to reoriginate the subject. This limit is usually about 5%, although it may sometimes be possible to achieve a 10% variation. Because the dots are etched by a hand process (ferrocyanide applied with a brush), there comes a point when exaggerated corrections will begin to show on the proof — either as uneven patches or with defined edges to the etched portion. To see whether the proof has been incorrectly inked on the proofing press, check the colour control bar on the edge of the sheet (see p94).

Proofs should also be checked for register, blemishes, scratches, acid stains and broken screens. Use a magnifying glass to see whether the screen is damaged. If it has been, it may be necessary to remake the subject, although highly skilled retouchers can sometimes work wonders. A subject that is out of register is one that has two or more colours appearing 'out of sync' with the others, although the edges of the illustration are clean and in perfect register with each other. If the edges are also out of register, then the film has merely been incorrectly stripped together for proofing purposes and can easily be adjusted — though a further proof will be necessary.

Finally, it is vital to check that the pictures are the correct size, and that they are the right way round and not reversed. If the latter happens, the picture has to be 'flopped'. This is not just a simple case of turning the separated film upside down; a new contact film has to be made so that the emulsion is on the correct side of the film, depending on the platemaking process the printer uses. The emulsion, whether on negative or positive film, has to come into contact with the surface of the plate or block.

When marking corrections on proofs it is best to be as explicit as possible. If you do not know how to achieve the desired end result, tell the origination house what effect is required — they will know what needs to be done. Colour correction symbols are particularly useful if there is a language barrier as when the origination house is abroad, which is frequently the case.

Paste-up The stage at which proofs of type and pictures are assembled together on a page is called paste-up. This term usually refers to the final state of paste-up as given to the typesetter or printer, but it is preceded by a preliminary stage, or rough paste-up, in which galley proofs and picture proofs are assembled together on layout sheets so that everything can be checked for size before the final paste-up begins.

Final paste-up takes two forms, depending on what the typesetter or printer is contracted to supply. Many typesetting systems now incorporate a facility whereby the copy, having been keyed-in and issued with various typeface instructions, can be arranged in page position on a special screen and produced as page film from the typesetting machine. In such cases, the paste-up will consist of galleys and pictures pasted up accurately together on the same piece of board, with everything that is to appear in print — body text, captions, headlines, folios and rules — clearly marked up for any special requirements such as colour. The thicknesses and length of rules must be specified. Accuracy is obviously extremely important as anything positioned in the wrong place will appear wrongly positioned on the final film.

The other form of paste-up is that which is placed directly under the camera and photographed to produce final text film. This is called 'camera-ready' paste-up, or 'mechanicals'. With this method, only type and rules should appear, since if illustrations were incorporated onto the same surface, they would have to be masked out for final film to be made. The most expedient way of producing camera-ready paste-up is to paste the picture proofs onto the printed grid baseboard, with all type, rules and other matter to be photographed being positioned accurately on a draughting film overlay. Any areas to print as a tint should be marked clearly on the baseboard, whereas type or rules to print in a different colour should be marked on a tracing paper overlay, which also serves as a protective covering. Typesetting proofs used for camera-ready paste-up are generally called reproduction pulls (repro), but more specifically bromides or PMTs (for film or photo typesetting) and barytas (metal composition). Repro should not lift or curl at the corners, so it must be securely stuck with an adhesive that is reliable, but also one that permits the designer to remove or reposition it without damage. There are several proprietary brands of spray adhesive and rubber solutions suitable for this purpose. Small pieces of repro — such as individual words — can be secured with double-sided adhesive tape, but this is difficult to remove.

Printing The next stage is for the text film to be matched with the illustration film. This can be done by the typesetter, origination house or printer, depending on how film is supplied or who has been contracted to do the job. For instance, the typesetter will produce final page film of the text — working from the designer's paste-up — and receive illustration film from the origination house. The two are assembled together. The origination house, on the other hand, may have made film separations in page position and will then receive either page film from the typesetter or camera-ready paste-up from the designer. The process of assembling film in page position is usually called 'stripping'. Each individual piece of illustration film is stripped in position onto a much larger support film. This will eventually be photographically converted by way of a contact print into a single, flat piece of final film.

Before final film is made, a proof is made from the stripped-together film. This proof is called a dyeline or ozalid. It is sometimes referred to as a 'blueprint' because of its blue colour. Text and illustration can now be seen together, in the positions that they will be printed. This is the last stage at which any corrections can reasonably be made. Once the printing plates have been made, making corrections is a costly process. In some cases, especially in commercial work, pages are proofed up after the ozalid stage and before machine plates are made.

The main purpose of the blueprint is to serve as a positional check for the designer, since illustrations can easily be repositioned even at this stage as they are individually taped to the carrier film. Textual changes can also be made, although the printer will have to cut up the film manually to position new type — or reposition old. The ozalid should also be read to ensure that the film is free from marks and that no broken type needs to be repaired. Ozalids of four-colour jobs will usually only consist of film of the black printer plus illustration film of one — or occasionally two — of the other colours.

After the return of the ozalids, final, 'clean' film is produced and this is used to make plates. Any machine proofs after the ozalid stage are checked to see that each piece of colour film has been correctly assembled, the alterations carried out and that the film has not been damaged prior to platemaking.

Ideally, when printing starts, the designer should be there to view the illustrations, particularly if colour is involved. Even at this stage, colour can be corrected through manual alteration of the inking process. This is done by regulating the ducts which control the amount of ink passing from the ink reservoirs onto the rollers and thence the plates. Colour can only be corrected in strips parallel to the direction the sheets of paper come off the machine, and great care must be exercised to make sure that, by adjusting the colour on one section of the sheet, the balance of colour in another part is not upset, especially where two halves of the same illustration appear in opposite corners of the sheet (see Imposition, p135). In any case, the printer will be on hand to offer advice although, once the running sheets have been adjusted and pasted, more formal approval will be required, usually the designer's signature on the printed sheet. This is quite normal, and while it absolves the printer from any recriminations by a dissatisfied customer, it puts all the responsibility firmly and squarely on the designer's shoulders. An added difficulty for the designer is that any decision about whether colour needs adjusting must be made almost instantly; presses print extremely quickly and stopping one is very expensive. The production of a book varies according to its type and how it is to be printed. For instance, producing a book that consists entirely of text — such as a novel — is relatively simple.However, the moment pictures are introduced, the procedure becomes much more complicated. The most difficult type of book to produce is probably an illustrated reference book but there are quite a few procedures that are applicable to all book production.

Also, in addition to the basic printing features already described, book production has added features of its own.

Book production One of these is at the earliest stage, where, as opposed to the rough, the design concept is normally presented in the form of a dummy book, or 'bulking' dummy. A blank book is ordered from the printer to show its proposed size, bulk (the thickness determined by the number of pages and the quality of paper) and binding. Inside this, a number of dummy pages are pasted, and these can either be 'live' (with real type and artwork), make-believe, or a mixture of the two — real pictures with dummy text, for instance. In any case, these pages should show the style and level of the projected contents, such as the proportion of illustration to text.

Depending on the scale of the project, presentation spreads (two pages together) are sometimes made by preparing flat sheets mounted on board and protected by transparent acetate film to accompany the bulking dummy. Again, these can be dummy, live or a mixture.

A book can be the most complex job a designer has to put together — especially if it contains a large number of pages or if it involves distribution of full-colour, two-colour and black-and-white pages — so it must be carefully planned in advance. This is done by drawing up a flat plan, showing the chapter breakdown, number of pages devoted to the end matter and preliminary pages, where colour pages fall, and so on. The most complex flat plans are called flow charts, and these serve as a visual contents list, giving an idea of what will appear on every page of the book. Flat plans consist of pages drawn in miniature, showing text and illustration on every page, and they are often used more for sales rather than editorial purposes.

Binding and budgetary considerations also have to be taken into account, especially when planning the colour distribution. If a book is to be bound in 16-page sections, the designer has to work in multiples of 16. That is, each block of 16 pages must be consistent within itself — either four-colour throughout ('four backed four'), or four-colour spreads alternating with two- or one-colour spreads 'four backed two', 'four backed one'). It may be the case that, while a book is to be bound in 16s, it will be printed on sheets of 32 pages — 16 on one side and 16 on the other ('16 to view') — in which case each block of 16 pages of one treatment must be matched by an identical block of 16 elsewhere in the book. It does not matter if those blocks are not consecutive since the sheets can be cut ('slit') after they are printed. It is possible to divide a 16-page section in two — say eight pages of four-colour followed by eight pages of one-colour. In this instance, the printer uses a procedure known as 'work and turn', whereby both sides of the 16 pages appear on one plate which is used to print both sides of the sheet, thus printing two copies on one sheet.

Book jackets The design of a book jacket is often thought just as important to the publisher as the inside of the book, because it not only has to convey its quality and content instantly to the prospective buyer, but also has to project this information boldly from the midst of a vast array of books on what may well be the same subject. The section of jacket designs is usually made by several people comprising the sales, marketing, editorial and managing aspects of a publishing house. In many instances the final decision will be compromise since a combination of opinions tend to rule out intuitive judgements. For this reason, it is a mistake for the designer to consider a book jacket merely as a design exercise. It is not. Certainly, the designer always starts with the premise that the solution that looks aesthetically pleasing is the one most likely to appeal to the prospective buyer, but what may appeal to the designer may not appeal to the market at which the book is directed, and vice versa.

Market research is rarely, if ever, carried out on a book or book jacket prior to its publication, and any reasons a publisher may have for preferring one jacket design over another is very often based on precedent — if particular types of jacket have worked

1	2	3	4	5	6	7	8	9	10	11	12	13	14	15	16
17	18	19	20	21	22	23	24	25	26	27	28	29	30	31	32
33	34	35	36	37	38	39	40	41	42	43	44	45	46	47	48
49	50	51	52	53	54	55	56	57	58	59	60	61	62	63	64
65	66	67	68	69	70	71	72	73	74	75	76	77	78	79	80
81	82	83	84	85	86	87	88	89	90	91	92	93	94	95	96
97	98	99	100	101	102	103	104	015	106	107	108	109	110	111	112
113	114	115	116	117	118	119	120	121	122	123	124	125	126	127	128

1

1	2	3	4	5	6	7	8	9	10	11	12	13	14	15	16	A
17	18	19	20	21	22	23	24	25	26	27	28	29	30	31	32	B
33	34	35	36	37	38	39	40	41	42	43	44	45	46	47	48	B
49	50	51	52	53	54	55	56	57	58	59	60	61	62	63	64	C
65	66	67	68	69	70	71	72	73	74	75	76	77	78	79	80	C
81	82	83	84	85	86	87	88	89	90	91	92	93	94	95	96	A
97	98	99	100	101	102	103	104	105	106	107	108	109	110	111	112	D
113	114	115	116	117	118	119	120	121	122	123	124	125	126	127	128	D

2

One colour Two colours Four colours

1	2	3	4	5	6	7	8	9	10	11	12	13	14	15	16
17	18	19	20	21	22	23	24	25	26	27	28	29	30	31	32
33	34	35	36	37	38	39	40	41	42	43	44	45	46	47	48
49	50	51	52	53	54	55	56	57	58	59	60	61	62	63	64
65	66	67	68	69	70	71	72	73	74	75	76	77	78	79	80
81	82	83	84	85	86	87	88	89	90	91	92	93	94	95	96
97	98	99	100	101	102	103	104	105	106	107	108	109	110	111	112
113	114	115	116	117	118	119	120	121	122	123	124	125	126	127	128

3

4

Wraps   Inserts   Wraps

5

A flat plan is essential whenever printing in more than one colour combination. The plan ensures the combination works in terms of the number of pages to be printed in two passes through the press. The first three examples show a 128-page job, using four sheets of paper with 64 pages printing on each sheet. The pages are arranged in 16-page strips, since they will be bound in 16-page sections, or signatures. When planning the colour fall on a book specified to print in four-colour and 64 pages of single-colour, the simplest method of achieving even distribution throughout

the book is to arrange the colour so that one side of the sheet prints in four-colour and the other in one-colour. The result is that every alternate double-page spread is in four-colour (1). The distribution can be varied by, say, arranging four-colour to be printed in two blocks of 16 pages — 32 pages in each block — to make up the 64 pages available. These 32-page blocks can be located anywhere in the job, provided that each 16-page section matches up with another 16-page section, so that 32 pages always print complete (2). Another possible variation is 48 pages of four-colour, 32 pages of two-colour and 48 pages

of one-colour, remembering, again, to work in matching 16-page sections (3). The basic determining factor is the number of pages on each side of the sheet — this book was printed 24 pages to view — and the binding requirements (4). Wraps and inserts are used when colour is less evenly distributed than in the other examples show here. Here, a 160-page job is printing as 128 pages of single colour and the separate insert of 32 pages of four-colour can be wrapped around, or inserted into, each section in blocks of four pages. Wraps and inserts are frequently inserted when the sheets are folded and gathered.

Paper bulk (after binding)	8	10	11	12	14	16	17	19	22mm
Spine width (with 3mm boards)	14	17	19	19	21	22	24	27	30mm

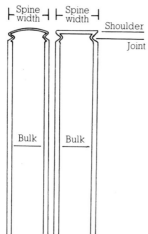

When designing a book jacket, it is always preferable to work from an accurate bulking dummy to establish the spine width. This is because the paper bulks less when bound and, unless this is taken into consideration, the jacket will not fit properly. The thickness of the boards must also be taken into account. On book jackets, flaps should not be forgotten; they should normally be about 75mm wide. The most accurate way of assessing the size of jacket is to wrap paper around a bulking dummy and mark off where it folds round the foredges and spine of the case. It is essential that the dummy is made to the exact specification of the intended book, so check that the trim size, the number of pages, the thickness of the boards and the weight of the paper are all correct.

for a particular audience in the past, then further designs on that subject are likely to fall within those parameters already known. These precedents will often extend to such things as preference for one colour over another, and even these preferences will vary from publisher to publisher — for instance, one may have had considerable success with predominantly black jackets, while another may not.

Individual taste is another important factor in book jacket design whether it is based on precedent or not. A designer who is familiar with the likes and dislikes of the personalities involved in decision-making is more likely to find a design accepted.

As with most design jobs, the level to which a rough jacket design is drawn depends largely on the criteria for making final decisions — an inhouse designer, for instance, may only have to satisfy an art director, in which case a fairly rudimentary visual, showing the intent rather than the final effect, will suffice. In any other circumstances, however, the only way to put across the total impact of a design is to present a full-scale mock-up, complete with actual photographs or illustrations and type, covered with self-adhesive film laminate to give the impression of proper lamination, and wrapped around a bulking dummy.

Magazine design Editorial procedures in magazine production roughly parallel those of book production although on a much larger labour-intensive scale, depending on the frequency of the publication. Magazines are put together as a result of constant discussion between the editor, art editor and picture editor as well as various feature editors and staff writers. The largest single influence on the number of editorial pages available is that of the number of advertisements sold in any one issue, since most magazines rely on advertising for their profit.

Having decided what is to go into an issue, the pictures are obtained first, since most magazine features cannot be laid out without the pictures. Two or three main features will then be assembled as layouts and if any of them are disliked they are discarded at this stage. More features are prepared than are actually needed for a single issue just in case any are rejected. Those that are acceptable may be held over for a subsequent issue. Magazines usually rely heavily on picture libraries for main features such as sporting events, and also for back-up material. Many articles will require specially commissioned photography. If this is to be done in a studio, the designer should try to be present at the shoot.

The method used for printing a magazine is a major factor in determining its design limitations, as is, of course, the market at which the magazine is aimed. If, for instance, a magazine is printed by offset lithography, roughly the same principles and limitations apply as those of book production. On the other hand, magazines printed by gravure require special considerations; design for gravure-printed magazines needs to be much bolder than for litho not least because everything — including type — is screened. This means that more delicate designs may start to break up or even disappear entirely. Also, subtle detail in pictures is much more difficult to control in gravure printing, while very deep blacks can be achieved, any detail in dark areas will disappear. Even the degree of blackness in a picture can be somewhat variable — the result is just as likely to be very thin as it is to be very black. These technical limitations thus affect the size at which a picture can be satisfactorily reproduced, whereas an image to be reproduced by litho can retain a certain amount of detail at sizes of one inch or even less. Two or three inches is probably the smallest size that gravure can handle before the readability of an image becomes difficult. It is interesting that although the results achieved by gravure-printed magazines can be somewhat unpredictable, postage stamps — which require the highest standards of technical reproduction — are also printed by the gravure process, but at much slower speeds and on equipment that can produce much greater technical tolerance.

The reasons for using one printing method as opposed to the other rests solely with the quantity of magazines to be printed. While the quality of offset litho is much higher than that of gravure, litho plates will generally only print up to about 1000,000 copies before the image quality becomes unacceptable and the plates need to be remade, whereas gravure cylinders can print an almost limitless number. Some weekly magazines may be printing up to about four or five million copies.

Speed is another important factor when deciding which printing process to use — gravure machines run at much faster speeds than web offset. It is becoming increasingly common for some magazines to be printed by a mixture of gravure and litho, the latter normally being used for regional inserts. This enables advertisers to aim at selective, localized markets, without having to pay the considerably higher rates for national coverage.

Having obtained the material for a feature, the designer sets about making a rough scheme of the layout. The pictures are sized up and printed on black-and-white document paper straight from the transparency. Areas of type are indicated by using cut up text from previously printed issues; this is so that everyone working on the magazine knows exactly where the type is going to be and how much is required. Colour images are normally sent down to the printer about six weeks before the magazine is due to appear, the deadline for monochrome pictures being about four weeks before publication. It is possible for last-minute features — on a current, topical theme for instance — to be put together within two or three hours and sent to the printer as late as one week before publication, but if it can be avoided this rarely happens due to cost of printers' overtime.

The fall of colour pages throughout a magazine is determined by the printer in consultation with the production editor, but this is never so rigid that the designer is not permitted to make last minute changes provided, of course, that this does not affect the location of advertisements — the main criterion in deciding colour imposition.

One or two days after the colour has been sent off, the text copy is marked up and headlines are specified. These are then typeset, assembled in position with the colour pictures by the printer and returned as black-and-white photoprinted page proofs. At this stage the position of colour pictures cannot be changed, but alterations can be made to the type. Correction marks are then made on the proofs and sent back to the printer, who makes the corrections and returns them. These latest proofs are called 'as to press' and it

Right These symbols are widely used to mark corrections on proofs. Always write instructions neatly and make any expansion to the marks clear (**below**). A subject marked for reproofing (**2**) normally requires reorigination unless the whole sheet is unacceptable. Detail and modelling (**5**) refers to highlights and details that need enhancing. Hardness (**6, 7**) refers to subjects where edges of colour, shape or tone are too hard or too soft. An out-of-register subject (**10**) is one in which the film for each colour has been wrongly stripped. Its edges should be in register; if they are not, the film was positioned incorrectly on the plate. Slur (**11**) is a proofing defect which enlongates halftone dots. **Far right** These proofs of the same subject show some of the things that can go wrong.

Instruction	Marginal mark
1 Passed for press	
2 Reproof	
3 Reduce contrast	
4 Increase contrast	
5 Improve detail or modelling	
6 Too hard, make softer	
7 Too soft, make sharper	
8 Rectify uneven tint	
9 Repair broken type, rule or tint	
10 Improve register	
11 Correct slur	

Process colour	Increase	Reduce
Yellow	Y +	Y −
Magenta	M +	M −
Cyan	C +	C −
Black	B +	B −

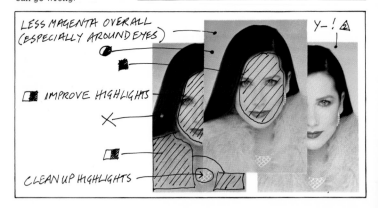

LESS MAGENTA OVERALL (ESPECIALLY AROUND EYES)

Y − !

IMPROVE HIGHLIGHTS

CLEAN UP HIGHLIGHTS

is extremely difficult to make any changes at all at this stage.

The as-to-press proofs are returned to the printer who then makes colour proofs of the pages — but without any type appearing unless it is to be in colour. These colour proofs do not contain any monochrome pictures either — the next time they are seen is on 'running' copies (the actual printed copies of the magazine).

The proofs are then colour corrected and, when all the corrections have been done, the gravure cylinders are put onto machine and printing commences. Once the magazine is being run (printed), it is very difficult to make last minute colour adjustments — not because of technical difficulties, but because any adjustment may affect the colour of an advertisement. Since it is the advertisers who provide the financial backing for producing most magazines, they must be satisfied with the quality of their advertisements. If they are unhappy with results, advertisers simply will not pay the bills, even though they will already have had the opportunity to reject any unsatisfactory proofs.

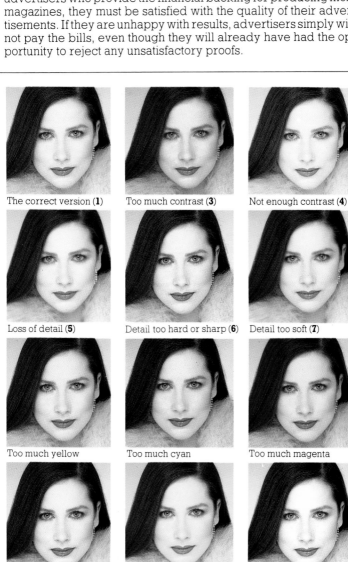

The correct version (**1**) Too much contrast (**3**) Not enough contrast (**4**)

Loss of detail (**5**) Detail too hard or sharp (**6**) Detail too soft (**7**)

Too much yellow Too much cyan Too much magenta

Too little yellow Too little cyan Too little magenta

4
PHOTOGRAPHY AND DESIGN

Photography for reproduction/
Black-and-white film/Colour film/
Film speeds/Film formats/Lenses/
Lighting/Studio effects/Prints from
transparencies

After typography, photography is perhaps the next most important and widely used element in graphic design, and the designer's involvement with it takes many forms. For instance, a photographer will often be working from layouts produced by the designer, and if the job in question is particularly complex the designer's presence may be required at the shooting session. This is necessary because instant decisions may be needed concerning changes if the actual photograph will not fit the layout. In such cases, it is the designer who controls the compromises needed to convert the initial concept to the finished picture.

The other extreme is when the designer's job is simply one of selecting pictures from a mass of stock material. This frequently involves considerable compromises when the layout must be manipulated to fit the picture, taking into account that uncommissioned photography can range from the superb to the unacceptable.

For design purposes, photographs are used either to provide an illustrated record or to add to or enhance an editorial or promotional concept. Success is achieved in the first case by the photographer's skill in recording a sharply-defined, evenly-lit and correctly exposed image. Secondly, success depends upon close communication between photographer and designer and, in particular, upon the designer's understanding of the way in which photography and photographic reproduction work.

Photography for reproduction Among the many qualities that photographs to be used in design work should have, the most important is what is termed the reproduction ratio. In theory, a photographic original can be enlarged to a huge extent and yet remain intelligible — for instance, on a cinema screen a 35mm format is enlarged by more than 30,000%. In the context of a printed page, however, the same original would begin to look blurred and weak in colour at an enlargement of only 1000%. The typical enlargement ratio for a 35mm transparency ranges between 100% (same size) and 1500%. At an enlargement of 1000% a 35mm transparency would cover this entire spread, while a 5 x 4in would require 247% enlargement, and a 10 x 8in would be slightly larger than same size at 112%. Since the grain size of film of a particular type and speed is the same regardless of format, larger sizes of transparency produce a clearer definition when reproduced.

Black-and-white film All general-purpose black-and-white camera films are panchromatic; they react to all colours in the visible spectrum though not to quite the same degree in each case Although this wide range of sensitivity is generally considered desirable, in certain cases the use of filters may be necessary in order to distinguish certain colours more clearly from the surrounding colours, or even to eliminate one completely. A yellow filter, for instance, will enhance the appearance of white clouds in a clear blue sky by reducing the amount of blue light reaching the film. Consequently, the sky area appears darker on the resulting print, producing a greater contrast with the white clouds. Alternatively, coloured stains on a document can be weakened or eliminated in a photographic copy by the use of a suitable filter, such as a filter of the same colour as the stain.

Colour film Reversal ('slide' or 'transparency') and negative films both contain three layers of light-sensitive emulsion — a blue-sensitive layer forming a yellow dye, green-sensitive forming magenta and red-sensitive forming cyan. Most colours, with the

35mm | **2¼square** | **5 x 4**

561%

367%

159%

640%

556%

254%

1200%

737%

333%

Most design work calls for the enlargement of photographs, so take into account what effect this will have on the qualities of the original pictures. The greater the enlargement, the more detail that will be lost and the more grainy the printed image. The strips here show the same image photographed in different formats — 35mm, 2¼in square and 5 x 4 — and the effects of varying degrees of enlargement. It is clear that the larger the original format, the more it can be enlarged, while preserving clarity and detail.

All designers should have a basic understanding of the nature of black-and-white film and how it works when faced with the problem of recording colour. When black-and-white film is used in this way, there are obvious anomalies in the way the various types react. The graph (**below**) shows some of these variations by contrasting the colour sensitivity of film to that of the human eye. Although the eye reacts most strongly to green, for instance, film, in comparison, over-reacts to the blue end of the colour spectrum. Orthochromatic film does not respond at all to red, as the graph shows, while modern panchromatic film covers the full range of visual colours. This point is emphasized in the bar diagram (**bottom**), where the response of various black-and-white films to colour is clearly demonstrated. Again, panchromatic is on the whole the most faithful. The chart (**right**) details some of the major black-and-white film types available today. Special films like Agfacontour are intended for darkroom use.

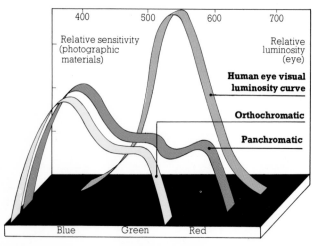

400   500   600   700

Relative sensitivity (photographic materials)

Relative luminosity (eye)

Human eye visual luminosity curve

Orthochromatic

Panchromatic

Blue   Green   Red

Colour   **Panchromatic**   **Orthochromatic**

Black-and-white film	Speed (ASA)	Sensi-tivity	35mm	Roll	Sheet	Comments
Normal Contrast						
Adox KB17	40	0	●			100ft rolls
Ilford Pan F	50	P	●			
Kodak Panatomic X	32	P	●	●		
Adox KB21	100	P	●			100ft rolls
Agfapan 100	100	P	●	●	●	
Ilford FP4	125	P	●	●	●	
Kodak Plus X	125	P	●	●	●	
Agfapan 400	400	P	●	●	●	
Ilford HP5	400	P	●	●	●	
Ilford XP1	variable	P	●			Final image in dye
Kodak Tri X	400	P	●	●		
Kodak Recording 2475	1000	P	●			
Kodak Royal X Pan	1250	P		●		
Kodak Prof Copy	25	0			●	Available USA only
Kodak Gravure Pos	20	0			●	
Agfapan Vario-XL Prof	variable	P	●			Final image in dye
High contrast						
Kodalith type 3	12	0	●		●	35 mm in bulk rolls
Kodalith Pan	40	P			●	
Specials						
Agfacontour		0			●	Special effects
Afga Dia-direct	100	P	●			Reversal slide film

0 = Orthochromatic   P = Panchromatic

Grade 0

Grade 1

Grade 2

Grade 3

Grade 4

Grade 5

When ordering black-and-white prints, it is vital to specify the paper they are to be printed on, since each paper has its own particular characteristics. The prints here show the effects of printing on

Grade 0 paper (**top left**) through to Grade 5 paper (**bottom right**), 0 is very flat and intended for use with high-contrast negatives; 5, on the other hand, is extremely hard and is used with soft negatives. The softer the

grade, the greater the amount of detail. While the hard grades make full use of the paper's tonal range, they produce harsh images with no detail at either end of the scale.

Any designer commissioning black-and-white photography should be aware of the importance of filters and the effects they can have on photographs. The shot in colour was re-photographed without a filter, with a yellow filter, a blue filter and a red filter to make this point.

No filter

Yellow filter

Blue filter

Red filter

Black-and-white photography relies on filters to create the necessary contrast. In colour (**right**), the tomato contrasts clearly with the lettuce. In the black-and-white print (**below left**), a red filter allowed red light to pass to the negative, while green light was blocked. Thus, the tomato prints lighter and the lettuce darker. With a green filter (**below right**), this is reversed.

exception of fluorescent ones, can be produced by combinations of the final processed dye layers. It is important that the correct type of colour film is used for the conditions in which the shot is being taken, such as 'daylight' and 'artificial' light types.

All reversal film types are fundamentally the same, but substantive varieties such as Ektachrome can be processed by the user. Non-substantive films such as Kodachrome — which is usually sold process-paid — require special treatment and so they have to be returned to the manufacturer for processing.

The capabilities of the two types of film are more or less the same, except that because it cannot be specially developed, non-substantive film is of no use if circumstances dictate that the film must be uprated ('pushed') to a faster speed. This can, however, be achieved with substantive films during the developing process, although this is not altogether desirable, since pushed film will result in a loss of picture quality with increased graininess and contrast, as well as degraded colour rendering.

Because the manufacture of reversal colour film is such an exacting process, the reaction of films from different prodution batches to the same subject may not be identical. For this reason, film boxes are stamped with the batch code and expiry date so that films required for the same shooting session can be matched together.

Negative colour film is generally only used to produce prints for presentation purposes such as in dummy packs or books. Negative duplicating film is used to make master originals in the mass-production of transparencies for audio-visual use.

Film-speeds The speed of a particular film depends on the size of the grains of silver in their chemical structure — the larger the grains the faster the film. One of the fundamental rules when either black-and-white or colour film is used is that an increase in film speed inevitably leads to a loss of quality in the final image, although modern film technology is reducing the differences between quality of films of different speeds. The speed of a particular film can usually be recognized by the rating given to it by the American Standards Association, thus the term 'ASA'. German 'DIN' (Deutsche Industrie Norm) is also used, but both this and ASA are being gradually replaced by ISO (International Standards Organization). Camera films range in speed from 32ASA to 1250ASA, although this upper limit can be extended to about 3000ASA by forced development.

The choice of film speed is influenced not only by the amount of light available but also by the subject, the context and degree of enlargement in reproduction and the chosen format. In addition, some purely mechanical factors must be taken into consideration such as the distance from the camera the subject comes into, and goes out of, focus. The limits within which the portion of the photograph remains in focus is called depth of field, and this can be regulated by the size of aperture in the camera lens through which the light passes. The smaller the aperture ('stop', shown on the lens control as an 'f' number), the greater the depth of field.

If a greater depth of field is required, the lens aperture can be stopped down (on 35mm cameras the lens f-numbers normally range from f1.2, the largest, to f32, the smallest — depending on its focal length), but because the same amount of light must reach the film in order to make a perfect exposure, the camera shutter must be set at a slower speed. At slower speeds, subject or camera movement, or both, may degrade the image. Alternatively, a

Though photographers argue that there is little difference between the results produced by different colour films, the enlargements here clearly show the difference. This knowledge is particularly important to the designer, who will be frequently asking for original prints and transparencies to be enlarged. The Kodachrome 25 transparency remains clear and sharp; there is virtually no graininess. The colours are well-saturated, the reds and yellows being particularly true to life. The Ektrachrome 400 transparency is flatter and more grainy by comparison, with poorer colour saturation. This is partly caused by its extra speed. In addition, it is slightly bluer overall, which makes it more suitable for photographing tungsten-lit night scenes. The test strips (**right**) show the colour qualities of various reversal films. The two Kodachrome examples differ from the others in that the colour dyes are added during processing. This reduces graininess. In general, the basic rule is the faster the film, the more grainy the result.

Ektachrome 400

Kodachrome 25

Kodachrome 25

Kodachrome 64

Ektachrome 200

Ektachrome 64

Agfa CT18

Ektachrome 400

Fujichrome 100

Agfa CT21

3M 400

Fujichrome 400

1/30sec f4 = +3 stops

1/30sec f16 = −1 stop

1/30sec f5.6 = +2 stops

1/30sec f22 = −2 stops

1/30sec f8 = +1 stop

1/30sec f22 = −3 stops

1/30sec f11 = Through-the-lens reading

1/30sec f22 = −4 stops

It is important when directing photography to realize that colour film inevitably reacts to different quantities of light and that there are strict exposure latitudes. Time wasted on location, for instance, means more expense if the results have to be re-shot and the delay may jeopardize schedules. The examples here show how a strip of Kodachrome 64 produced very different results when the exposure was deliberately varied from the through-the-lens reading of an exposure of 1/30sec at f11 (**bottom left**). As the number of stops was increased from +1 to +3, the picture changed noticeably. An extra stop made the sky less intense and gave it a slight green tinge. Two stops bleached large areas of highlights to white, while three stops produced a totally over-exposed result. There are virtually no hues, while almost all detail is lost. The shots in the righthand column show the effects of decreasing exposure from −1 stop (**top**) to −4 stops (**bottom**). As the exposure is progressively reduced, the more features disappear from the shadow areas. From the designer's point of view, underexposure is usually preferable to overexposure, since, though the choice is subjective, under-exposure is generally more acceptable.

faster film can be used, thus permitting a faster shutter speed, but the resulting increase in grain size may prove unacceptable.

Changing to a lens of shorter focal length such as a 28mm (wide-angle) lens will give a greater depth of field than a standard 50mm lens set at the same aperture, but it will also reduce the size of the subject within the film frame. Moving closer to the subject with the wide-angle lens to make it large enough may result in an undesirable exaggerated perspective because of the change in viewpoint. A smaller lens aperture would be possible if the subject could be lit with brighter lighting, but this may be difficult to achieve except in a large studio. Similar, and generally more complex, problems usually face the photographer in all but the simplest commissions.

Film formats Apart from jobs which require the photographer to have mobility — travel and reportage photography for instance where the norm is 35mm — the choice of format is usually a compromise between cost and definition. The larger the format, the more expensive photography becomes — in terms of equipment, film, processing, lighting and studio space required, and sometimes the photographer's fees. However, it is important to remember that, to achieve the highest quality, the format must match the printed application wherever possible.

35mm The most widely used format is the 35mm system, especially the single-lens reflex,which produces a frame size of 24 x 36mm. This system is far more flexible than any other and is often used in preference to the others even when considerable enlargement is required. The photographer is thus able to work at high speed if necessary, and because a wide range of film emulsion is available at a relatively low cost, a high degree of experimentation and intensive subject coverage is possible. The motor-drive of the 35mm camera — firing the shutter and moving the film forward at up to five frames per second — means that a photographer can snatch the opportunity of a completely fortuitous shot with comparative ease without having to judge the right moment.

Finished transparencies must be handled with great care so that they are prevented from being damaged. Individual frames, whether mounted or unmounted, should be sealed in transparent sleeves. The mounts themselves should be of a type which permits easy removal of the transparency as the scanning method of colour separation requires that transparencies be removed from their mounts. Glass mounts are intended for projection only and are unsuitable since they break easily and could well damage the transparency.

The 120 system Cameras using 120 and 220 rollfilm fall into three groups: the twin-lens reflex types such as Mamiyaflex and Rollei and the single-lens reflex such as the Hasselblad. Both these types produce 2¼ x 2¼ in (60 x 60mm) images, but the advantages of this square format are not fully realized in reproduction since most designs seem to call for rectangular shapes. This is where the third group of the 120 system — the single-lens reflex such as the large format Pentax and Mamiya RB67 — comes into its own. Two frame sizes are produced. The first, the so-called 'ideal format', measures 60 x 45mm, and the other, larger size is 60 x 70mm. Both these formats are becoming increasingly popular.

Larger formats Because studio conditions can be controlled with powerful lighting equipment, and cameras can be mounted in fixed positions, large film formats are used so that the highest standards of reproduction can be achieved. Of the several available, three formats are particularly popular: 5 x 4in, 7 x 5in and 10 x 8in.

The film is supplied in packs of single sheets — hence the name 'sheet-film' — which is loaded into a double-sided, light-tight holder as required. This holder, or 'dark slide', displaces the camera's focusing screen when the desired composition has been made, and a movable sheath is slid back ready for the film to be exposed to the light when the camera shutter is opened. A Polaroid film holder can also be fitted to allow a preview of the finished photograph. The photographer will normally have one sheet of film processed before the final shot is taken or, alternatively, two or three sheets of different exposures will be processed before the set is dismantled.

Cameras using large film formats are very versatile and image shapes can be manipulated by using the built-in movements of lens and film planes. Use of these formats also allows a scaled drawing of the required design on tracing paper to be taped directly onto the focusing screen as a final compositional check.

Lenses The 'normal' lens for any particular format is that which is the nearest to normal human vision. A photographic image is totally unlike one perceived by the eye — not surprisingly as a camera only has one lens, but people have two eyes thus enabling surroundings to be perceived in three dimensions as opposed to the two dimensions of a photograph. The overall 'angle of view' of the

A view camera can be used to manipulate the shape and sharpness of an image. Here, the vertical tilt of the film back means the sides of the front surface do not appear parallel.

By tilting the lens panel back, the shape of the cube stays the same, but the distribution of sharpness alters. Here the panel is almost vertical.

human eye is about 180°, far more extensive than the 45° of the normal lens, but the eye's area of focus is comparatively small.

Any deviation from the normal lens will begin to distort or alter perspective — close-up shooting with a wide-angle lens distorts the features of the face, for instance, while a long-focus lens will compress perspective. This compression is an illusion, since the image presented by a long-focus lens is simply a magnification of a portion of the same subject as seen by a normal lens from exactly the same viewpoint. The distortion is less if a wide-angle shot is reproduced large, or if a telephoto shot is reproduced small.

The magnifying property of a lens is described by its focal length. In the 35mm format, a 50mm or 55mm lens is normal, 28mm format or less is wide-angle and 90mm, 135mm or more is long-focus. With larger formats these figures increase — 80mm is normal for 2¼ x 2¼, 150mm for 5 x 4in and so on. Variable focal length (zoom) lenses can replace a number of fixed focal-length lenses in the 35mm format but, because they usually contain a large number of lens elements, contrast and definition may be substantially reduced. They have the added disadvantages of smaller apertures and bulk.

There are a variety of specialist lenses at each end of the focal-length scale. For instance, ultra-wide-angle lenses for 35mm cameras — such as 20mm or less — produce increasing degrees of

Swinging the camera back to the left means the sharpest focus runs diagonally. The cube's shape is distorted and its position altered slightly.

Swinging the lens panel to the left does not affect the cube's shape, but alters the plane of sharpest focus to the diagonal running from near left.

linear distortion, whereas the fish-eye lens with curvilinear (barrel) distortion, produces a circular image of everything in front of the camera and even slightly behind it. More compact long-focus lenses such as telephoto lenses are shorter and mirror lenses even more so. The latter have only limited application since they have no conventional diaphragm, so exposure can only be controlled by changing the shutter speed of the camera. Pictures produced by mirror lenses can be recognized by the circular 'doughnut' form out-of-focus highlights in the background. Generally, all longer and heavier lenses need to be supported by a tripod to avoid camera shake.

When extreme close-up work is required, the camera lens must be moved further from the film plane than the ordinary focusing mechanism allows, and special focusing mounts, extension tubes or bellows allow magnification of up to about three times life-size. 'Macro' lenses have a specially-long range of focusing movement, and will magnify without any accessories. Extra case must be taken when lighting close-up subjects since the lens itself may get in the way and cast a shadow on the subject. Some lenses have been developed to overcome this problem, such as the medical Nikkor which has a built-in ring flash which gives shadowless frontal illumination.

Shutter speeds The photographer's usual aim is to keep exposure time as short as possible since exposures longer than 1/30 second, on a hand-held camera, will almost certainly allow time for the camera or even subject to move. The safest lower limit on a hand-held camera is probably 1/125th second, depending on the focal length of the lens.

Slow shutter speeds can be an effective way of describing speed in an otherwise static medium. By focusing on a speeding car, for instance, and provided that the camera is travelling at the same relative 'speed' as the subject, a slow shutter speed will produce a background blur of horizontal lines, while the car itself will remain sharp.

The fastest shutter speeds on conventional cameras are usually 1/1000 second, sometimes 1/2000 second, and even 1/4000 second, and movement at these speeds becomes frozen in a picture. Even faster speeds, enabling faster-moving subjects to be captured, such as a drop of falling liquid, can be achieved by electronic flash exposures. In this case, the duration of the flash is shorter than the fastest shutter speed on the camera.

Lighting The way in which a subject is lit, as well as the amount of light reaching the film, is the most important variable in successful photography. The eye responds automatically to changes in lighting quality, colour and direction, whereas camera film does not. To record every bit of detail of a subject, it must be lit in a way that eliminates shadow areas, thus exposing the detail. In natural, daylight conditions, lighting can still be controlled to a certain extent. For example, details in deep shadows, cast by direct sun, can be retained to a limited extent by using diffusers and reflectors to reduce the contrast.

Artificial lighting primarily sets out to imitate natural light and, for this reason, the basis of most set-ups is typified by a single diffused high-intensity light. Additionally, fill-in lights, diffusers, reflectors and even mirrors are required to retain sufficient detail in areas of shadow cast by the main light. Care has to be taken, however, when using a group of lights because shadows cast by more than one can quite easily destroy the unity of the picture.

Many of these basic 'rules' can be broken in order to achieve visual effect and drama — for instance, a shot may be lit with high contrast to emphasize one small area.

There are two types of artificial photographic light source — continuous tungsten and electronic flash. The first group comprises the basic photoflood — a more powerful version of the domestic tungsten lamp — spotlights (more or less the same as those used in the theatre), and quartz-iodine lamps.

But the most widely used source is electronic flash, comprising a single (or more) control console which can power up to eight studio flash units, or 'heads'. Some types of flash unit are self-contained, providing their own charge.

It is impossible to observe the effect of lighting during a test firing of the flash because of its speed and intensity. Instead, each head is equipped with a continuous 'modelling' light, usually in the centre of the tube itself, so that an approximation of the final result can be seen. Flash light can be controlled by setting individual flash heads to give much lower charges than their rated output. A variety of attachments similar to those used on other lights will also modify their effect.

The 'correct' exposure of a flash-lit subject is determined by the use of a special meter, most of which give a direct indication of the precise f-stop to be used. On static subjects a cumulative exposure can be made by firing the heads repeatedly with the shutter remaining open until the total exposure reaches the required level. To light large areas, several heads are required. These are often assembled into a large mobile housing faced with diffusing gauze, the whole assembly being called a 'fish-fryer'. These are used extensively to simulate natural daytime lighting conditions on table-sized sets. Even larger sets can be lit with an assembly called a 'swimming pool'.

There are flashes for special applications, such as the ring flash — developed for medical use — where the flash encircles the camera lens and gives shadowless results at close range. A ring flash is also quite effective at portrait range if the subject is placed close to a flat background, creating an intense rim-shadow. Since all these devices operate at very high voltages and generate considerable heat, safety is of paramount importance in their use.

Studio effects Reality can be subjected to much trickery in the studio by the use of optical camera techniques, filtration, the use of scale models as substitutes for the real subject, illusory backgrounds and a wide range of effects borrowed from stage and film techniques.

The basic item required for studio photography is a background 'sweep' — a wide roll of paper placed behind, and often under, the subject. This can be up to 12ft (3.6m) wide and in any of up to 40 different colours.

A neutral coloured background may be required for smaller-scale work, such as with glassware, where objects can be placed on a light box or even a glass-faced fish-fryer, giving uniform, soft, shadow-free lighting. A refinement of this technique can be used to create an impression that an object is floating in space. This is achieved by placing the subject on transparent glass or acrylic sheet, taking care that potentially reflective equipment, including the camera, is carefully masked in order to avoid spoiling the illusion. An object can also be 'suspended' by attaching a black rod to the back of the subject, with the other end of the rod being fixed to the background immediately behind so that it is unseen.

Top lighting/spot	Top lighting/diffuser	¾ lighting/spot	¾ lighting/diffuse

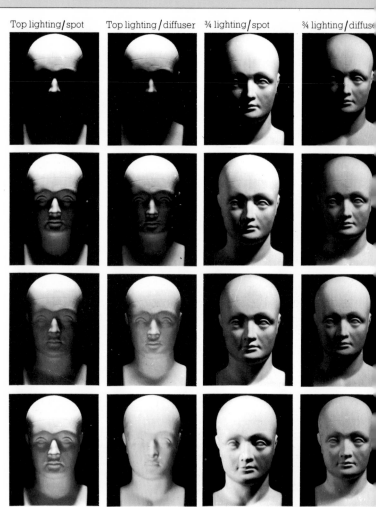

Many other situations, evoking 'characterful' settings such as those required in food photography, can be achieved by the extensive use of props, with kitchen sets invariably being built in the studio. Entire room sets can also be built, complete with carpets, doors and windows, any naturalistic effect — such as a view through a window — being created by the addition of foliage and the projection of scenes onto a screen beyond the window. Projection can be from the front or rear.

A back-up of special equipment is used on subjects to rectify flaws or to enhance effects in the studio. An aerosol of dulling spray, for instance, will deaden strong highlights or reflections, while oil or glycerine will restore the glaze to food covered by an unappetizing film caused by cooling. Another useful hint is to use a mist sprayer of plain water to revive a tired lettuce or enhance water droplets on a cooled glass of liquid. A fizzy drink can be livened up with a burst of carbon-dioxide gas.

Precise photography may often exaggerate flaws in badly made objects, and for this reason manufactured subjects must be carefully chosen or examined before they are photographed — cardboard packs, for instance, should be carefully folded from

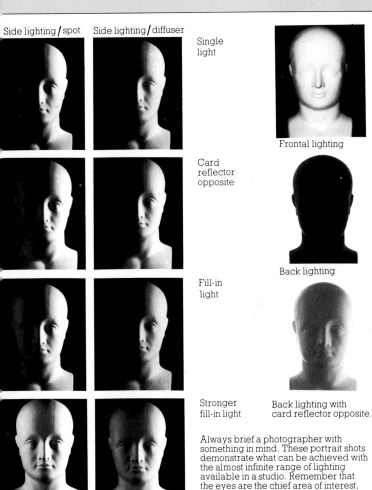

Side lighting/spot Side lighting/diffuser

Single light

Frontal lighting

Card reflector opposite

Back lighting

Fill-in light

Stronger fill-in light

Back lighting with card reflector opposite.

Always brief a photographer with something in mind. These portrait shots demonstrate what can be achieved with the almost infinite range of lighting available in a studio. Remember that the eyes are the chief area of interest, so they should be used as the starting point.

flat blanks taken from the production line, and labels stuck onto bottles should not be creased or have glue around the edges.

Prints from transparencies There are two distinct methods by which colour prints can be made from transparencies. In the first, an intermediate copy negative ('interneg') is made by a contact print produced from the original transparency. This negative is used to produce what is called a 'C-type' print. The second is a direct process, called an 'R-type' print, in which the original transparency is projected directly onto printing paper.

With the direct process, prints tend to give a contrasting result, and if the original itself shows excessive contrast the end result may prove unacceptable. Modifications can be made to a print by using the conventional black-and-white printing techniques of 'dodging' and 'burning-in', and employing these techniques with coloured filters extends the range of controls yet further. Special papers can be used to make black-and-white prints from both transparency and negative originals. With black-and-white prints for reproduction it is important that the highest possible quality of print is attained because detail can be lost and the image degraded by the halftone process.

5
DESIGN EQUIPMENT
Pencils/Pens/Fibre and felt-tipped
pens/Inks/Airbrushes/
Photocopying/PMTs

All graphic designers need a wide range of the best possible quality of equipment to enable them to work to the deadlines and to the high standards demanded today. This equipment ranges from tools which have changed little since their invention to those which have been recently developed for specific purposes using the latest technology. For example, while wood-cased pencils are very similar to those used in the eighteenth century, precision engineering has improved the reliability of clutch and propelling pencils. Erasers have also been developed to erase not only pencil, but also many inks.

Basic equipment for the graphic designer includes a good drawing board, good light, suitable measuring equipment — an inch and millimetre scale, a type scale and a steel straight-edge are essential — set squares (the adjustable kind are the most versatile), drawing equipment including a stylo-tipped fountain pen with a variety of different width nibs, and a basic variety of brushes. With deadlines to meet, the designer must be able to work quickly and accurately, so any device which can speed up work is invaluable.

Drawing pencils As many as 19 grades of pencil are available, ranging from the softest — EE, EB, 6B to B, HB — through F, which is of medium hardness, and from H to 9H — the hardest.

Carbon pencils A recommended carbon pencil is Wolff's, available in degrees ranging from HH to BB. There are three degress of black Conté pencils — No 1 medium (HB), No 2 soft (B) and No 3 extra soft (BB).

Coloured pencils Three main types of coloured pencil are widely available. Firstly, those with thick, comparatively soft leads are both waterproof and lightproof and can be bought in a wide variety of colours — Derwent produce 72 shades and Eagle 62. They do not smudge or erase easily, nor do they need to be fixed.

Secondly, the Veri-thin variety has, as the name implies, a thin, non-crumbling lead, which is useful for fine detailed work. They are also waterproof, but only 36 to 40 shades are generally available. They do not smudge but only a few colours are manufactured which are completely erasable.

The third group are those which are water-soluble. Used with water to produce washes of colour, these are something of a cross between pencils and watercolours and are made by various manufacturers with either thick or thin leads and in ranges of up to about 36 colours.

Clutch pencils A development of the propelling pencil, clutch pencils consist of a holder made of plastic or metal, or both, inside which is a sleeve which holds and protects the lead. The lead is secured in position by a clutch lock which is released to project the lead forward by pressing a button at the end of the holder. Leads are available in a wide variety of softnesses and widths, the smallest of which is 0.2mm.

Pens Apart from the traditional quills, reed-pens and dip-pens, fountain pens — particularly the stylo-tipped variety — are the most useful for the designer. Stylo-tipped fountain pens are useful not only because of the wide range of 15 widths but also because they draw a line of consistent and unvarying width. Osmiroid drawing pens — now adapted to take black non-clogging waterproof drawing ink — are extremely useful. They range from those with broad italic nibs to ones with fine, flexible copperplate nibs.

Reservoir pens are popular among draughtsmen and illustrators alike, in that their chief attraction is that they can be used with waterproof drawing inks of any type, for which there is a wide range of colours. Of this type Pelikan 'Graphos' pens have a range of 19 nibs which are quickly interchangeable and so just as useful as stylo-tipped pens.

Fibre and felt-tipped pens These are now produced in a vast range of types, mostly with a large selection of colours. Their main virtue is that they produce a dependable, flowing and consistent

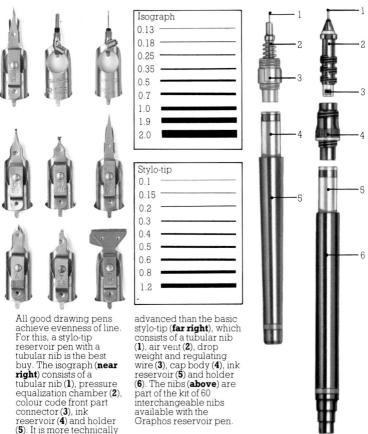

Isograph
| 0.13 |
| 0.18 |
| 0.25 |
| 0.35 |
| 0.5 |
| 0.7 |
| 1.0 |
| 1.9 |
| 2.0 |

Stylo-tip
| 0.1 |
| 0.15 |
| 0.2 |
| 0.3 |
| 0.4 |
| 0.5 |
| 0.6 |
| 0.8 |
| 1.2 |

All good drawing pens achieve evenness of line. For this, a stylo-tip reservoir pen with a tubular nib is the best buy. The isograph (**near right**) consists of a tubular nib (**1**), pressure equalization chamber (**2**), colour code front part connector (**3**), ink reservoir (**4**) and holder (**5**). It is more technically advanced than the basic stylo-tip (**far right**), which consists of a tubular nib (**1**), air vent (**2**), drop weight and regulating wire (**3**), cap body (**4**), ink reservoir (**5**) and holder (**6**). The nibs (**above**) are part of the kit of 60 interchangeable nibs available with the Graphos reservoir pen.

line, while their width sensitivity makes working with them similar to drawing with the tip of a brush. Many are made for specific uses, such as drawing on film for overhead projection purposes. They are also available in water-soluble and spirit-based permanent varieties, as well as in an almost daunting range of tip thicknesses.

Inks Artists' drawing inks are waterproof and dry to a glossy film. They are available in an impressive variety of colours: for example Grumbacher offer 17, Pelikan make 18 and Winsor and Newton have 22. The range of black drawing inks, sometimes called Indian, is similarly impressive. Pelikan make a variety of special coloured inks in filler bottles for use in Graphos and stylo-tipped pens, as well as special drawing inks for use on polyester drawing films.

Bottles of ink should always be shaken before use, since the pigment tends to settle at the bottom of the bottle if it is left unused for some time. Ink may evaporate slightly in summer while uncorked during a day's work, with the result that the colour becomes deeper and the ink thicker; the addition of just a small amount of distilled water (not a heavy dilution) will thin it again and cause an easier flow.

Airbrushes There are two types of airbrush mechanisms — single-action lever and double-action lever. Single action is the simplest form of airbrush, in which the only way of altering the pattern of spray is to increase or decrease the distance between the brush and the surface being sprayed. Though simple to maintain, this type of airbrush is only suitable for general background work.

By contrast, the double-action brush is essential for the precision and detail required in much technical illustration. Its main advantage is that it gives the user the ability to control the proportions of paint to air; as the lever is depressed air, not paint, is released through the brush, and only when it is pulled backwards does paint meet the airstream — the further back, the greater the amount of paint released. There are a wide range of airbrushes on the market today, and choice of a suitable instrument will depend upon what it is to be used for.

The Aerograph Super 63 A-504 is a double-action lever model, giving precision control suitable for most types of work. The Super 63 E-504 is similar to the A-504, but has a coarser nozzle and a larger reservoir, so allowing a greater area to be covered in a shorter time. The Sprite is a simpler double-action type and, consequently, is less precise on line work. The Conograph is a single-action lever brush with detachable cups.

The Wold A1 is a double-action lever brush with two air caps — one coned and one flared. It can be used for work ranging from fine line rendering to broad wash tones. The Wold A2 is similar to the A1, but with an improved air cap assembly, while the M type has double the capacity of the A series, as it is fitted with a 1oz or 2oz jar, with interchangeable cups for any colour changes. The K-M is single-action with a wheel control that predetermines the volume of spray, handling large quantities of colour in a short time.

The Thayer and Chandler models AA and A are both double lever brushes which produce fine lines and broad coverage of tones. The C type's 2oz capacity makes it ideal for large areas, while the E and G1 models are ideal for display artists.

The Paasche AB is capable of producing the finest hairline thickness or dots and so it is ideally suited to freehand drawing and photographic retouching. The Paasche H1, H2 and H3 types are single-action control lever brushes with separate controls which can be pre-adjusted for colour and air. The air caps and colour nozzles are interchangeable to provide a range from fine line to broad spray. The Paasche V1 and V2 are both double-action, the former being suitable for fine work and the latter for medium rendering, and both being good for vignetting. Each has a micrometer line adjuster giving rapid setting from very fine to broad. The Paasche air eraser holds an abrasive instead of paint, which can erase ink and paint without streaking or smudging. It can also be used for blending highlights and shadows.

An airbrush is an extremely expensive item of equipment and should be treated with the utmost care. It should be thoroughly cleaned after use because, for example, dried paint may distort the shape of the air cap or even damage the nozzle, thus affecting the quality of spray. Dried paint can even render an airbrush ineffective if it gets into the workings.

The air supply to an airbrush should be maintained at an average pressure of 30 pounds per square inch (2 kilograms per square centimeter) and is available in a variety of sources — in an aerosol can, a refillable canister like that used by underwater divers, by a foot pump (hard work) or by an electric compressor. The last is the most efficient method because the air is supplied at much more constant pressure.

Photocopying Some kind of reprographic equipment, whether it be a simple photocopier or a more versatile photomechanical Transfer (PMT) machine, is an essential modern design tool, for, without it, it would be impossible for the designer to produce artwork of the best possible quality.

The most useful photocopying machine for the designer is one that will produce prints to A3 size — the equivalent of two facing pages of A4 format. There are two basic types of photocopier — thermal and electrostatic. In the former, a paper negative is used, which produces prints on the same special paper. The electrostatic copier needs no negative, and will print onto any paper, and even onto transparent film.

One of the oldest copying systems, the dyeline process, has recently undergone a number of improvements — including substitution of the unpleasant smelling ammonia by another chemical. In this process, a transparent original is placed over sensitized paper and exposed to ultraviolet light. Dyeline is particularly suitable for copying engineering or architectural drawings, with a range of sizes extending up to A0.

A sophisticated version of the dyeline technique, the Safir SC process, enables the final appearance of a piece of artwork to be checked without going to the expense of getting it colour-proofed. Light passing through film-based images of the artwork — at its final size — activates a photo-sensitive coating on a white polyester base. Dye sticks to the exposed areas and successive layers of colour can be built up.

Photographic copying equipment — as distinct from photocopiers — using transparent or paper negatives, produce high-quality prints which can be used as successfully for reproduction as the original artwork, and, unlike cruder photocopies, can be made at any size within its maximum format.

One of the most popular systems, the PMT machine produces an excellent quality of reproduction, is cheaper to use than conventional photographic systems, and some types do not require a darkroom for processing. A large variety of different screens are available, and halftones can be produced which, although not as

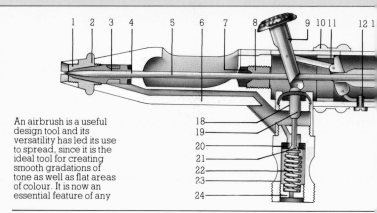

An airbrush is a useful design tool and its versatility has led its use to spread, since it is the ideal tool for creating smooth gradations of tone as well as flat areas of colour. It is now an essential feature of any

When selecting an airbrush, the most important factor to take into account is the type of work it will be expected to do. There is a wide range of models on the market, from the simplest which can do little more than colour surfaces quickly and apparently evenly to extremely complex versions. Some airbrushes, for instance, can produce lettering as fine as six-point type if required. If an airbrush is to be used for detailed graphic work, it is a false economy to select a cheaper model; if, on the other hand, the airbrush is to be used primarily for spraying large areas of colour, or for simple stencil patterns, an elaborate version is an unnecessary expense. Whichever the model, accuracy and evenness of spray depend on two main factors. These are the principles of internal or external atomization — the former is more sophisticated than the latter — and whether the lever controlling the spray is single-or double-action. The Super 63 Aerograph (**1**), the Sprite Aerograph (**2**), the Badger 100 (**3**) the Paasche VI (**4**), the Paasche VL (**5**), the Thayer and Chandler A (**6**), the Olympos (Iwata) 100A (**7**), the Olympos (Iwata) SPA (**8**) and the Thayer and Chandler C (**9**) all have independent double-actions. The Conopois F (**10**), the Humbrol 1 (**11**) and the Grafo 11B (**12**) have fixed needles and double-action. The Paasche Turbo AB (**13**) allows the medium to air ratio to be altered by the artist.

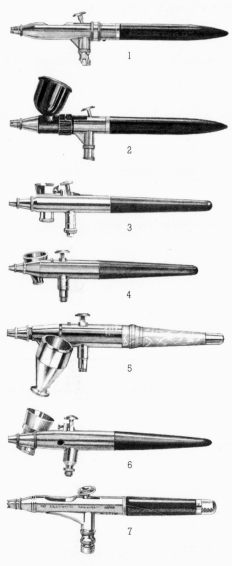

well-equipped art studio. The model shown here in cross-section is the Aerograph Super 63. Its features include (**1**) air cap guard; (**2**) air cap; (**3**) nozzle; (**4**) nozzle washer; (**5**) fluid needle; (**6**) model body assembly;

(**7**) needle gland washer; (**8**) needle packing gland; (**9**) lever assembly; (**10**) cam ring; (**11**) cam; (**12**) fixing screw; (**13**) square piece; (**14**) needle spring; (**15**) needle spring box; (**16**) needle locking nut; (**17**)

handle; (**18**) diaphragm nut; (**19**) diaphragm assembly; (**20**) air valve washer; (**21**) air valve stem; (**22**) air valve spring; (**23**) air valve box; (**24**) air valve spring retainer.

When removing the air cap from an airbrush, always remove the needle first. If this simple precaution is ignored, there is the risk that both needle and air cap will be damaged.

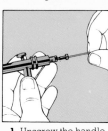

1 Unscrew the handle and loosen the nut locking the needle in position. Take the needle out about 1in (25mm).

2 Unscrew the air cap and remove the nozzle carefully.

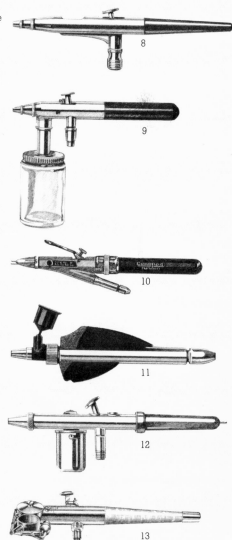

fine as those made by photoengraving, are quite adequate for low budget work or for reference prints.

The PMT machine can also be used to simulate colour in a design without having to go to the expense of a colour proof. First, the subject is printed onto a film base which is processed to give a colour simulation known as a colour key, and then a dye is used to develop the image in one of several stock colours. Since both the colours and the film base itself are transparent, they can be superimposed to create the appearance of two or more colours printed in line or halftone. Duotones and even four-colour effects outside the standard printing colours can be simulated as well.

The colour key technique also enables a designer to make a single copy of a simulated colour image in the form of a self-adhesive dry transfer, which can be applied to presentation material such as package designs, to give a customer an impression of how the finished job will look. Recent technological developments in photocopying have increased the quality and capability of most machines, thus widening the areas of application, particularly in the design field.

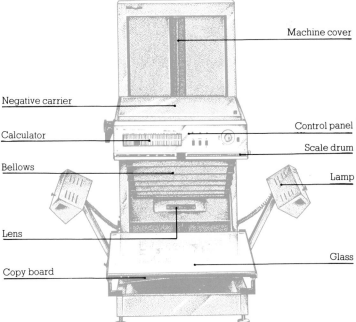

Machine cover

Negative carrier

Calculator

Control panel

Scale drum

Bellows

Lamp

Lens

Glass

Copy board

Vertical cameras or PMT (photo-mechanical transfer machines) are extremely versatile process cameras (**above**). They can convert black to white and vice versa, convert colour to black-and-white and reverse left to right. The negative is placed on the copyboard and the negative paper on the lens. When the negative is ready, it is placed on to positive paper. The machines can also be used to produce screens. In screening, continuous tones are reduced to thousands of dots, varying in size, shape and number. The screen selected for use varies, according to the surface of the paper, the type of printing plate and the quality of the printing press and printing inks. The examples (**left**) show some of the various types. These include denim (**1**), dot (**7**), concentric circle (**9**), random dot (**2**), straight line (**3**), weave plus highlight mask (**4**), wavy line (**5**), fine mezzo (**6**) and cross screen posterized (**8**). All produce striking effects. Other advantages of PMT machines include their ability to convert artwork and lettering into instant transfers, or autotypes, of any colour. They can also be used to produce cells. In this technique artwork is printed on to clear film, so that it can be manoeuvred easily on a layout. A final benefit is time; the process takes about 10 minutes.

6

TYPESETTING
Strike-on systems/Hot metal/
Photocomposition/Page make-up
systems

Methods of typesetting fall into two groups — direct and indirect. In the former, the image or impression of the letter-form is created directly from the pieces of type that have been assembled, or, in the most basic example — typewriters — as the result of keys being struck. The oldest method of direct typesetting is where individually cast, or punched, pieces of type were assembled by hand and subsequently printed.

The indirect method involves keying matter into some kind of storage system from which it is subsequently converted — either by metal, photographically or by digitized computer — into an image. The storage system can be either punched paper tape or, for instance, in the case of computer-controlled phototypesetting or digitized image-formation, on magnetic discs.

Strike-on systems and typewriters The cheapest way of producing typeset matter is with what amounts to nothing more than a sophsticated electric typewriter. These typewriters, for instance the IBM Composer, are used with interchangeable typing heads ('golf balls'), each being a different typeface. Unlike the ordinary typewriter which has fixed character spacing, these machines produce variable character spacing with up to four different widths. They can also be linked to computers which give the added facility of end-of-line (hyphenation) decisions and justification. However, even with computer-assisted decisions, the quality of output of these strike-on systems can be inconsistent and does not match that of metal or photocomposition. Nevertheless, with jobs in which minimal costs are more important than typographic quality, any typewriter can produce acceptable results — and can even be used to dramatic effect where appropriate, if used with aesthetic sensitivity.

Hot metal When type composition was mechanized at the beginning of this century it became known as hot metal composition because the type for each job is freshly cast from molten metal. The principal manufacturers are Monotype, Linotype, Ludlow and Intertype. With Monotype machines, text is converted into a punched paper tape from a keyboard. This is then used to control a casting machine which holds a matrix case of up to seven alphabets. The type is cast in lines of individual pieces of type. Linotype machines combine keyboard and caster and produce each line of typeset matter as one piece of metal.

Although still in use, hot metal machines are becoming increasingly rare, not least because of certain typographic limitations, such as their inability to reduce inter-character or inter-line spacing, even though combinations of certain characters have been designed to 'kern'. This is when part of a character overhangs its body and rests on the body of a neighbouring letter or space.

Photo-composition Although having reached a high degree of technical sophistication, photocomposition is, in some ways, still in a state of infancy, with new technology being developed at a rate almost too rapid for the designer to keep up with. Another problem is that because many phototypesetting systems can now be operated by people with little or no typographic knowledge, the designer must keep an eye on the quality of typeset matter. This means that designers today require a much greater understanding of the technological aspects of typesetting than ever before. The term phototypesetting itself is somewhat loosely applied, since newer systems barely use a photographic process at all, but any attempts at categorization within the overall label can easily become confusing.

Technical experts often talk of phototypesetting systems as being grouped in 'generations' — first, second, third, fourth and recently fifth generations are referred to — although this is slightly misleading since there are no universally defined parameters for each generation, and while one or two manufacturers may refer to their own third generation system, say, the equivalent by other manufacturers may be called their fourth generation.

It is more appropriate, therefore, to regard phototypesetters as being grouped according to their method of image-formation. Of these there are three: photomechanical, digitized cathode ray tube (CRT) and digitized laser. The photomechanical method produces typeset matter ('output') by light being shone through a film negative of the typeform onto photographic film or paper. Digitized CRT produces output either by a contact process — film or paper is placed over the front of the CRT itself (onto which the image is projected through a system of fibre optics) — or by optical transmission of the tube beams directly onto photographic film or paper. Thirdly, digitized lasers, as the name suggests, use a laser instead of a CRT to produce the image. Each group has its own advantages — from the hard-edged high-quality (but somewhat variable character spacing and alignment) letterform of photomechanical typesetters to the phenomenal speed of digital lasers (with subsequent poor image resolution — at present only suitable for high volume setting such as telephone directories). All in all, there is as yet no system which combines high resolution image quality, high quality character spacing and alignment and high speed.

All three categories of image-formation relate only to one stage in the phototypesetting process, since most systems involve three main components — keyboard, computer and (for image formation) phototypesetting unit. Because copy goes into the system by keying it in at one end ('input') and comes out at the other as typeset matter ('output'), the first and last parts of the whole system are referred to as 'front-end' and 'back-end' respectively.

Some systems can incorporate more complex arrangements including, for instance, a page make-up (or area composition) facility, while others may be a single unit combining all three components ('direct entry'). Systems in which the various components are interconnected are referred to as being 'on-line'.

The keyboard is used to input the matter to be set, with the copy being recorded on a punched paper or magnetic tape, or on a disc, depending on the system. This can subsequently be used either for editing or setting type or can be stored for later use. Floppy discs or 'diskettes' — similar in size to a 45rpm record — are becoming the most popular type of storage system as they hold more information than paper or magnetic tape, and, more importantly, they have the facility of 'random access'. This means it is possible to go instantly to any part of the keyed matter, as opposed to having to play the whole length of a tape through. This makes correcting and editing much easier.

On most systems, end-of-line decisions (hyphenation and justification, or 'H/J') are made by the computer after the matter has been input, but systems with more sophisticated 'counting' keyboards require their operators to make such decisions. To do this the operator must know the complete type specification for a job so that each line can be set within the limits of that particular specification. Counting keyboards are especially useful for setting complex jobs such as those involving runarounds and mathematical and scientific material.

Alternatively, less sophisticated 'non-counting' keyboards have the advantage of enabling matter to be input and stored before the type specification is known. A whole job, having already been set to a particular specification, can be reset to a completely different typeface, size, measure and leading simply by issuing a new set of instructions ('formatting code') and, without having to re-key the original copy. However, non-counting keyboards cannot display a preview of complicated setting, and jobs involving any complexities such as indents and run-arounds can often be achieved only by trial and error. Some typesetting firms input matter through a

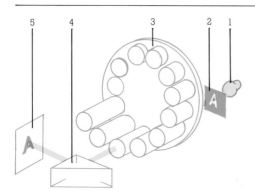

Photosetting (**left**) works on simple principles. In many systems, a high intensity light (**1**) flashes through the negative type images on a spinning disc (**2**). In others, the light moves while the disc remains stationary. The characters are then projected through a lens turret (**3**), which establishes type size, and a moving prism (**4**), which fixes the type position on the photosensitive film or paper (**5**).

Most typesetting systems include in their typeface range faces which, although well-known, are specially designed for each manufacturer and their final appearance can vary considerably as these alphabets(**right**)set in Times Roman clearly show. For this reason, it is always necessary to ask for sample setting on the machine that will actually be used to typeset the job before finalizing the choice of typeface.

abcdefghijklmnopqrstuvwxyz
Photon

abcdefghijklmnopqrstuvwxyz
APS 4

abcdefghijklmnopqrstuvwxyz
Bobst Eurocast

abcdefghijklmnopqrstuvwxyz
Linotron 202

abcdefghijklmnopqrstuvwxyz
Monophoto 2000

abcdefghijklmnopqrstuvwxyz
Linocomp

'blind' keyboard (one without a visual display unit, or 'VDU'), formatting codes being issued later on a different keyboard.

Wherever it occurs in the system, the computer is used to refine the input (make end-of-line decisions, for example), and to instruct the phototypesetter to produce output. The quality of the appearance of the output depends as much on the level of programming ('software') as on the optical sophistication of the equipment itself ('hardware').

Apart from the facility of controlling character spacing, word spacing, kerning and other typographic subtleties, the most important aspect of software is the degree of sophistication of its automatic wordbreak, or H/J, program. There are a variety of program levels by which wordbreaks are controlled, the simplest being 'hyphenless' — one that will not break words at all, with its consequently poor effect on character and word spacing.

A 'discretionary' program is one that uses a hyphen only if it is in a word that falls at the end of a line, the operator having first hyphenated all particular words that may need it. A 'logic' program has a specific — but limited — set of rules governing hyphenation; all words ending *ing*, for example (with obvious shortcomings, such as *s-ing*!). To avoid this happening and also to prevent poor hyphenation, computers are often programmed with an 'exception dictionary' which will cope with words that are exceptions to the computer's rules of logic. Alternatively — though less common — a 'true dictionary' may be used, where words of six or more letters are hyphenated according to 'correct' English usage and stored as a guide in the computer's memory. The success of any dictionary, however, depends upon the number of words included within it, and this can vary considerably.

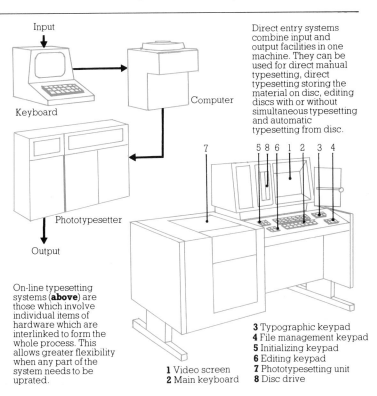

Input

Keyboard

Computer

Direct entry systems combine input and output facilities in one machine. They can be used for direct manual typesetting, direct typesetting storing the material on disc, editing discs with or without simultaneous typesetting and automatic typesetting from disc.

Phototypesetter

Output

On-line typesetting systems (**above**) are those which involve individual items of hardware which are interlinked to form the whole process. This allows greater flexibility when any part of the system needs to be uprated.

1 Video screen
2 Main keyboard
3 Typographic keypad
4 File management keypad
5 Initializing keypad
6 Editing keypad
7 Phototypesetting unit
8 Disc drive

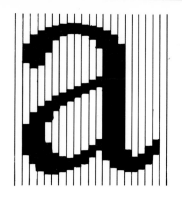

This character was set on a CRT (cathode ray tube) typesetter. These work in either of two ways. In the first, data is stored in the computer and the type generated electronically from a digital fount on to the video tube. From there, it is transferred to photosensitive paper or film. In the second, a photographic fount is scanned by the machine to recreate the characters. In both, the characters are made up of dots or lines (**left**).

Dictionaries can also be used to check that words have been correctly spelt, or — with a 'search and replace' mode — they can be used to convert words of one spelling style into another — English to American spelling, for example (this is not infallible such as if, in changing the word *post* to *mail*, the computer is instructed to search and replace each word beginning *post* with results like *Mail-Impressionist*).

The typeset matter, or output, is provided by the phototypesetting unit. In the photomechanical group these are units that carry a fount — or founts — in the form of negative images through which light is shone onto photographic film or paper which, in turn, is later passed through a processor to develop the image. The way in which the image is exposed varies from system to system. For instance, the fount may move while the light source remains stationary, or vice versa.

The founts themselves come in a variety of forms, each one being incompatible with the others. They can be in film strips, discs or segments of discs, and most will carry more than one fount, enabling typefaces or weights to be mixed — light, light italic, medium and bold, for instance — without changing founts. Some units carry more than one disc or film strip, so giving greater flexibility in typeface selection. The type of fount dictates the number of characters, which in turn determines the extent of its range — small caps, ligatures, foreign accents and so on. The range of type sizes also depends on the system being used — one may use a master to set sizes from 5 point to 10 point and another master for 11 point to 36 point, while a different system may use only one master to set all sizes.

Most digital CRT and laser typesetters generate characters which have been electronically stored in the computer's memory, although some recreate a photographic image on the tube by a process of scanning. CRT typesetters are now producing a more acceptable image resolution and, in addition to high-speed output, they have the added advantage of being able to store a vast number — as many as 1200 — digitized typefaces in their memory.

The CRT character itself is generated either as lines or, though more rarely, as linked-together dots — both methods being imperceptible to the eye at small sizes.

Unlike conventional galley pulls from metal typesetting which are made on sheets of paper of uniform size, photocomposed output is made on a continuous roll of paper or film and can be awkward to handle as repro because of its inconsistent lengths. However, galley proofs of photocomposed matter can be made by photocopying onto uniformly sized paper.

The cost of photocomposing systems can be massive, and for this reason, typesetting companies frequently concentrate their investment onto whichever end of the system is most important for the predominant type of work they produce. A company typesetting mostly for advertising, for instance, will tend to have a more sophisticated back-end to their system, whereas those producing high-volume work will concentrate on the front-end of their system.

The quality of typesetting depends not only on the system being used, but also on the designer's knowledge of it. While the lens system, accuracy of the machine and software programs account for a large part of the quality of output, the difference between typefaces designed for conventional metal setting which are then converted for photographic use can be considerable. The tendency is for photoset type to be set comparatively closer than their metal equivalents, but there are some faces, such as Univers, which have been specially designed to set with wider-spaced letters and consequently tend to read better when set as the designer intended.

Another facility of photocomposition is the ability to distort the appearance of type by introducing prisms into the light path. Depending on the nature of the prism, type can be condensed, expanded or inclined to form an italic as required, although the appearance of type set by this method may be less acceptable than faces specifically designed for each purpose.

Page make-up systems Variously called area composition, video layout, and composition and layout systems, page make-up systems are basically sophisticated input terminals, although 'raw' copy will normally have already been input through a photocomposing keyboard or a word-processor. Its function is to manipulate matter into the position it will finally appear as a complete page before anything has actually been output, thus eliminating the process of manual make-up or paste-up.

As with photocomposing systems, the variety and scope of page make-up systems is wide, their capabilities being related almost directly to their cost. A major limiting factor is the cost of manufacturing video screens large enough to display entire large-format pages or double page spreads. Some are operated by keyboard controls, some by a graphics tablet and some by a combination of both of these.

A simple, low-cost system will merely enable the operator to position copy which has already been issued with a formatting code, displaying it on a video screen in a uniform face, size and weight regardless of its final appearance. Conversely, a high-cost system will allow the operator to edit copy and to alter any of its variables — typeface, size, weight, line length and so on — and some can display the matter in a simulated near-facsimile of the final result. Rules of any thickness and shape — even circular — can also be 'drawn' in. Proofs can be produced on a line-printer and final page film is output from a phototypesetting unit.

Although having mostly been used for jobs requiring less sensitive typographic treatment, such as directories and small ads, page make-up systems will soon be available that will enable the designer to produce tight, sensitive layouts on-line, thus eliminating the sometimes cumbersome time-consuming procedure of manipulating typographic elements of the paste-up process by hand.

7
REPRODUCTION

Halftone image formation/Colour
reproduction/Scanners/Colour
separation/Colour tint charts

In its broadest sense, reproduction is the duplication of an image by any means. However, in the printing business, it is generally used to describe the photomechanical conversion of an illustration or photograph so that it can be used in any of the various printing processes.

Halftone image formation When printing by letterpress, lithography or screen, ink is transferred to the surface to be printed in a layer of uniform density. This is fine for areas of solid colour, but if gradations of tone are required, such as in a photograph, the original must be broken up into a pattern of dots. Each dot varies in size to give the optical illusion of continuous tone when printed small enough not to be detected when viewed at a normal reading distance.

The conversion into dots is made by placing a screen between the original subject and the film negative. The screen itself can be one of two types: a conventional glass cross-line screen or a vignetted contact screen. The cross-line screen is comprised of two pieces of glass, each one having had parallel grooves etched into its surface, these being filled with opaque pigment. The two pieces are sealed together with the lines intersecting at right angles to create square windows in a lattice pattern of opaque lines. This is placed a few millimetres in front of the photographic film thus allowing incoming light to spread slightly behind the screen. The gap between film and screen is crucial since it is the spread of light — dictated by its intensity as reflected from the subject — which determines the final size of the dot. For instance, the highlights from a subject reflect the most light and the resulting image on the film — in negative — will be an opaque area with pinpricks of tiny windows which will eventually print — in positive — as small dots, the area surrounding them being predominantly white. The opposite happens in the dark areas of the original. The same principle applies to all the intermediate tones but in varying proportions; the illusion of different tones of grey in a printed subject is the result of the arrangement of different size dots, their centre points being exactly the same distance from each other.

Vignetted contact screens employ the same principle of converting the intensity of light into different sized dots but in a different way. Instead of a lattice pattern of lines the screen is comprised of dots — each one being vignetted (solid at its core, but fading away gradually towards its circumference until it disappears

A screen is used to reproduce a halftone original (**above**). If this is enlarged (**right**), the halftone dots become clearly visible. The lightest areas are black dots on white, and the shaded parts are white on a black background.

A screen angled at 90°

A screen angled at 45°

Left Halftone screens have to be placed at an angle of 45° so that the pattern of dots cannot be detected by the eye. If the screen is placed at 90°, the lines of dots form a noticeable pattern. Screens vary in coarseness (**below**) ranging from 55 lines per inch through to 300 lines per inch.

55 lines per inch
20 lines per centimetre

65 lines per inch
26 lines per centimetre

85 lines per inch
35 lines per centimetre

100 lines per inch
40 lines per centimetre

120 lines per inch
48 lines per centimetre

133 lines per inch
54 lines per centimetre

150 lines per inch
60 lines per centimetre

175 lines per inch
70 lines per centimetre

200 lines per inch
80 lines per centimetre

altogether). This screen is placed in direct contact with the film emulsion, the size of dot being determined by the intensity of light passing through each dot. In monochrome reproduction, the screens are positioned with the rows of dots running at 45° to the page as this makes them less noticeable to the eye.

The distance at which dot centres occur between each other on a screen is measured in terms of their frequency per inch or centimetre. Thus a screen with 133 rows of dots (lines) to each inch (54 per centimetre) is referred to as a 133 screen (54 screen), but because of the wide use of both imperial and metric measurements it is usually safer to be specific. Screens are available in a variety of sizes ranging from 5 lines per inch (20 lines per centimetre) to 200 lines per inch (80 lines per centimetre). The finer the screen, the finer the detail in a printed subject.

The coarseness of a screen depends entirely upon the printing process and the porosity and smoothness of the paper to be used.

1 Black-and-white halftone

2 Second colour halftone

3 20% tint of second colour

4 Tint over black-and-white halftone

There are a number of ways in which the designer can achieve a wide variety of effects when reproducing images by combining colour and black tints. The most basic type of halftone is black-and-white (**1**). In this, the subject will obviously only appear in shades of black. In a colour halftone (**2**), the black is replaced by whichever second colour has been selected. The result is an image in shades of the colour and white. The colour tone itself (**3**) is chosen by looking at a range of percentage screened tints. To create a flat tint halftone (**4**), a black-and-white halftone is combined with a flat second colour tint. This gives the combined effect of an image in both colour and black-and-white.

Black halftone

20% colour halftone over black

40% halftone over black

60% halftone over black

80% halftone over black

Full value colour halftone over black

Pictured above are a selection of duotones of the same image. A duotone is a print with a two-colour halftone made from a photograph which has been screened with a second colour. To create a duotone, two plates have to be made. First, the black plate is shot which will give a black-and-white image. This provides the required tones of light and shadow in the picture. The second shot is for the colour which is used to create all the middle tones. These two plates are then combined to give an image in the full range of tones.

Generally, duotones look best when they are in pastel shades. This also ensures that the contrast in the picture is not dominated. Grey is also a useful second colour when a greater range of tones is required in a black-and-white picture.

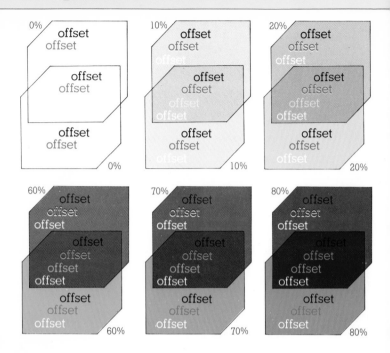

Newsprint, for instance, with its high absorbency, is only suitable for coarser halftone screens of say, 65 lines per inch (26 lines per centimetre), whereas very smooth coated art paper can produce a high quality reproduction with screens as fine as 200 lines per inch (80 lines per centimetre).

Colour reproduction In its crudest sense, the term 'colour printing' can be applied to anything which is printed in more than one colour — and in some cases anything printed in any single colour except black. More often it is used to denote the reproduction of full-colour originals. Because each colour in the printing process has to be applied by a separate printing surface, reproduction is

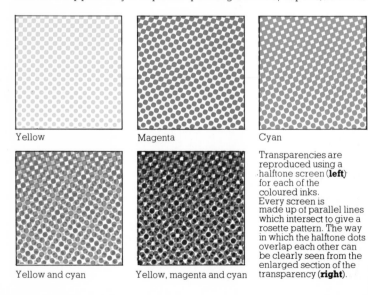

Yellow

Magenta

Cyan

Yellow and cyan

Yellow, magenta and cyan

Transparencies are reproduced using a halftone screen (**left**) for each of the coloured inks. Every screen is made up of parallel lines which intersect to give a rosette pattern. The way in which the halftone dots overlap each other can be clearly seen from the enlarged section of the transparency (**right**).

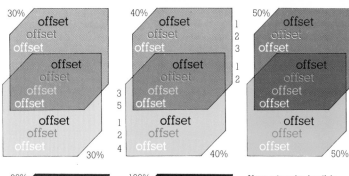

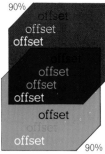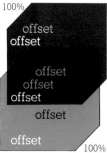

If type is to be legible, tints placed beneath it must be chosen with care. These diagrams show the varying strengths from 0% to 100%. The lettering has been printed as follows: solid black (**1**), solid magenta (**2**), white reversed out of black (**3**), white reversed out of magenta (**4**), and white reversed out of black and magenta (**5**).

achieved by the use of three 'process' colours — yellow, magenta and cyan, with black also being used to add finer detail and greater density in dark areas. Consequently, any original that has been presented in colour first has to be separated into pieces of film, each one representing a different colour.

Originals for colour reproduction can be grouped into two main types — those consisting of solid areas of colour without intermediate tones ('line originals') and those comprising a subject which appears as full-colour continuous tone. The latter can exist as any form of hand-created art — such as a watercolour painting — on a flat surface (called 'flat artwork' or 'flat copy'), as full-colour prints on photographic paper, or as colour transparencies. A flat original is reproduced by light being reflected from it, whereas light is shone through a transparency.

In printing, nearly all colours can be obtained by mixing yellow, magenta and cyan inks in their correct proportions, which are determined by the size of the halftone dots on each piece of film. Photographic colour originals produce more faithful reproduction since the same principle of simulating full colour is employed, colour film emulsion being comprised of yellow, magenta and cyan dyes.

In some high-quality reproduction work such as fine art pain-

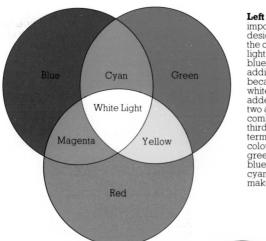

Left It is extremely important for the designer to be aware of the colour properties of light. Red, green and blue are known as additive primaries because they produce white light when they are added together. When two additive colours are combined, they create a third colour which is termed a subtractive colour. Thus, red and green will make yellow; blue and green make cyan; and red and blue make magenta.

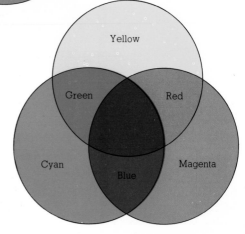

Right In the same way that two additive primaries combined will produce a subtractive primary, two subtractive primaries mixed together will create an additive primary. In other words, cyan and yellow make green; yellow and magenta make red; and a mixture of cyan and magenta makes blue. Unlike the additives which produce white light, when combined, the three additives together make black.

tings, the standard 'tri-chromatic' process colours cannot achieve faithful results and need to be supplemented by one or two — and, though rarely, even more — additional colours such as lemon yellow because this colour cannot be achieved with process yellow alone.

The simplest use of colour printing is by reproducing line originals as solid colours. Depending on the limitations of the job specification, there need be no restriction on the number of colours used, since any number of inks — each applied by a separate plate or block — can be used to match the original. If the design is to be printed in a publication restricted to the process colours, overlapping solid colours can be used to create more than just yellow, magenta, cyan and black — yellow and cyan, for instance, can be used to produce green. Different shades of the solid colours can even be achieved by using screen tints.

The easiest way of presenting line artwork for colour reproduction is to produce a black representation of each respective colour on a transparent overlay. If the original is presented in full-colour, a separation process must be used. To separate a colour original into its process colour components, it is necessary to make a negative for each respective colour by photographing the original through a colour filter which has been matched to the standard

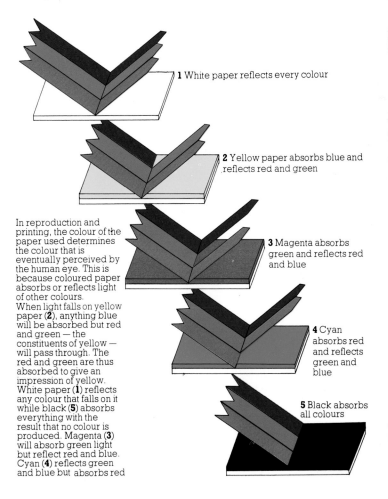

1 White paper reflects every colour

2 Yellow paper absorbs blue and reflects red and green

In reproduction and printing, the colour of the paper used determines the colour that is eventually perceived by the human eye. This is because coloured paper absorbs or reflects light of other colours.
When light falls on yellow paper (**2**), anything blue will be absorbed but red and green — the constituents of yellow — will pass through. The red and green are thus absorbed to give an impression of yellow. White paper (**1**) reflects any colour that falls on it while black (**5**) absorbs everything with the result that no colour is produced. Magenta (**3**) will absorb green light but reflect red and blue. Cyan (**4**) reflects green and blue but absorbs red

3 Magenta absorbs green and reflects red and blue

4 Cyan absorbs red and reflects green and blue

5 Black absorbs all colours

Colour scanning is rapidly superseding traditional camera methods of reproduction because it is speedier, more accurate and more flexible. In principle, the way it works is simple. Images are scanned by a high-intensity light or laser beam, which, via colour filters and a computer, converts them into individual screened films for each colour. These films can be either positive or negative, according to requirements.

Scanning transparencies The first step is to tape the transparencies to the glass cylinder or drum of the scanner. Since the process is expensive, it is cost-effective for the transparencies to be batched so that the optimum number of whatever size can be fitted to the drum at the same time. Their densities, however, should also be similar, since the scanner will be set to average this out. In addition, the accuracy of a modern scanner means that the slightest flaw or scratch on a transparency will be picked up and magnified. This is a particular risk with 35mm transparencies and, for this

reason, it is common for such transparencies to be floated in oil on the surface of the drum if an enlargement of more than 500% is required.

The operator then keys in the percentage reductions or enlargements required on the scanner's computer. These are expressed in two dimensions, or factor numbers, which are calculated from the master chart supplied by the manufacturer. At the same time, the screen percentage is set. This dictates how many lines of dots appear per inch on the final film.

The drum is then fitted to the scanner and rotated at high speed. The light or laser passes through a system of lenses to be angled by a mirror set at 90° to illuminate the images, which are then analyzed as the scanning head moves along the surface of the drum. The signals are passed to the computer via the colour filters and the computer transmits this in digital form to the film. This is held in 20in (50cm) x 16in (40cm) cassette form, of which 19½in (49cm) x 15½in (38cm) is the image area. The

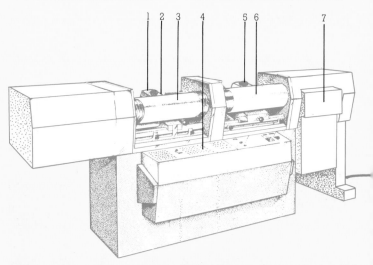

Scanners can be programmed deliberately to produce extremely striking effects. The racing car (**above**) was stretched horizontally to increase the impression of speed by the operator setting the horizontal enlargement to a greater amount than that of the vertical. They also have the ability to correct out-of-focus originals (**near right**) to a certain degree (**far right**). The computer modified the signal by increasing the contrast across the adjacent areas of detail.

film used is hard-dot film. Its use means that, if the dots are slightly etched away in colour correction, their area remains the same, as opposed to soft dots which become smaller.

The film is removed and processed by rapid access developing. This takes 90 seconds, as opposed to five minutes or more in traditional photolitho processing. Many operators can tell the accuracy of the colour by visual examination of the film even before proofing. Normally, very little correction is needed, though proofs are correctable up to between 5% and 10% on hard film (20% on soft). The reason why colour correction is still necessary — even with this sophisticated system — is simple. With the pigments currently available, it is impossible to produce a perfectly pure printing ink, since each ink absorbs some of the light it should reflect. Colour correction compensates for this undesirable absorption of colour by the inks.

Often, it is quicker and cheaper to re-run the images than correct. The entire process — from mounting the

transparencies to proofing can take as little as five hours, but the normal time is around 10 days.

Scanning artwork The scanning of artwork is carried out in exactly the same way as the scanning of transparencies. However, it is important to remember that the scanner is even more sensitive, because of the amount of light artwork will reflect. Certain colours, too, are difficult or impossible to reproduce. These include turquoise — a slightly warmer colour than cyan — and orange-reds. Lemon yellow and fluorescent colours are impossible, while excessive amounts of process white tend to make the colour read-out, the basis for computation, inaccurate.

When preparing artwork for the scanner, it is vital to use flexible board as the base, so the artwork can be wrapped around the drum without damaging it. If artwork is incorrectly presented, the operator may try to strip it off so that it can be mounted, with the consequent high risk of tearing. If paint is applied too thickly, it may also crack.

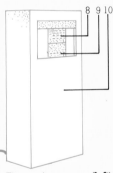

Electronic scanners (**left**) include a scanning head (**1**), optical colour system (**2**) — scanning drum (**3**) — seen in action (**right**) — colour computer (**4**), recording head (**5**), make-up drum (**6**), film cassette (**7**), dimension keys (**8**), screen keys (**9**) and computer shell (**10**).

inks and also to the respective parts of the colour spectrum.

To explain this, some understanding of the colour components of light is required. White light is formed by a combination of all of the colours of the spectrum, and these can be broken down into three main colour sectors — red, green and blue. Since these colours are added together or overlapped to create white light, they are known as 'additive' primaries. If one of the primary colours is taken away, a different colour is produced. Hence the combination of red and green, without blue, makes yellow, whereas red and blue without green produces magenta, and green and blue

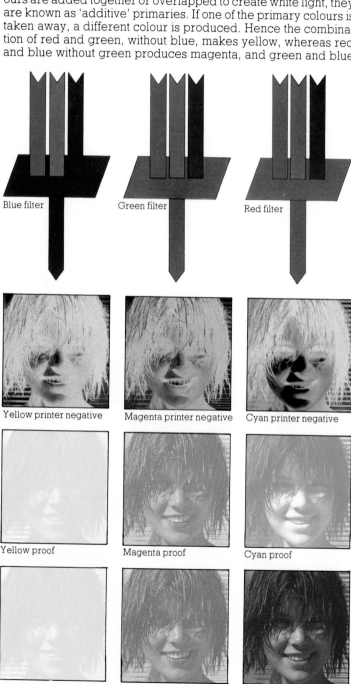

Blue filter

Green filter

Red filter

Yellow printer negative

Magenta printer negative

Cyan printer negative

Yellow proof

Magenta proof

Cyan proof

Yellow proof

Yellow plus magenta

Yellow, magenta plus cyan

without red give cyan. The three colours made in this way — magenta, yellow and cyan — are known as 'subtractive' primaries.

Thus, related to colour separation, the negative for each of the process colours (subtractive primaries) requires the use of a filter of the respective additive primary colour. Thus to make a negative record of the yellow component of the original a blue filter is required, the effect of which will be to absorb all wavelengths of light reflected from the yellow components. The result is that yellow is not recorded on the photographic emulsion — whereas the blue reflects light and *is* recorded. Similarly, a green filter is used to

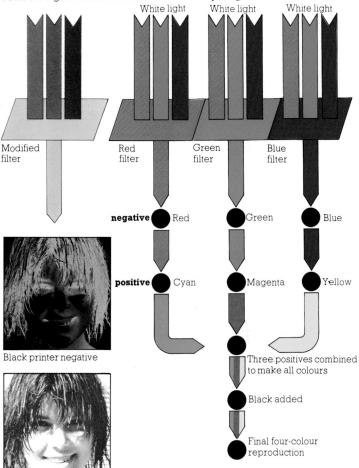

White light   White light   White light

Modified filter

Red filter   Green filter   Blue filter

negative   Red   Green   Blue

positive   Cyan   Magenta   Yellow

Three positives combined to make all colours

Black added

Final four-colour reproduction

Black printer negative

Black proof

Yellow, magenta, cyan plus black

Yellow, magenta, cyan and black are the process colours employed in colour printing. They initially print as tiny dots of colour which are eventually combined to give the colour of the original. The reproduction is broken down into many stages (**left**) before the colour negative can be made. The original is photographed four times through coloured filters to produce a separation

negative for each colour. For example, a blue filter creates a separation negative which prints in yellow. Once the colour separation process has been carried out, positives are made from the separation negatives (**above**). Depending on which colour filter is used, these will print in cyan, magenta or yellow. All the positive images are combined in printing to produce a full-colour image. Black is nearly always added at the end,

One of the most important aspects of printing is ensuring that all the screens have been positioned correctly, otherwise moiré can easily occur. When an image is being printed in two-colour (**1**) the black screen should be placed at an angle of 45° — the least visible angle — and the second-colour screen should be at 75°. These two screens remain at the same angles for three-colour printing, but an additional screen (for the third colour) is placed at 105°. In four-colour printing, the black screen is angled at 45°, the magenta at 75°, the cyan screen at 105° and the yellow one at 90°. This is the most visible angle and for this reason yellow — the lightest colour — is always positioned there. The way in which the four process colours overlap to give full-colour reproduction of an image can be clearly seen in the illustration (**below**). Here all the dots are show at a greatly enlarged size but they become invisible and impossible to distinguish when the picture is reproduced at the correct size.

1 Two-colour printing

Second colour 75° / Black 45°

2 Three-colour printing

Third colour 105° / Second colour 75° / Black 45°

3 Four-colour printing

Cyan 105° / Yellow 90° / Magenta 75° / Black 45°

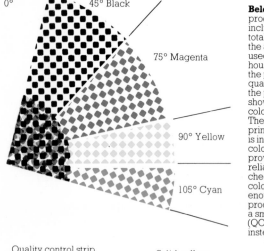

0° — 45° Black

75° Magenta

90° Yellow

105° Cyan

Below Most colour proofs have a colour bar included on them. This is totally independent of the actual image and is used by the origination house, the designer and the printer to check the quality of the colours on the proofs. The bar shows the process colours in various forms. The amount of ink the printer should lay down is indicated by the solid colours. Colour bars provide a fast and reliable method for checking the strength of colour. If there is not enough room beside a proof for a complete bar, a smaller quality control (QC) strip can be shown instead.

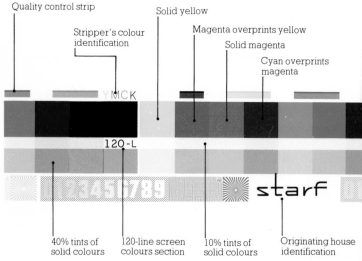

Quality control strip

Stripper's colour identification

Solid yellow

Magenta overprints yellow

Solid magenta

Cyan overprints magenta

Y M C K

120 - L

starf

40% tints of solid colours

120-line screen colours section

10% tints of solid colours

Originating house identification

Occasionally when a halftone is photographed through a screen a moiré effect occurs (**right**). This gives the image a characteristic but undesirable chequered pattern. The reason moiré happens is because two halftone screens have been superimposed incorrectly at the wrong angle. To correct the problem, the screens should be repositioned so that there is at least an angle of 15° between them. If a moiré effect needs to be removed, this should be marked up on the colour proof when it is being corrected. The designer should also check that colours have not been transposed. This is normally detectable on progressive proofs which show the progressive combinations of each process colour in their printing sequence. Here (**below**) cyan is printing as magenta and vice versa. The corrected proof is **below right**.

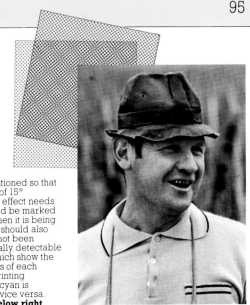

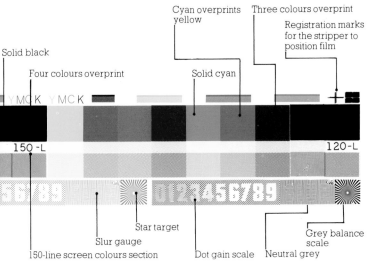

Cyan overprints yellow

Three colours overprint

Registration marks for the stripper to position film

Solid black

Four colours overprint

Solid cyan

Y M C K Y M C K

150 -L

120 -L

Star target

Slur gauge

150-line screen colours section

Dot gain scale

Neutral grey

Grey balance scale

record magenta (in negative), and a red filter for cyan. To separate black, either a combination of all three filters is used, according to the colour bias of the original, or no filter at all.

To produce separated negatives for printing, a halftone screen must be introduced. There are various ways of doing this, but they are all referred to as being either indirect or direct. The indirect method involves a two-step process. An accurate continuous tone record of the primary colours is produced as a 'continuous tone separation negative' which is then used to make a positive image, the halftone screen having been introduced at this stage. In the direct method the halftone screen is introduced at the initial separation stage, without first making a continuous tone negative. Thus, the negative is already screened.

It is always extremely difficult, if not impossible, to produce perfect colour reproductions when printing the separated subjects. This is because pigmented printing inks are not pure in that they do not reflect or absorb all incidental light accurately. Thus the colour must be corrected by adjusting the negative or positive separation films. This is done either by photographic 'masking', skilled hand-retouching (see p42) or, if an electronic colour scanner has been used, by programming corrections into the scanner.

To make colour halftone reproductions each colour negative or positive is photographed through the same screen. In order to avoid a screen clash, known as *moiré*, the screen lines are set at different angles to each other — usually about 30° between each. This produces the desired 'rosette' pattern — imperceptible except under a magnifying glass — giving the appearance of smooth variation in tones when viewed at a normal reading distance.

Most types of original can be used for colour halftone reproduction (though not colour negatives), and an unwanted colour bias — if slight — can usually be corrected at the filtration stage, especially if a scanner is being used. Contrast can also be improved

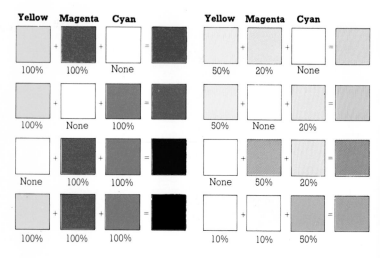

The four process colours — yellow, magenta, cyan and black — can be printed in a wide number of combinations to produce the appearance of flat colours. In the first four columns (**above**), various combinations of solid colour are shown, together with the colour that they will produce when printed. To the right of these columns are percentage tints with combinations. Process colours are mainly used to reproduce full-colour continuous tone originals, but the wide variety of possible tints puts the four-colour facility to its fullest use.

although never up to the standard that a perfect original would produce. Generally, transparencies produce better results than reflective flat originals because the light path is direct, and does not suffer from the subsequent degradation suffered by reflected light. The best results are obtained from transparencies in which the density range is not too great, the details clear in both the shadows and highlights, definition good and finally, the colour balance neutral, with no bias in any particular direction.

Tint charts

Many jobs involving colour reproduction require the use of flat areas of colour. These are made up from cyan, yellow and magenta — the three process colours. Such tints are created by screening the solid colours into percentages, usually in 10% increments, and then combining them with one, or both, of the other colours. To make a tint selection, a chart showing the complete range of combined colours must be used. Such charts, however, are extremely difficult to come by and those that are available tend to be extremely expensive. This is because accurate charts must be printed with a high degree of scientific precision, since normal good printing may deviate from the precise colours by as much as 10% in either direction up or down. There are also other factors to be taken into consideration. One is the type of paper upon which the chart is printed; most charts are printed upon two types of paper — art (glossy) and matt art. The other is the inks that are used to print them.

The tint charts on the following pages are as accurate as a normal conventional print run will allow. Indeed, the virtue of this is that the charts show reasonably accurately how tints will actually look when printed. There are 1100 tints using the three process colours alone, plus a further 300 showing tints of each of the process colours combined with black.

The tint charts on the following pages are vital to designers working in full-colour and they are simple to use. Once the designer has looked through charts and selected the tint he or she prefers, this must be specified for the printer. The traditional way to do this is in the order yellow, magenta, cyan and black, as the colours are printed in this sequence. The percentage of yellow in a tint is given in the top left corner of the chart, magenta is given along the top and cyan is printed down the lefthand edge. In the example here, the chosen tint consists of 50% yellow, 10% magenta and 30% cyan. Thus it should be specified as 50Y + 10M + 30C.

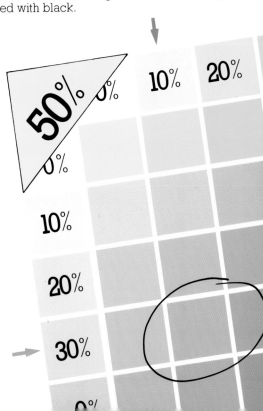

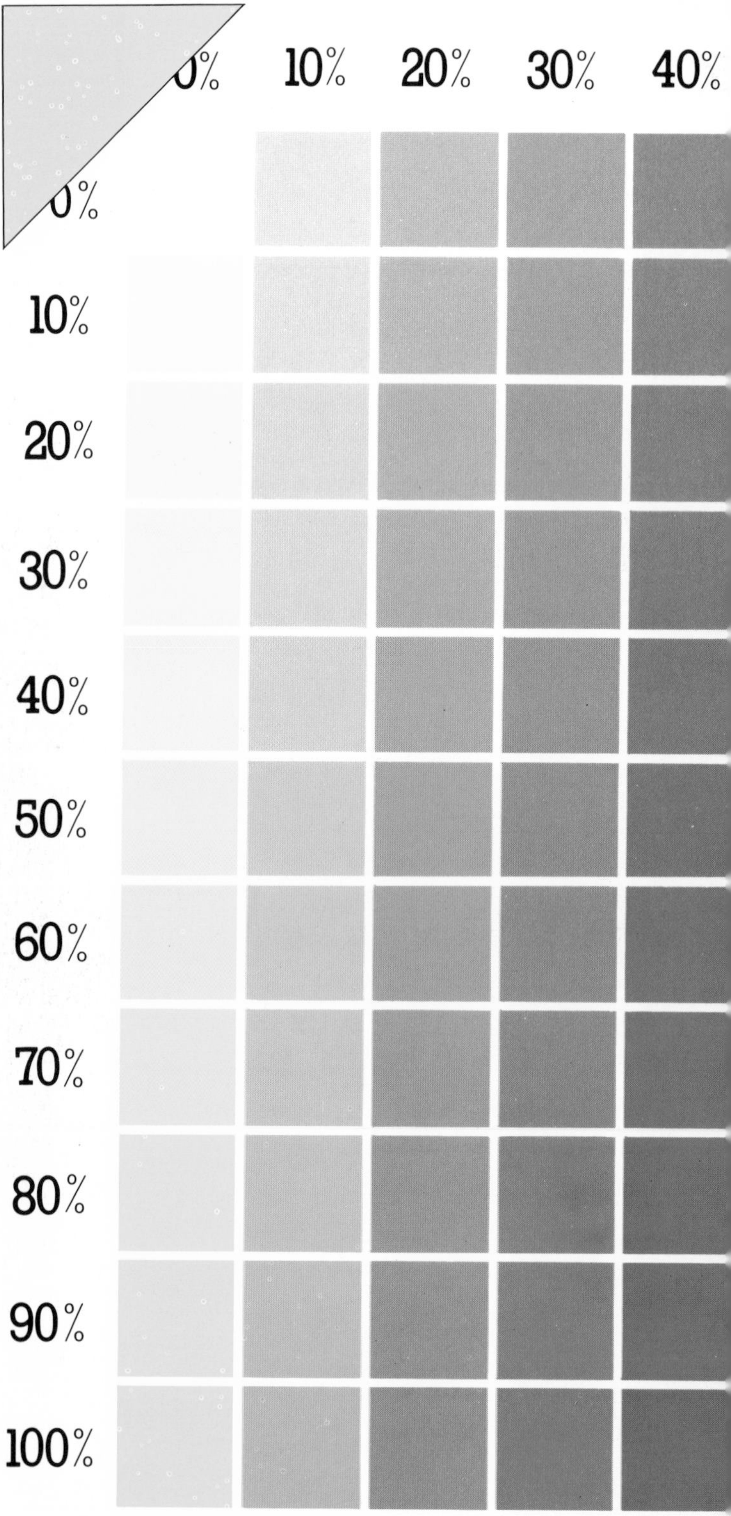
0%
10%
20%
30%
40%
0%
10%
20%
30%
40%
50%
60%
70%
80%
90%
100%

50% 60% 70% 80% 90% 100%

| | 0% | 10% | 20% | 30% | 40% |

50% 60% 70% 80% 90% 100%

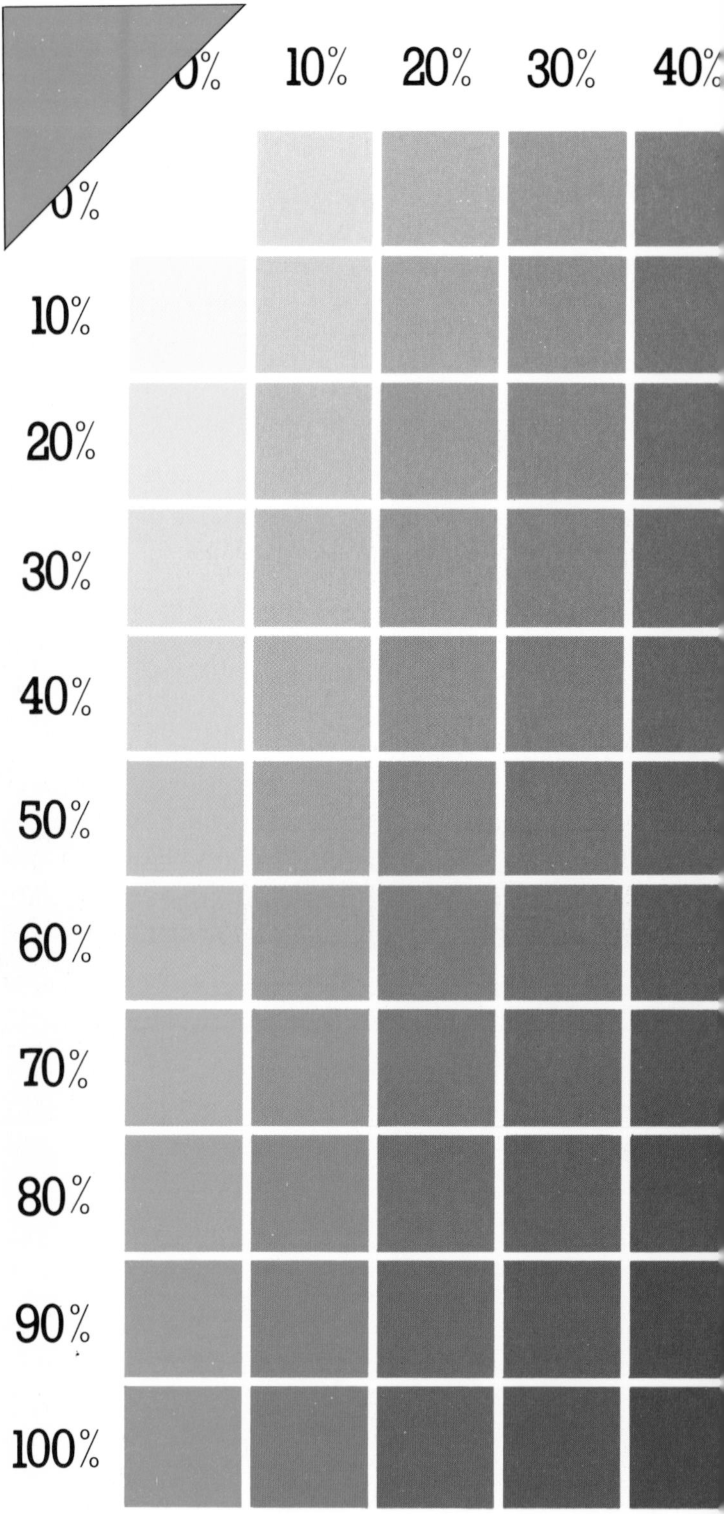
10%
20%
30%
10%
20%
30%
40%
50%
60%
70%
80%
90%
100%

50% 60% 70% 80% 90% 100%

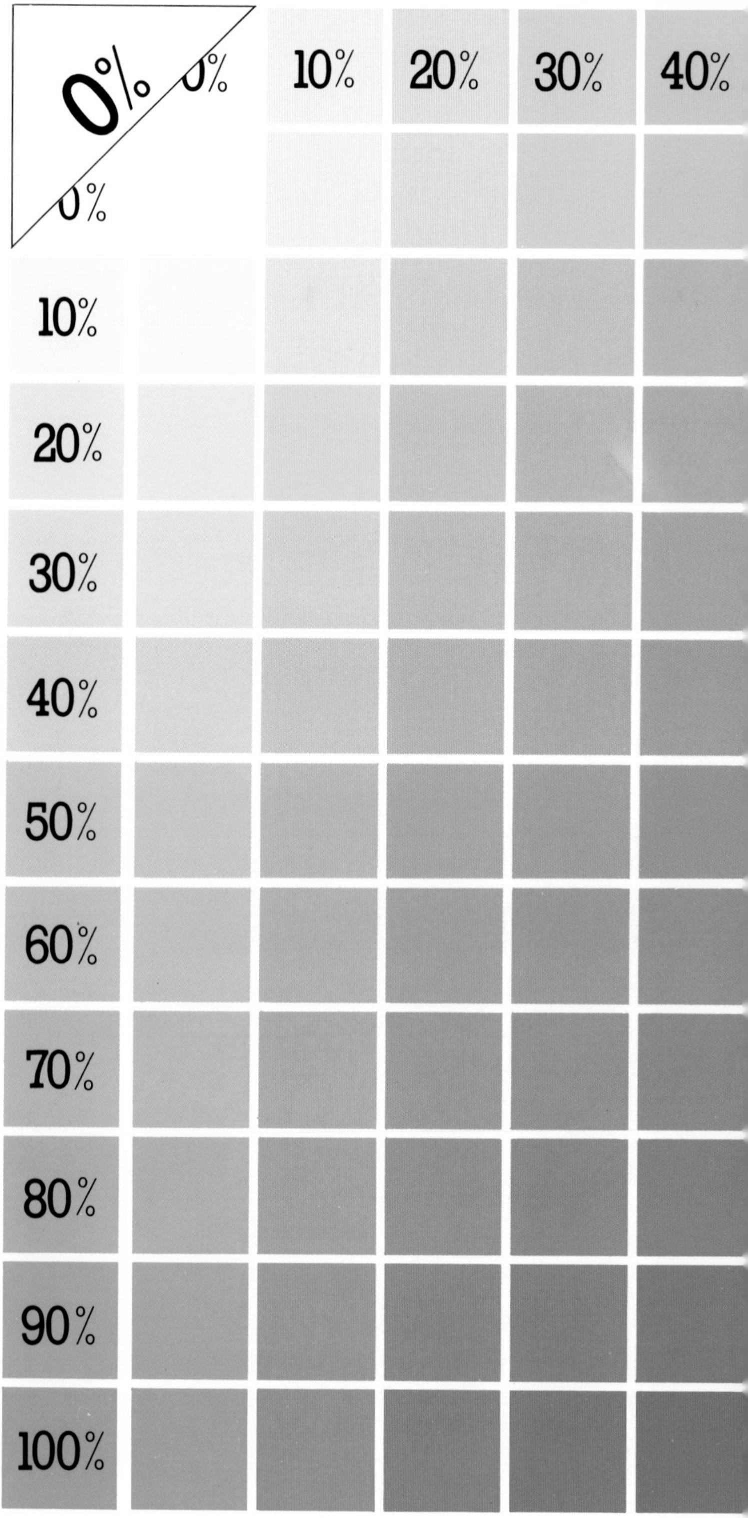
0%
10%
20%
30%
40%
10%
20%
30%
40%
50%
60%
70%
80%
90%
100%

| 50% | 60% | 70% | 80% | 90% | 100% |

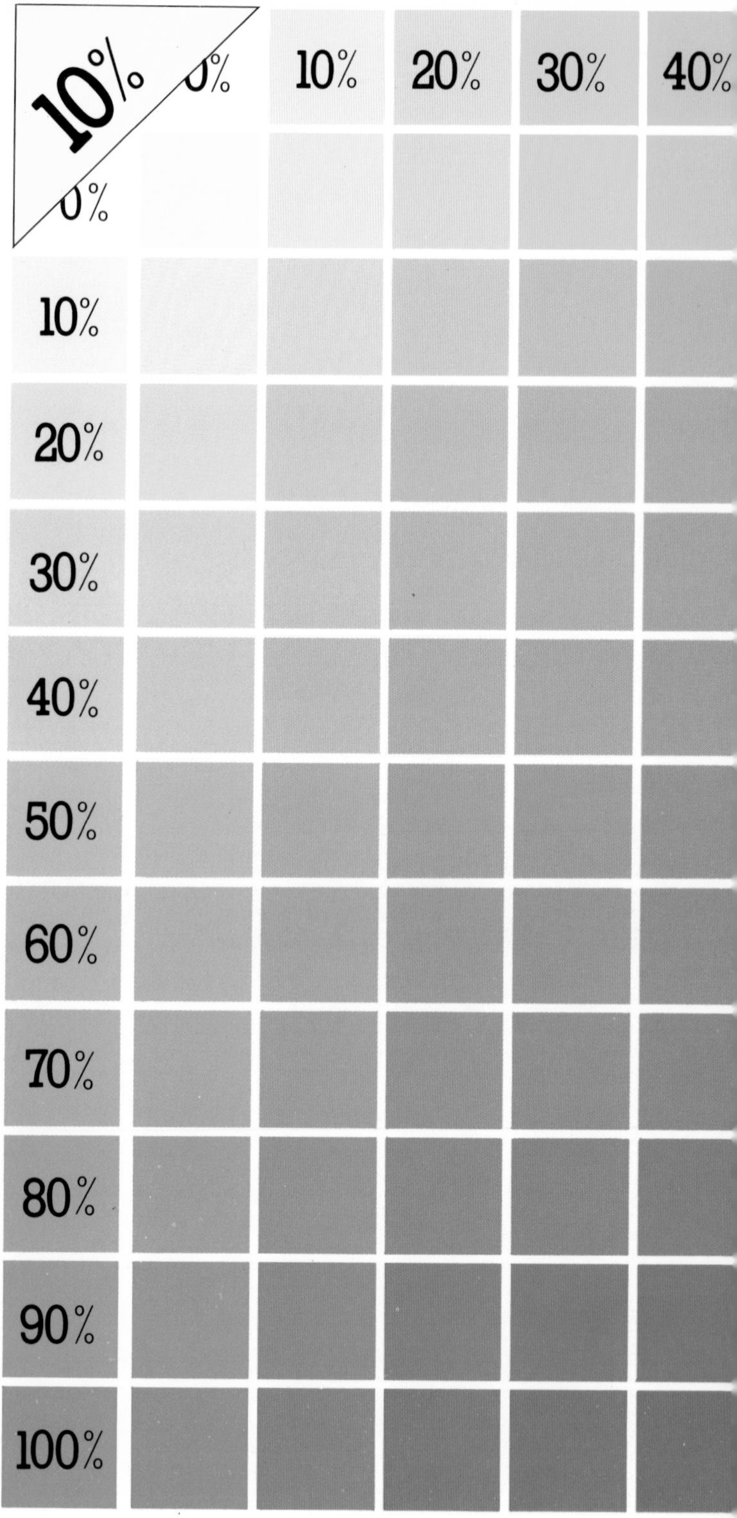
10%
0%
0%
10%
20%
30%
40%
10%
20%
30%
40%
50%
60%
70%
80%
90%
100%

| 50% | 60% | 70% | 80% | 90% | 100% |

	0%	10%	20%	30%	40%
0%					
10%					
20%					
30%					
40%					
50%					
60%					
70%					
80%					
90%					
100%					

| 50% | 60% | 70% | 80% | 90% | 100% |

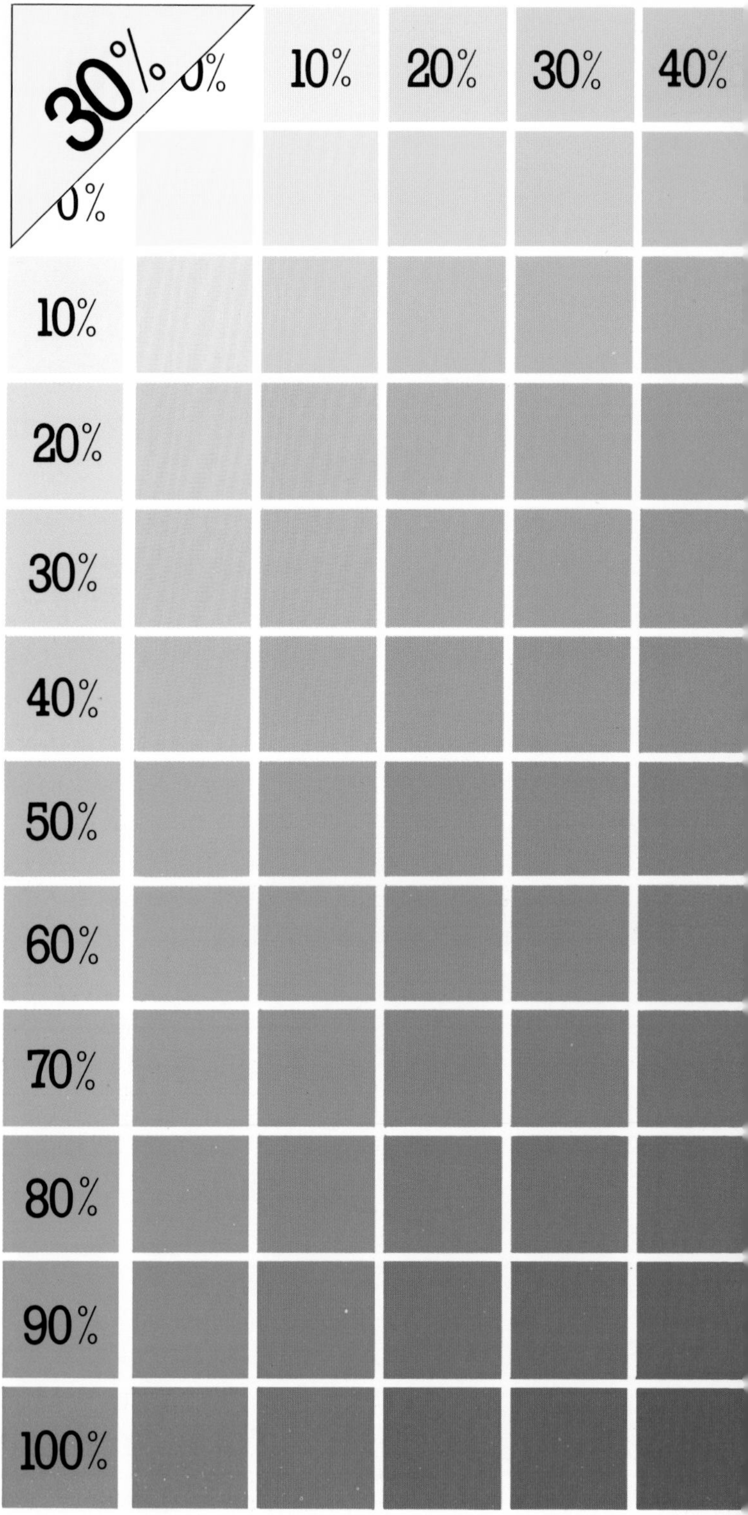
30%
0%
10%
20%
30%
40%
0%
10%
20%
30%
40%
50%
60%
70%
80%
90%
100%

50% 60% 70% 80% 90% 100%

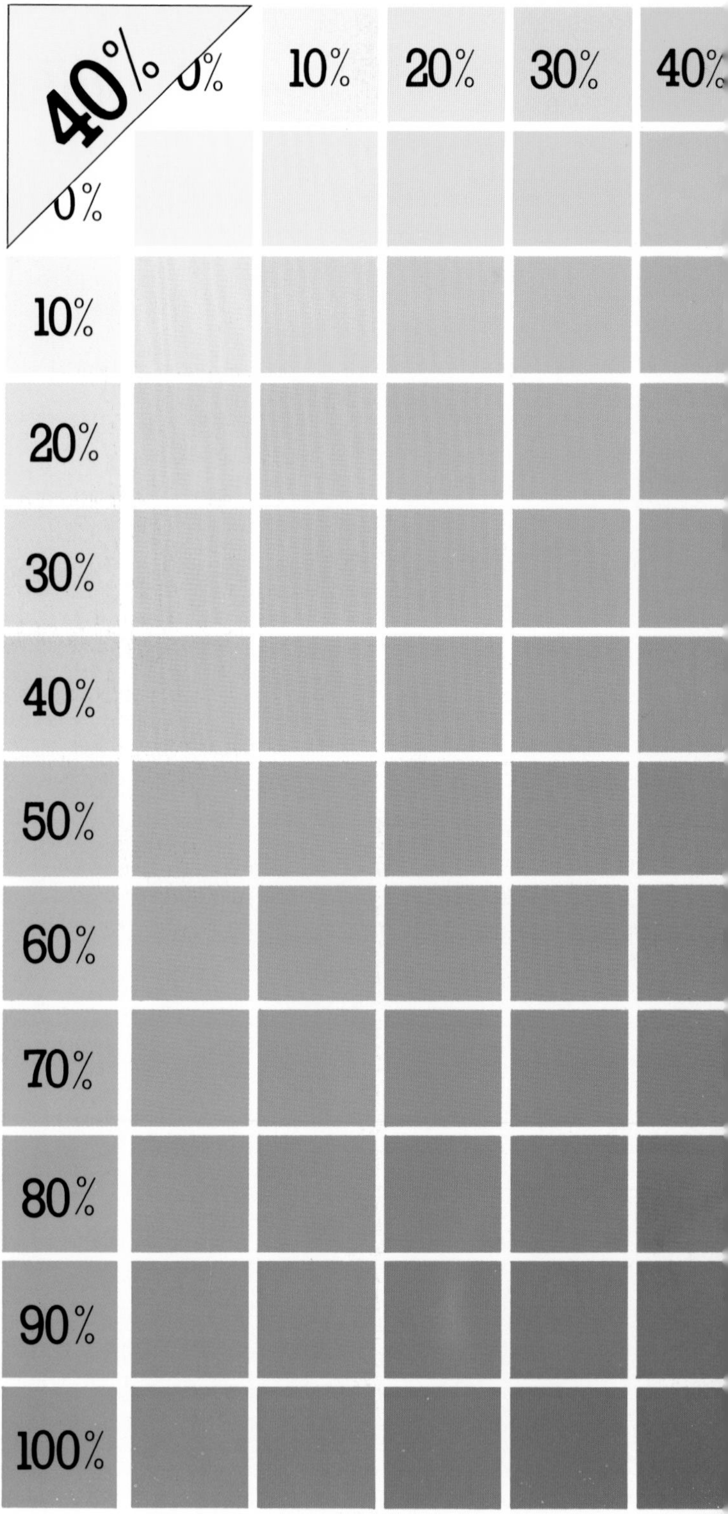
40%
0%
0%
10%
20%
30%
40%
10%
20%
30%
40%
50%
60%
70%
80%
90%
100%

| 50% | 60% | 70% | 80% | 90% | 100% |

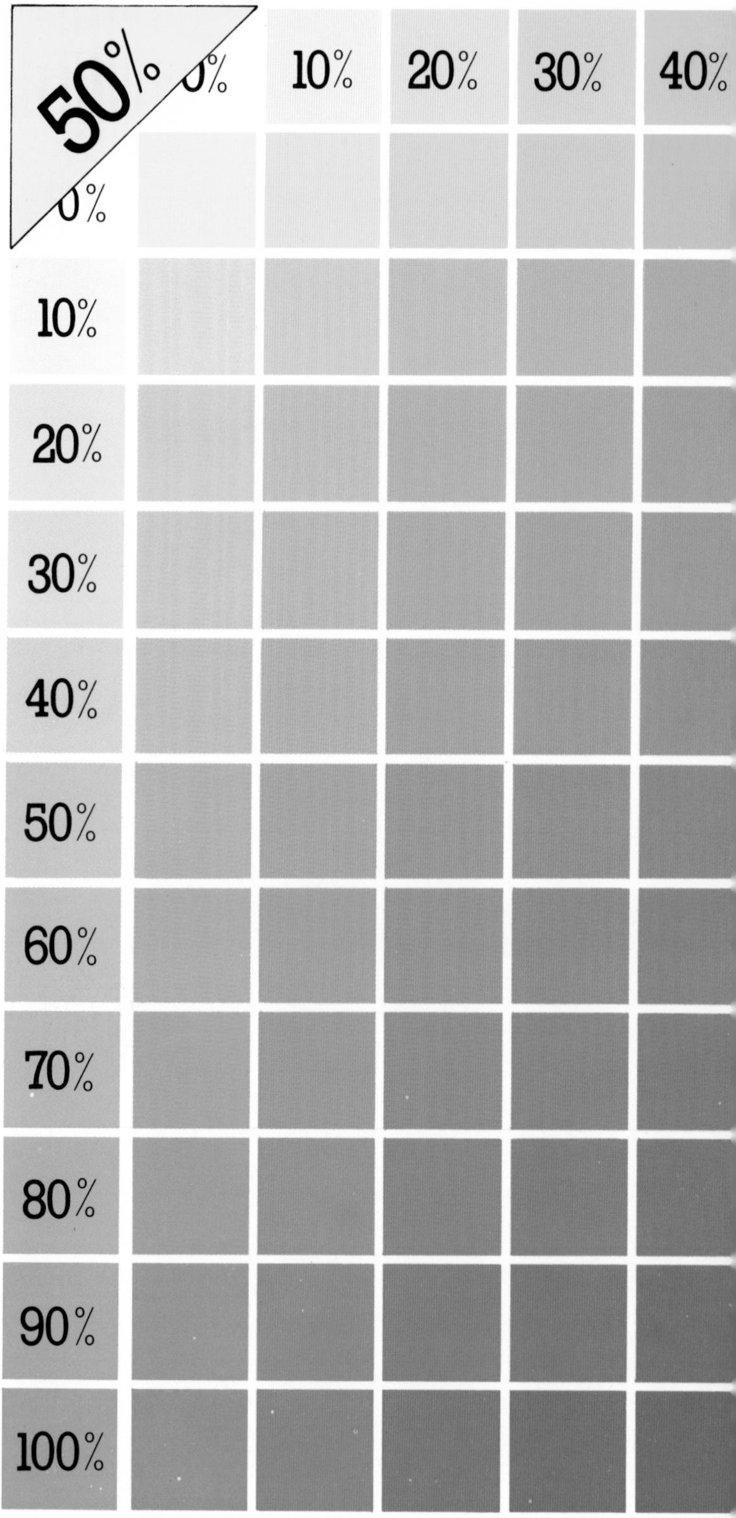
50%
0%
10%
20%
30%
40%
0%
10%
20%
30%
40%
50%
60%
70%
80%
90%
100%

| 50% | 60% | 70% | 80% | 90% | 100% |

60%	0%	10%	20%	30%	40%
0%					
10%					
20%					
30%					
40%					
50%					
60%					
70%					
80%					
90%					
100%					

| 50% | 60% | 70% | 80% | 90% | 100% |

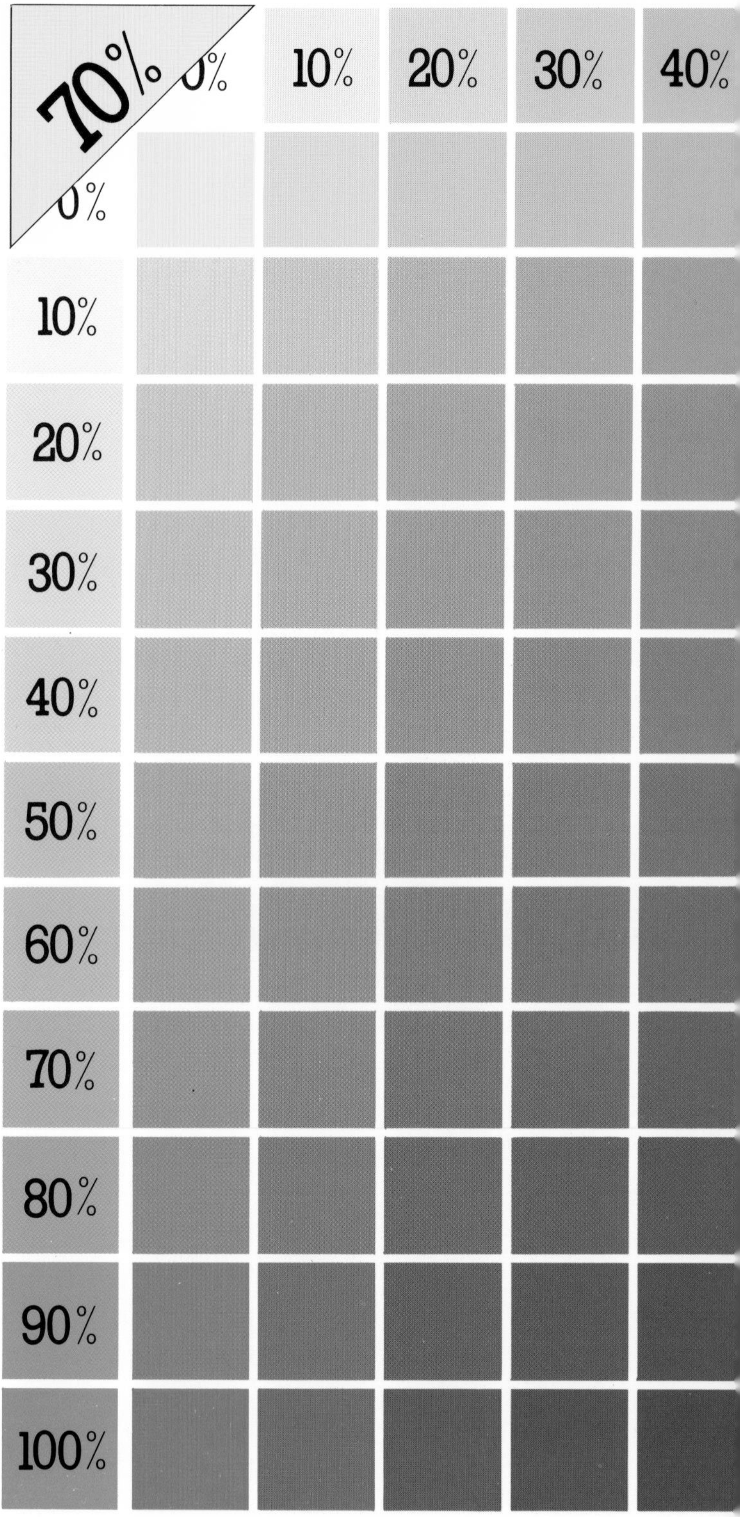

70%
10%
20%
30%
40%
10%
20%
30%
40%
50%
60%
70%
80%
90%
100%

| 50% | 60% | 70% | 80% | 90% | 100% |

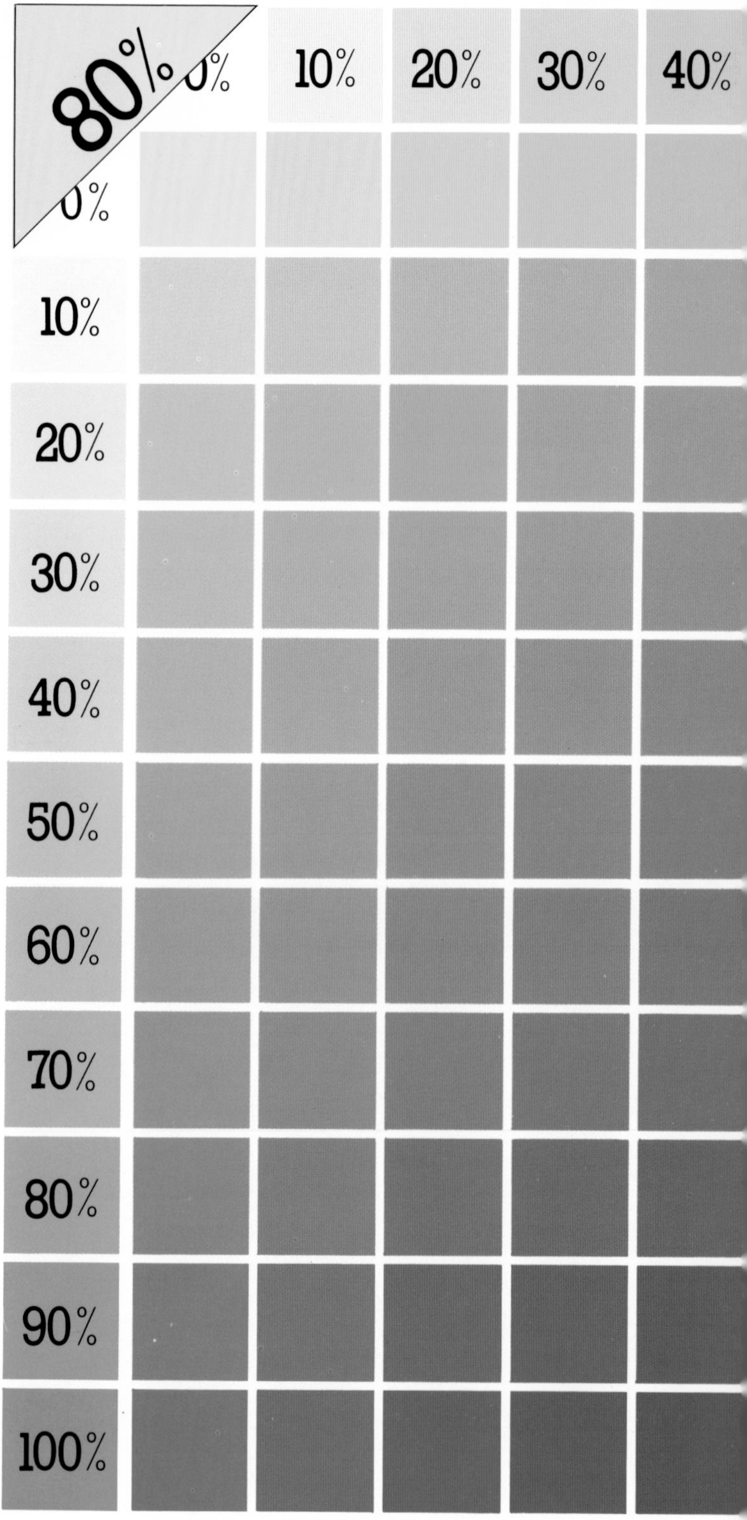
80%
0%
10%
20%
30%
40%
0%
10%
20%
30%
40%
50%
60%
70%
80%
90%
100%

50% 60% 70% 80% 90% 100%

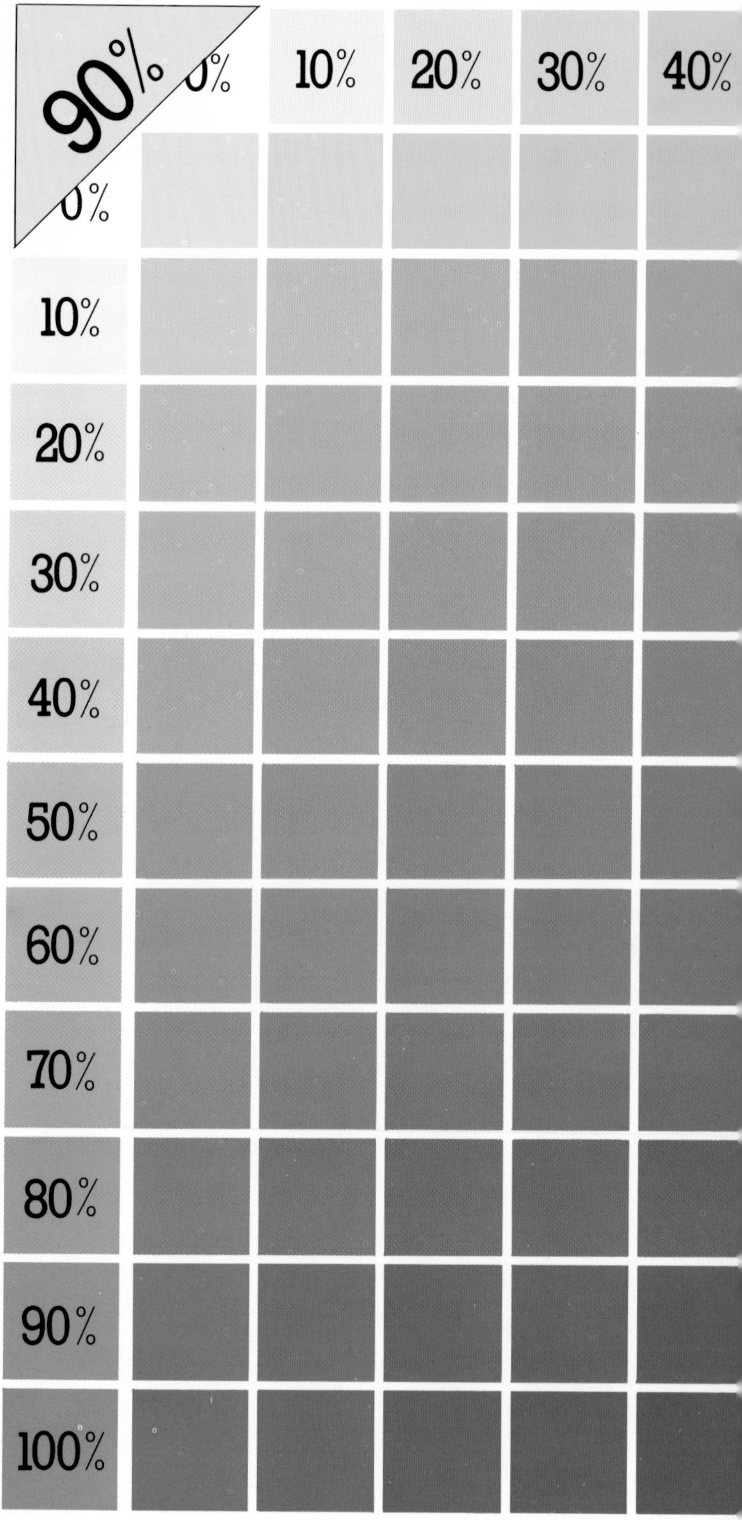
90%
10%
20%
30%
40%
10%
20%
30%
40%
50%
60%
70%
80%
90%
100%

| 50% | 60% | 70% | 80% | 90% | 100% |

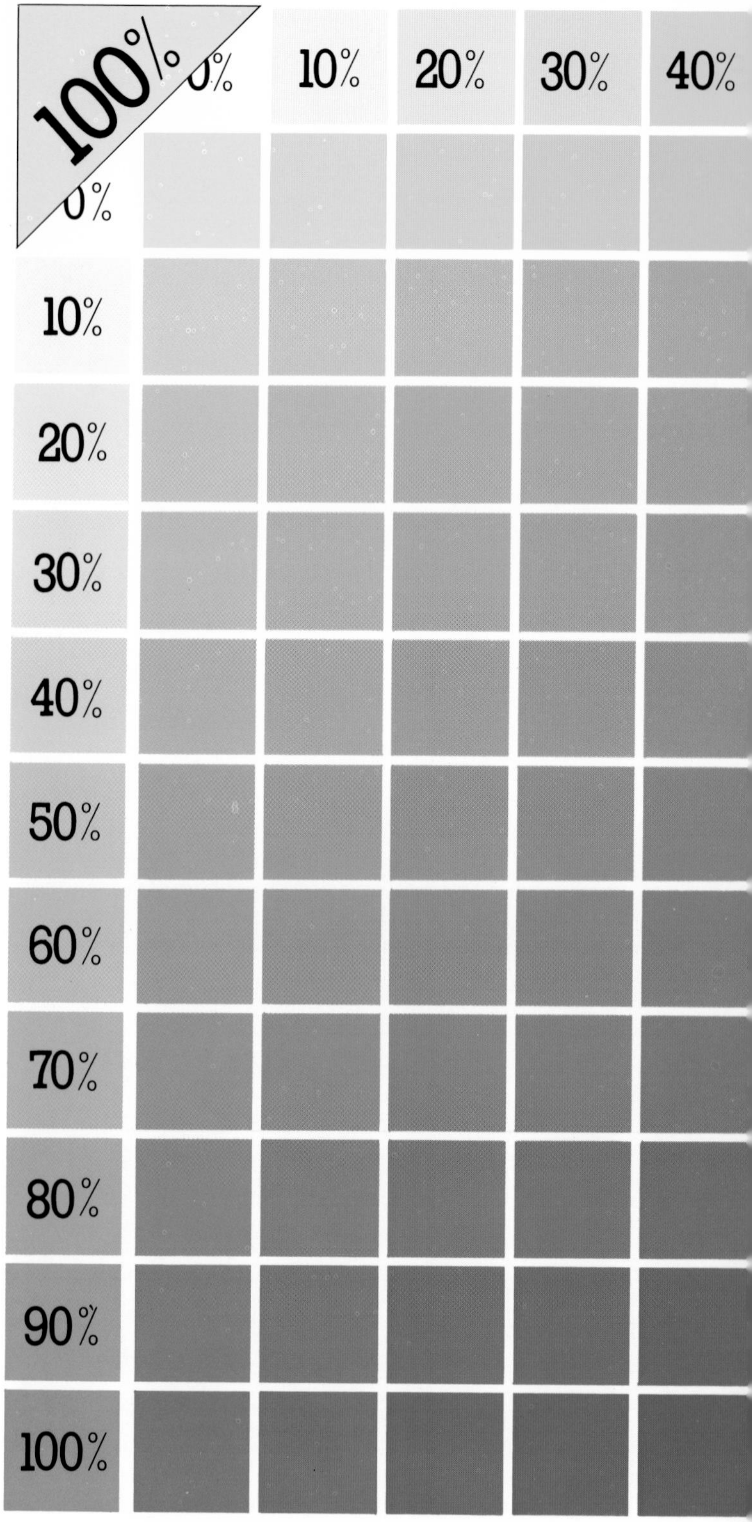
100%
0%
10%
20%
30%
40%
0%
10%
20%
30%
40%
50%
60%
70%
80%
90%
100%

| 50% | 60% | 70% | 80% | 90% | 100% |

8

PRINT PRODUCTION

Letterpress/Lithography/Gravure/
Screenprinting/Collotype/
Flexography/Thermography/Die-
stamping/Imposition/Scoring and
folding/Stitching/Binding/Blocking/
Paper

There are four principal methods in which ink can be transferred onto a surface in order to duplicate an image — by
relief, planographic, intaglio or stencil printing.

In the relief method, paper is pressed onto raised areas of wood
or metal, the surface of which has been inked. Commercially, this
process is called letterpress printing. Planographic printing, or
lithography, works on the principle that grease and water do not
mix — image areas are made to attract ink and non-image areas to
repel it. Intaglio printing employs a process of transferring ink onto the paper from very small cells of different depths which are
recessed into the printing surface. Gravure is the commercial process using the intaglio principle. Printing from stencils is possibly
the earliest known form of duplication — ink is simply passed
through the remaining apertures of a cut-out shape. These shapes
are held by a fine mesh, or screen, and consequently the process
is called screen printing.

Letterpress A letterpress printing surface may consist of just
pieces of type or, alternatively, the type can be used in conjunction with photoengraved plates. These plates — which may be
zinc, magnesium, copper, or plastic — are used if a line or halftone
illustration is to be included. They are usually produced by a
specialist firm of platemakers, and, having been mounted on to a
base material — the whole assembly being called a 'block' — they
are locked up together with the type in a framework called a
forme.

A line plate is coated with a layer of light-sensitive material
which, when dry, is exposed to a powerful light source through a
photographic negative of the original subject. The areas of coating
struck by the light become hard and will not dissolve in acid,
which is subsequently used to etch away the non-image areas. The
coated areas are left in relief so that the plate image is formed.

To make halftone plates, the photographic image is screened to
break the subject up into a pattern of dots which vary in size, thus
producing a range of different tones. Plates can be duplicated by
making a mould, or to produce plates made of a thermoplastic
material — PVC, for instance — on a hydraulic press. The resulting
plates are flexible and can be wrapped around a cylinder for
rotary letterpress printing.

To print letterpress, the type of machine used is either platen,
flat-bed or rotary. The platen press is the simplest machine which

operates by bringing two flat surfaces together. The forme is secured in the bed of the press and is inked by rollers when the platen opens. The paper is held on another flat surface and when the platen is closed, it brings the paper into contact with the forme under pressure.

With the flat-bed press, the forme lies on a horizontal bed and travels under the inking rollers, the paper being pressed against the type by a rotating impression cylinder. Apart from being used for almost every quality of printing job, flat-bed presses are also used, with modifications, by carton manufacturers for cutting and creasing.

A two-colour flat-bed press carries two formes, two inking systems and two impression cylinders, the paper being passed automatically from one cylinder to the other. Flat-bed perfecting presses are similar to two-colour flat-bed presses, but the paper is turned over for the second printing. These machines are frequently used for printing books.

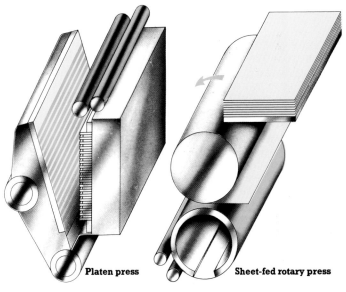

Platen press **Sheet-fed rotary press**

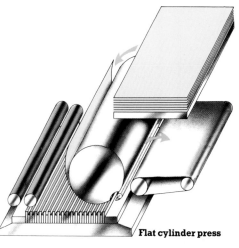

Flat cylinder press

Letterpress printing methods vary; here, three are shown. The platen press is the simplest letterpress machine. In it, the forme is held vertically. When the platen opens, the rollers ink the forme and, when it closes, the paper is pressed against the inked surface. The sheet-fed rotary press is a cylinder press with a curved printing surface, which can print single sheets of paper at high speed. The forme in the flat cylinder press lies on a flat bed, which travels under the inking rollers. The paper is pressed against the type by a rotating pressure cylinder.

The rotary press, like the flat-bed press, employs the use of an impression cylinder, but, as it is designed for high speed work, it prints on every revolution of the cylinder from a curved form on another cylinder, as opposed to every other revolution as with the flat-bed press.

Rotary presses can be sheet-fed or web-fed (printing on both sides of a continuous web of paper passing from one cylinder to the other), and can produce a fine-register high-quality work at speeds making long runs extremely economical. Sheet-fed presses can produce up to 6000 impressions per hour, while web-fed presses operate at speeds of more than 500 metres per minute. A modern development of letterpress printing is the wrap-around rotary press, which prints from a one-piece shallow relief plate fastened around a press cylinder. It is ideal for general commercial printing, folding cartons, labels and business forms.

Lithography The most important and widely used printing process today is lithography, with applications ranging from small office duplicating presses to massive machines used to print magazines, books and newspapers. Unlike letterpress, the image areas on the printing surface do not stand up in relief. This is because the principle of lithography works on the basis that grease — on the image areas — attracts ink, while water — on the non-image areas — repels it. Thus, water plays as important a part as all the other elements in the lithographic process since the plate must first be dampened before it is inked.

Lithographic ('litho') presses use a rotary method of printing, with the printing plate — made of strong, thin sheet metal, plastic or even paper — being wrapped around a revolving cylinder. Although plates can be made from a great variety of materials, the most common are those made of aluminium — combining strength, lightness and excellent lithographic qualities with economy.

The printing image on all commercial litho plates is produced by photographic methods, the plate is first coated with a light-

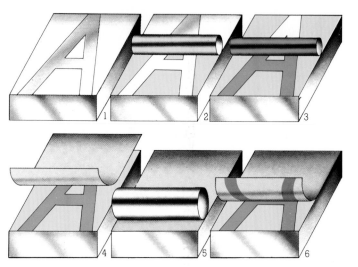

Lithography, or planographic printing, is based on the mutual repulsion of grease and water. The part of the plate to be printed is treated with a greasy medium (**1**) and rinsed. The plate is then dampened with rollers (**2**) and coated with ink (**3**), which sticks to the greasy image. Paper is positioned (**4**) and the plate run through the press (**5**) to produce the print (**6**).

sensitive material. Although many printers and platemakers still sensitize their own plates, it is now more usual for them to use pre-sensitized plates.

To prepare a plate, a light-sensitive photographic medium is applied to the surface, usually in a 'whirler' — a machine which spins the plate to ensure that it is evenly coated. Next, the sensitized plate is placed in contact with a photographic film image and exposed to high-intensity light. The types of coating on a plate can be 'negative-working' or 'positive-working', depending on whether it is exposed to a negative or positive film image.

After exposure the plate is treated with an emulsion developer which consists of lacquer and gum-etch in a solution of acid. After developing, the plate is thoroughly rinsed with water to leave a hard stencil image on the plate, which is then coated with a protective solution of gum arabic. The finished plate is mounted or wrapped around the plate cylinder of the press and clamped into place. In the press it comes into contact with two sets of rollers — one for dampening, the other for inking. The dampening rollers apply a solution of water, gum arabic and acid to the plate; this prepares the image to accept the ink when it comes into contact with the ink roller, and to repel it on the non-image areas, which are damp.

The plate then comes into contact with the 'blanket' cylinder which, being made of rubber, prevents the delicate litho plate from being damaged through contact with an abrasive paper surface. The rubber responds to irregular surfaces, making it possible to print on a wide variety of papers — from newsprint to heavily textured papers to fine art papers. Because the printing plate does not come into actual contact with the paper, the process is widely known as 'offset' litho.

Offset litho printing relies as much on its chemical as on its physical properties. Therefore successful results depend not just on mechanics and on the skills of the printer, but on such things as

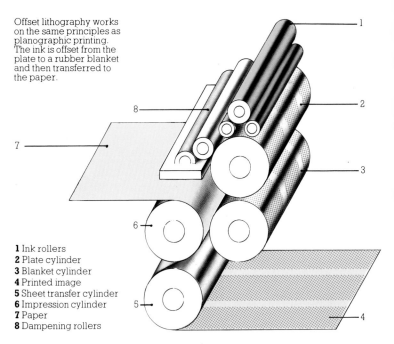

Offset lithography works on the same principles as planographic printing. The ink is offset from the plate to a rubber blanket and then transferred to the paper.

1 Ink rollers
2 Plate cylinder
3 Blanket cylinder
4 Printed image
5 Sheet transfer cylinder
6 Impression cylinder
7 Paper
8 Dampening rollers

conducive atmospheric conditions. As already mentioned, water is a vital part of the process, and too much of it in the air can easily affect the print quality. Excess dampening of the plates may give the printed sheet a 'flat' quality, so that the colours are lacking in density and 'lift' (the degree to which ink appears to lie on the surface of the paper, as opposed to being absorbed into it).

The speed at which machines run can also affect the final quality more in offset litho printing than in other processes. This book, for instance, has been run at a relatively slow speed (5500 sheets per hour as opposed to the maximum of 10,000), producing a good result despite having been printed in a country with very high humidity. Of course, ink and paper qualities are also an important factor — this book is printed with Japanese inks on Japanese blade-coated cartridge paper. The machine used is a German-built Roland 6, which is capable of printing a sheet size of 1000 x 1400mm.

At the other extreme from four-colour, high-volume and high-quality lithographic printing presses are small offset duplicating machines, which are now common office equipment and are adequate for printing limited circulation material where sophisticated finished results are not essential. These machines are ideal for quick printing of price lists, forms, sales lists, wide circulation memos and so on.

Gravure Gravure is an intaglio printing process in which ink is drawn out from small cells sunk into the printing surface. This process can be used with equal success on papers of different qualities ranging from newsprint to coated art paper. Though used mostly for printing magazines and packaging, gravure is used for such diverse applications as printing cellophane, decorative laminates, wallpaper, postage stamps and reproductions of fine art pictures.

There are three main types of cell structure — conventional gravure, variable area direct transfer, and variable area, variable depth. With conventional gravure, the surface size of the

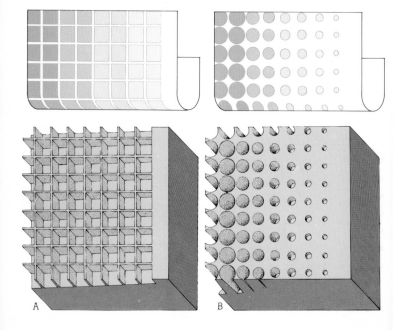

A   B

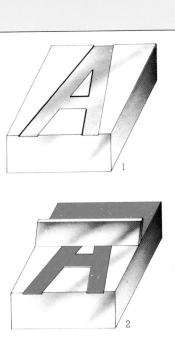

In intaglio printing, the image to be reproduced is etched or incised beneath the surface of the printing plate (**1**). Ink is applied with a roller and a thin, flexible steel blade, known as a 'doctor' is drawn across the plate to remove surplus ink from the non-printing areas (**2**). Paper is put on the plate (**3**) and pressure applied by a rubber-coated roller (**4**). This forces the paper into the recesses on the plate to pick up the image. The design is transferred and the finished print removed (**5**).

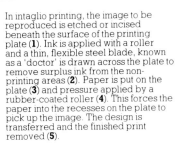

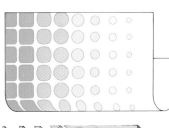

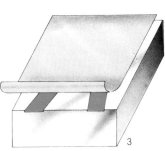

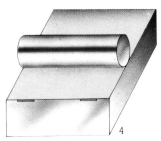

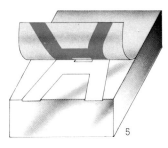

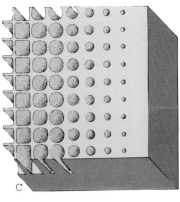

As well as its other uses, gravure printing (**left**) is particularly suited to the production of long runs because of the durability of the plates. On a conventional gravure plate (**A**), the cells vary in depth, but have the same surface areas. In variable surface variable depth gravure (**B**), the size of the cells varies as well as the depth. This form of gravure is suitable for long-run periodical printing. Variable area direct transfer gravure (**C**) is widely used in the printing of packaging and textiles. As the image areas do not vary in depth, only limited tones are available. The enlarged details above each example clearly show the individual effects of each method. They also demonstrate the basic gravure principle of printing in thousands of dots.

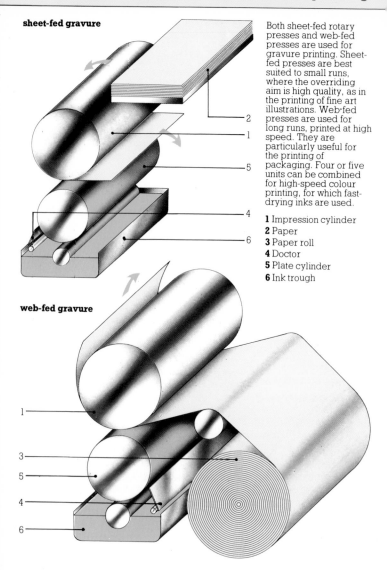

sheet-fed gravure

Both sheet-fed rotary presses and web-fed presses are used for gravure printing. Sheet-fed presses are best suited to small runs, where the overriding aim is high quality, as in the printing of fine art illustrations. Web-fed presses are used for long runs, printed at high speed. They are particularly useful for the printing of packaging. Four or five units can be combined for high-speed colour printing, for which fast-drying inks are used.

1 Impression cylinder
2 Paper
3 Paper roll
4 Doctor
5 Plate cylinder
6 Ink trough

web-fed gravure

cells are equal although the depth of each varies, and this is used for high quality jobs of short runs. Variable area direct transfer cells are all of the same depth but with different surface sizes; this process is used widely for packaging and textile printing. With variable area, variable depth cells (or invert halftone gravure) the size as well as the depth of the cells varies, thus producing wider ranging, more durable tones, particularly suitable for printing colour periodicals in large quantities.

There are various methods of engraving a surface. In electro-mechanical engraving a scanning head 'reads' the image to be reproduced, from which signals are used to control a diamond engraving head which cuts out the cells. Another method uses a laser beam to break up a selected area according to the strength of signal received from the scanning head.

Gravure printing surfaces are usually made of a thin, highly polished copper skin which has been electroplated onto a solid steel cylinder. This skin may be chromium plated after engraving to protect it against hard wear during long print runs. If the surface is to be engraved by conventional methods rather than by scanning, the image is transferred from positives of both text and pictures by the use of a sensitized gelatin transfer medium called carbon tissue. This is exposed to bright light in contact with a gravure screen (comprising transparent lines surrounding tiny opaque squares).

The positives are then exposed — in contact with the carbon tissue — to a diffused light which passes freely through the positive where the tones are light. Consequently, the gelatin on the carbon tissue becomes harder on these areas. The tissue is mounted onto the cylinder and when the paper backing is removed it is 'developed' in warm water to wash away any unhardened gelatin, the remaining gelatin forming an acid resist.

The cylinder is etched in solutions of ferric chloride, the rate of penetration depending on the thickness of the gelatin resist. A graded etching is produced by using a series of solutions of progressively decreasing concentration. The process etches the image below the surface of the plate so that it will retain the ink. It is at this stage that a first proof is usually taken, and corrections to tone and colour can be made by rolling-up the cylinder with a stiff ink. This permits local etching, needed to achieve the desired finish.

The finished cylinder is mounted onto the rotogravure press and 'made ready' — positioned and locked in register below the impression cylinder. Register can be controlled automatically by using an electric eye, which ensures accurate colour reproduction. The printing surface is inked by rotating the cylinder through a trough of printing ink. Any excess ink is removed from its surface by a flexible 'doctor' blade so that non-image areas remain clear.

In web-fed gravure, the paper is fed through the press continuously, passing between the etched cylinder and the impression cylinder, which has a hard rubber surface. This applies considerable pressure, forcing ink from the etched recesses of the cylinder onto the paper, thus transferring the image. Sheet-fed gravure presses employ the same method as web-fed machines, each revolution of the cylinder printing a single sheet. Gravure is an expensive process and alterations are difficult to make, so it is only really economical for long print runs.

Screen printing One of the simplest and cheapest forms of printing is by using stencils. A stencil is held in position by placing it on a fine mesh or screen which is stretched very tightly over a wood or metal frame. Traditionally the screen was made from silk and the process was called 'silkscreen printing', but synthetic materials are now used in preference to silk and so the process tends to be known as 'screen printing'.

In commercial screen printing, the most common method of producing stencils is by photographic means, although knife-cut stencils — cut directly from layouts — are still used occasionally. There are two methods of photographically-prepared stencil — direct and indirect. Direct stencils are made by exposing a screen mesh coated with light-sensitive emulsion to a film positive of the image by using ultraviolet light. The emulsion in the image areas is hardened by the light, leaving soluble emulsion in the image areas which is subsequently washed away with water. The same basic principle applies to indirect stencil-making, the difference being that the stencil is exposed and washed out or developed before it is applied to the screen.

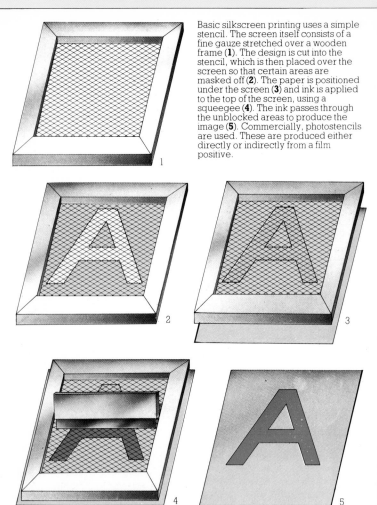

Basic silkscreen printing uses a simple stencil. The screen itself consists of a fine gauze stretched over a wooden frame (**1**). The design is cut into the stencil, which is then placed over the screen so that certain areas are masked off (**2**). The paper is positioned under the screen (**3**) and ink is applied to the top of the screen, using a squeegee (**4**). The ink passes through the unblocked areas to produce the image (**5**). Commercially, photostencils are used. These are produced either directly or indirectly from a film positive.

Once the screen has been prepared, it is scraped to remove any excess emulsion that may have built up. The paper to be printed is positioned accurately under the screen by aligning corresponding register marks in the corners. When the screen and the paper have been assembled on the frame, the actual printing process, known as 'pulling' the print, can take place. Printing ink is drawn across the screen with a rubber squeegee. The action of the squeegee presses the screen into contact with the paper — onto which the ink is forced through the unmasked areas of the mesh. Versatility is a major advantage of the process — it can be used to print on almost any surface including wood, glass, metal, plastic and fabrics.

One of the chief characteristics of screen printing is the thickness of the ink on the printed surface — sometimes up to 10 times as heavy as that of letterpress — but modern ink technology has reduced the ink film thickness considerably. Although screen printing equipment can be used to print at relatively high speeds and can be specially designed to suit almost any requirement, much of it is done on hand-operated presses.

Collotype Like lithography, collotype printing is a planographic process but it is not used on a large scale. However, this process is the only one which can produce high-quality black-and-white or colour continuous tone prints without the use of a screen.

The image is carried by a film of gelatin which has been made light-sensitive with potassium or ammonium dichromate. The gelatin, carried by a thick sheet of plate glass, is placed in contact with a photographic negative and exposed to light. The gelatin hardens according to the amount of light reaching it — the harder the gelatin, the more capable it is of accepting ink.

As with lithography, the process depends on water repelling grease, and thus the unexposed parts of the gelatin are kept moist with water and glycerine so that they repel the ink. This gives a result rather like that of a photograph in that it achieves gradations from the deepest black to the lightest tones of grey.

The machines used for printing are special collotype presses similar to litho machines, but they run at particularly slow speeds; it may take two days to produce 2000 copies — the maximum that can be taken from one plate. Despite this, the process can produce extremely high-quality results and is consequently used for printing small runs of fine art reproductions.

Flexography Like letterpress, flexography is a relief printing process but its printing surfaces are made of flexible synthetic rubber mounted round the press cylinder.

Flexography uses a very quick-drying fluid ink which may 'flood' halftone dots, making their reproduction difficult. The process is used extensively for packaging — especially that of foodstuffs, for which special inks have been developed. However, almost any material can be printed upon, provided it will pass through the press as a web. One exception is that highly absorbent paper should be avoided. This is because the process becomes uneconomical if too much ink is absorbed.

It is important that artwork for flexography is correctly prepared since distortions — both stretch and shrinkage — take place when the rubbers are mounted on the cylinders, and it is always advisable to seek advice from the printer before proceeding.

Thermography This process produces a glossy, raised image by using infra-red light. The image is first printed either by letterpress or litho using an adhesive ink which is coated with a fusible resin containing pigment or a metallic powder. When passed under infra-red light the coating is fused to give a hard image.

Die stamping This process also gives a raised printed image, but has the added advantage that designs can be 'blind embossed' — so the image stands out in relief, but is not inked. The process works by using two dies — a female die of engraved steel, and a male 'force' of plastic or card which presses the paper onto the male die to produce a bas-relief effect.

Imposition

Perhaps the most important aspect of print production to the designer is that of the position of the printed page on a sheet. The way in which pages can be 'imposed' (placed in position on a printing plate) vary considerably, and knowledge of how the printed sheets are to be folded is essential to ensure that the pages appear in the correct order.

This whole procedure can be particularly vexing to the designer, and before planning any job which involves complex colour fall — such as an uneven distribution of four-colour pages

Imposition refers to how the pages are arranged on each side of a printed sheet, so that they read correctly in the right order when cut, folded and trimmed. The illustrations (**below**) show the commonest forms of imposition scheme and the illustrations (**right**) show the corresponding folding methods. Sufficient margins are left for trimming — normally ⅛in (3.175mm) to ¼in (6.350mm).

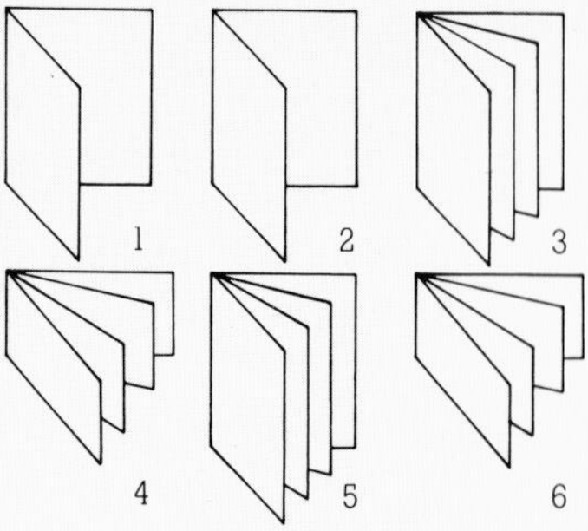

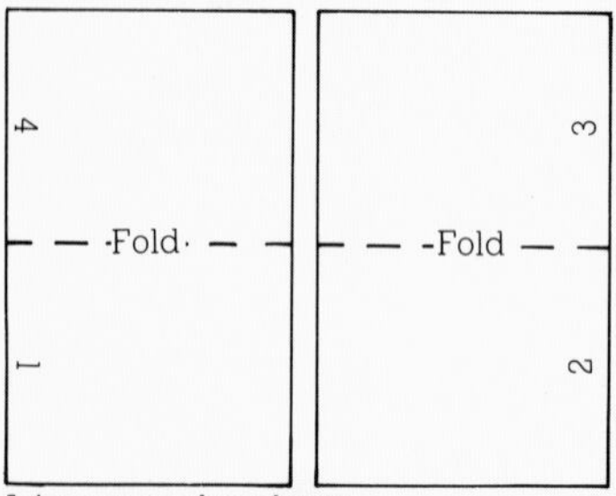

1 4-page work and turn

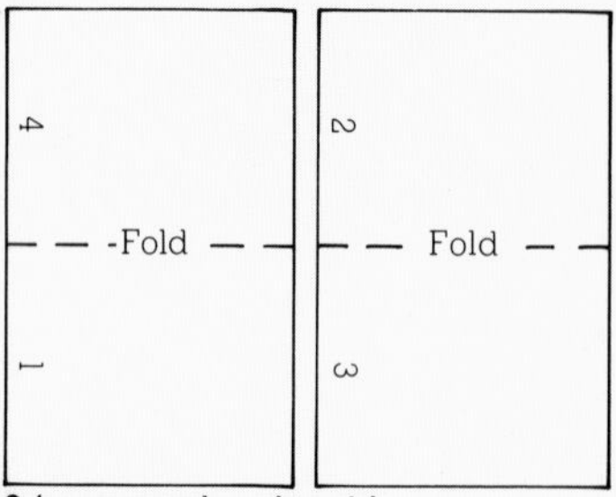

2 4-page work and tumble

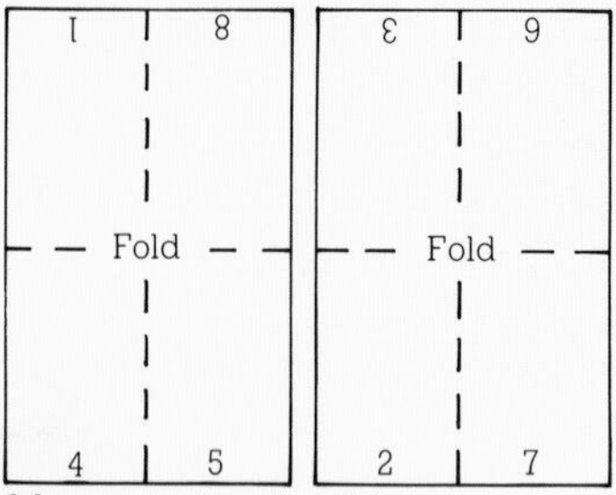

3 8-page work and tumble

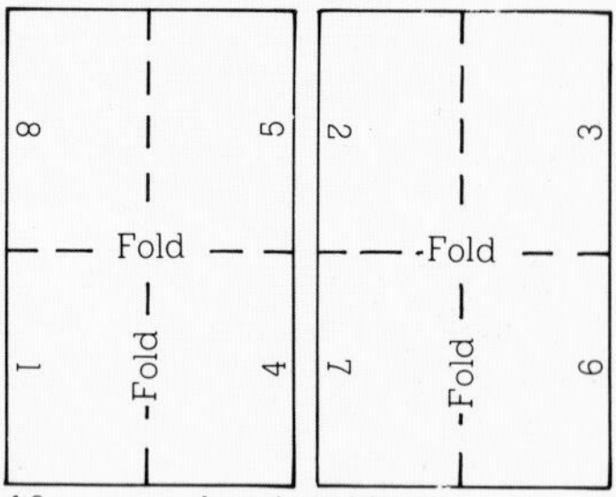

4 8-page work and tumble

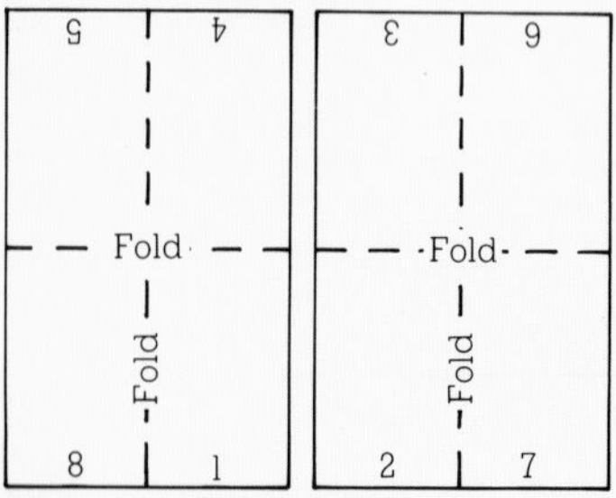

5 8-page work and turn

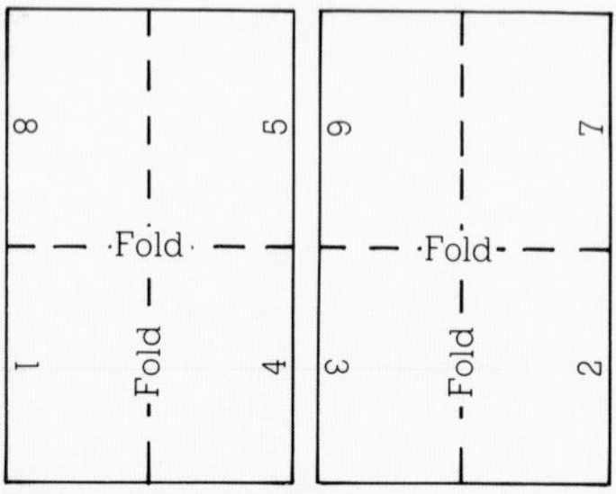

6 8-page work and turn

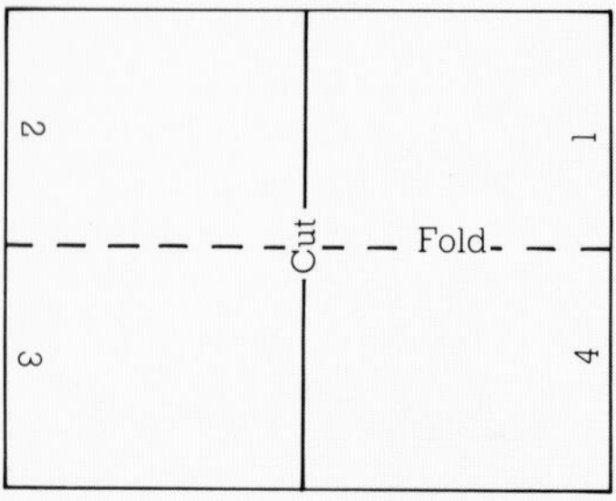

7 4-page work and turn one fold

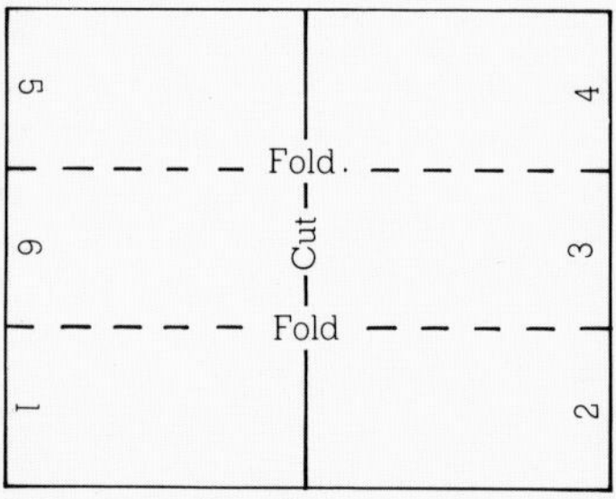

8 6-page work and turn

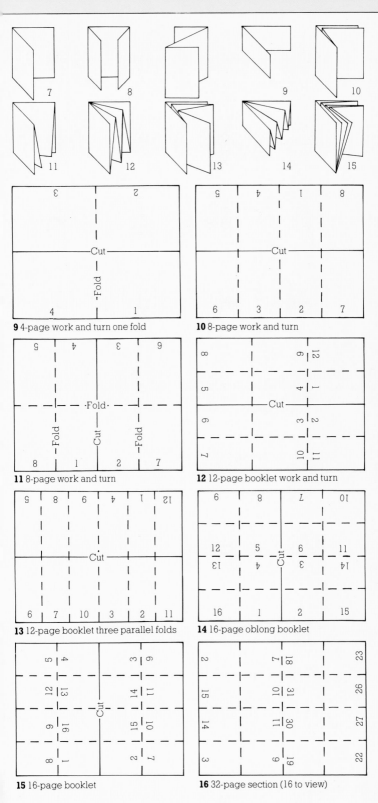

9 4-page work and turn one fold

10 8-page work and turn

11 8-page work and turn

12 12-page booklet work and turn

13 12-page booklet three parallel folds

14 16-page oblong booklet

15 16-page booklet

16 32-page section (16 to view)

among single-colour pages — the printer should be consulted first, since the size of the machine to be used will dictate how many pages can be printed on a sheet.

If a job is to print evenly — such as four-colour throughout — then imposition need not necessarily concern the designer, but if, say, a job is to print 'four backed two' (4x2 — four-colour backing onto two-colour pages) the actual fall of the colour is paramount to the design of the piece. Knowledge of imposition will reveal to the designer that a seemingly rigid distribution of 4x2 in fact allows considerable flexibility as to where those four-colour pages actually occur. For instance, a publication of 192 pages printing 4x2 (as this book is) means that the designer has 96 pages of four-colour and 96 pages of two-colour to play with. If the book is to be printed on sheets of 32 pages (16 pages on each side, or '16 to view') six sheets will be required to print the job. This means that the colour pages can be printed in a number of combinations with the two-colour. Three sheets, say, may be printed 4x4, leaving the remaining three to print 2x2, or, alternatively, one sheet may print 4x4, another 2x2 and the remaining four 4x2. This book is printed in two sheets of 96 pages, as 48 to view.

Further flexibility is possible if the sheets are slit after printing, or if the job is printed as 'work and turn'. This is when all the pages are printed on one side of the sheet which is then turned over to print the other side. A simple way of understanding imposition is to place a sheet of paper 'landscape' (the long edge towards the body) on a table and then fold it across the short side to bring the right edge to the left edge. Then fold it again to bring the top edge to the bottom. Next, place the folded sheet 'portrait' (the spine or the back to the left) and number the pages 1 to 8 in order, producing a folder with four leaves — eight printing pages. When the sheet is unfolded the complete scheme of the printed page layout can be seen on both sides of the sheet.

The number of pages on a sheet depends on the page size related to the sheet or machine size. While most printers print and bind in multiples of 16 pages, it is also common for them to work in multiples of 20 or 24.

Imposition not only affects the position of colour pages throughout a publication but also — because of the position of each page on the sheet — the degree to which colour can be corrected on machine. Balancing the colour of two halves of a double spread picture, for instance, can be extremely difficult if each half appears on opposite sides of the sheet and out of line from the direction the sheet comes off the machine. Colour correction is obviously easier to control if the two halves appear on a portion of the sheet passing through the same part of the inking process of the press.

Scoring and folding In order to fold a piece of paper without splits appearing, it must first be scored, or creased. Although scoring paper against its grain gives maximum endurance, a softer, smoother fold is achieved by scoring with the grain. Several methods of scoring can be used, depending on the type of paper to be folded, but the one applied most frequently is that which employs a round face scoring ruler locked in a forme on a printing press. The width of the rule is dictated by the thickness of the paper — the thicker the paper, the wider the rule. Scoring rules can also be attached to the cylinders of a rotary press.

Thick paper should not be used for folders of more than eight pages and these should be planned with great care. If a book is to include a fold-out page, allowance must be made for the page to fold-in, which must be slightly smaller — at least 0.25mm — than the trim size; the fold must not project beyond the trim size otherwise it will be trimmed off.

Stitching There are two principal methods of stitching — saddle-stitch and side-stitch (which is also called stab-stitch). Saddle-stitching is used for publications of up to 0.25mm in bulk. Folded sections are positioned on a 'saddle' underneath a mechanical head and a wire staple or thread stitch is forced through the spine of the book. Although a cheap method of binding, saddle-stitched publications will lie flat when opened.

For books of greater bulk, side-stitching is used. The folded sheets are gathered (placed one on top of the other) and the stitches are forced through from first page to last. The stitching is about 3mm from the spine — so it is important to allow for a wide inside margin on the pages — and will not permit the book to be opened flat.

Where books are to be case-bound the pages in each section are first sewn together. The sections are then gathered and sewn with thread. Sometimes glue is applied to strengthen the binding.

Binding Of the many different types of binding available probably the most common is 'perfect', or threadless, binding. In this, the folded and gathered sections have the back fold trimmed off and the pages are glued by their back edges to the cover. An allowance of ¼in (6mm) must be made for the trim at the backs and for the gutter margins. The minimum thickness for a perfect bound book is about ¼in (6mm) — any less and the pages may fall apart because they are insufficiently glued. Another problem is that a perfect bound publication will not endure constant use.

Covers for perfect bound work should only be laminated or varnished on the outside — glue will not adhere to a gloss-coated surface, unless a strip of uncoated paper has been specially left for the glue. Publications which have covers consisting of the same paper as its insides are described as having 'self' covers. These may be the same size as the text pages ('cut flush') or may overlap them, and in either case they may require some reinforcement. This can be achieved by a 'French fold' — double thickness paper, folded at the top — or as a 'wraparound' cover in which the paper is folded at the fore-edge and turned inwards. The latter may be given further support by wrapping the cover around a sheet of stiff card.

Case-bound work, in which the text pages are glued into covers made of boards wrapped in cloth, is used extensively for more expensive trade books. This method of binding can range from wholly-mechanized mass-produced publications to specialized hand-tooled work — although this is naturally very costly. A wide variety of finishes are available, from real leather to imitation cloth, such as Arlin. Alternatively, a case-bound book may have a printed cover which is glued onto the boards instead of cloth, and this may sometimes eliminate the need for a dust jacket (a printed and laminated paper sleeve which is loosely wrapped around the case).

Blocking The case of most books is impressed either with its title or a design, or both. This may be done by blocking (stamping) the case with a metal die forced into the cloth through gold or metallic foil. Metallic foils are available in a variety of finishes which are produced by vaporizing aluminium with coloured dyes. Black, white and other colours are also available — either in a matt or in a bright, polished finish.

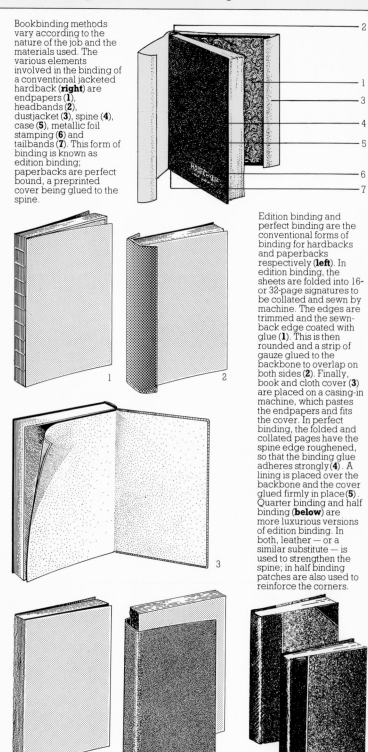

Bookbinding methods vary according to the nature of the job and the materials used. The various elements involved in the binding of a conventional jacketed hardback (**right**) are endpapers (**1**), headbands (**2**), dustjacket (**3**), spine (**4**), case (**5**), metallic foil stamping (**6**) and tailbands (**7**). This form of binding is known as edition binding; paperbacks are perfect bound, a preprinted cover being glued to the spine.

Edition binding and perfect binding are the conventional forms of binding for hardbacks and paperbacks respectively (**left**). In edition binding, the sheets are folded into 16- or 32-page signatures to be collated and sewn by machine. The edges are trimmed and the sewn-back edge coated with glue (**1**). This is then rounded and a strip of gauze glued to the backbone to overlap on both sides (**2**). Finally, book and cloth cover (**3**) are placed on a casing-in machine, which pastes the endpapers and fits the cover. In perfect binding, the folded and collated pages have the spine edge roughened, so that the binding glue adheres strongly (**4**). A lining is placed over the backbone and the cover glued firmly in place (**5**). Quarter binding and half binding (**below**) are more luxurious versions of edition binding. In both, leather — or a similar substitute — is used to strengthen the spine; in half binding patches are also used to reinforce the corners.

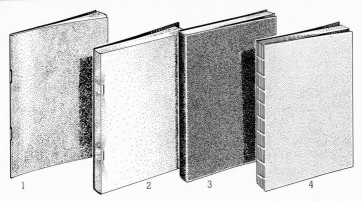

1   2   3   4

There are four main stitching methods (**above**). Saddle-stitch binding is the most common(**1**). In this, the book is opened over a 'saddle' and stapled along the back fold. In side-wire stitching (**2**), wire staples are inserted from the front, about ¼ in (6mm) from the back edge, and then clinched at the back. In thermoplastic binding, the gathered signatures are trimmed along the back edge and bound with a hot plastic glue (**3**). In sewn-thread binding (**4**), the gathered signatures are sewn individually, then sewn together again.

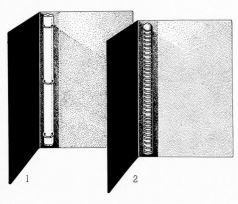

1   2

Ring binding (**left**) allows a book to lie absolutely flat when it is opened. The loose-leaf post or ring binder (**1**) is based on two or four rings, riveted to a stiff cover. These springs open so that ready-drilled paper can be inserted. The multiple ring binder (**2**) works on exactly the same principle, but uses many more rings.

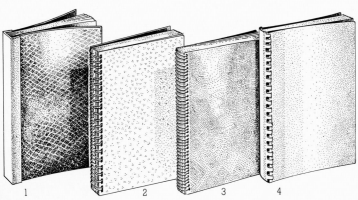

1   2   3   4

In one version of mechanical binding (**above**), a plastic gripper is fitted tightly over the spine to hold the pages together (**1**). In open-flat mechanical binding, holes are drilled through covers and pages, which are then bound together with a wire or plastic coil. Examples include the wire-0 (**2**), spiral (**3**) and plastic comb (**4**). Because the pages lie flat when the book is opened with these three forms of binding, they are ideal for reference manuals or notebooks.

The finesse of a blocked design much depends on the material onto which it is being stamped. A coarse canvas cloth, for instance, will respond better to a simple, clearly defined image, whereas a smooth, paper-covered board will accept designs with a high degree of intricacy.

Paper

The choice of paper for a printed work is as much an integral part of the design as every other aspect. Generally, paper types are grouped according to the purpose for which they are to be used and also according to the printing process that is to be employed. Of each group, or classification, there are hundreds of different qualities — each manufacturer may produce several different qualities of papers for the same specific use.

Understanding the characteristics of paper requires some knowledge of how it is made. One of the main constituents of paper is cellulose fibre which is normally obtained from either wood, rag or old paper, or any combination of these. In the past, many other sources of fibre were used, such as grasses, bamboo and sugar cane — the nature of the raw fibre determining the type of paper produced.

Softwoods such as pine, spruce and fir, have relatively long fibres, and this gives added strength to the paper. Timber is reduced to pulp either by mechanical or by chemical means. The former, being simpler and more economical, produces weaker, less permanent papers such as those used for newspaper printing. Chemically produced pulp gives a much stronger, brighter and permanent quality than mechanically produced ('groundwood') pulp; but the yield is smaller and more expensive.

The pulp is washed, screened for impurities, bleached and finally beaten. This breaks down the fibres and releases a gelatinous substance which helps to bond them together. The pulp is then delivered to the mill or factory in the form of bales of fibre. At the mill, fillers, size (glue) and dyes are added. The most common additive is china clay, which serves as a filler to add bulk to the more costly cellulose; it also improves the colour and opacity

Every designer should have a basic knowledge of the common types of paper and their suitability or lack of suitability for various jobs. Good quality halftones, for instance, should be printed on a coated art paper to reproduce to best effect. Conversely, rough surface antique papers, though they reproduce text well, are not suitable for halftones. The chart here gives a selection of common paper types and a guide to their best uses.

Paper	Comments	Uses
Antique	Subdivided into two types — antique laid, if mould marks show, otherwise antique wove	Text books. Not suitable for halftone reproduction or large line plates
Newsprint	Made from mechanical woodpulp. Cheap, discolours rapidly	Newspapers, cheap leaflets, proofing
Mechanical	Made from mechanical woodpulp. If polished, subdivided into super-calendered (SC), machine-finished (MF) and machine-glazed (MG), depending on how polishing is done.	Cheap leaflets, booklets, magazines. SCs print tones up to 100 screen; MFs to 85 screen
Woodfree	Does not contain woodpulp. Strong, with good colour. Bulks well.	General and magazine printing. Lithography if hard-sized
Art boards	Boards covered with lining paper on both sides	Packaging

of paper and is used to size the surface of high gloss papers.

The pulp is further broken down in a pulper, where it is mixed with a given quantity of water to form a slurry called furnish. This has a known consistency or percentage volume of fibre and water. After further mechanical and chemical treatment to break down the chemical structure of the fibres, the furnish is pumped into the first stage ('wet end') of the papermaking system. Here it is diluted again, then moved to a mechanism ('flow head' or 'head-box'), which feeds it onto an endles, moving wire. This conveys it through a series of presses, where most of the water is squeezed out.

It next moves to the drying section of the machine, which consists of a series of heated rollers — basically, hollow metal cylinders through which steam is passed, thus heating the surface of the cylinder so that the paper is dried as it passes over them. At the end of the drying section, the surface of the paper is smoothed and finished by being passed under chilled heavy iron rollers. These exert enough pressure to compress the surface fibres — a process known as calendering. The degree of the smoothness of the paper is determined by the number of calenders, or 'nips', the paper runs through — the more calenders, the higher the final gloss.

The finished paper is reeled up on bobbins until the roll reaches the required size. It is then removed without interruption of the continuous production process. Certain types of paper — particularly the more expensive, high-quality grades — are treated with fluorescing agents to increase their whiteness. At the end of the production line, these are exposed to an ultraviolet lamp to check the degree of fluorescence.

The whole papermaking operation, from pulp to the finished paper, can be performed as a continuous production process by automatic machines housed in a single factory or mill. All the various units may take up several hundred feet, but they can produce finished sheets of paper in less than two minutes. The end product is a continuous sheet of paper, known as a 'web'. This can be used at once, in reel form, for web-fed printing processes — newspapers, for instance — or it can be transferred to another machine which cuts it into sheets for sheet-fed presses.

Paper	Comments	Uses
Art	Coated with china clay to give it smoothness. In imitation art, the clay is mixed with the wood pulp. Often polished, though some are matt	Halftones, especially four-colour printing. Frequently used for offset lithography. Reproduces up to 150 line line screen; imitation art to 120 line screen
Chromo	Very smooth, usually matt and coated on one side	Proofing four-colour halftones. Reproduction proofs
Cast-coated	Very smooth, highly polished	Packaging, labels, booklet covers
Cover-papers	Strong, fold and wear well. Available in plain and embossed finishes. Usually coloured	Book and pamphlet covers
Cloth-lined board	One side lined with linen or cloth for strength. Depending on quality of paper, cloth can be sandwiched between lining papers	Covers
Cartridge	Tough wove, similar to Antique, although smoother. Offset cartridge specially designed for offset lithography	Booklets, brochures, drawings. Print litho well. Reproduce letterpress halftones to 85 screen

9
GLOSSARY

With the advance of new technology, the designer's dictionary has been extended to massive proportions. In order to include as many new terms as possible, some obsolete ones relating to older processes have been omitted. **Key:** *com:* computer; *pho:* photography; *pri:* printing; *typ:* typography/typesetting. Terms which have their own entry in the glossary are written in SMALL CAPS.

AA *abb* AUTHOR'S ALTERATION.

Absorbency The ability of a material to take up liquid or moisture.

AC *abb* AUTHOR'S CORRECTION.

Accent A mark added to a letter to denote pronunciation in a given language. The most common are boll å, grave è, acute é, cedilla ç, circumflex â, tilde ñ, bar∅, umlaut ä.

Accordion fold *(US)* see CONCERTINA FOLD.

Acetate see CELLULOSE ACETATE.

Acknowledgement Any statement expressing thanks for contributions to a work from organizations or individuals.

Acrylic A polymer based on synthetic resin. Most paints with an acrylic emulsion base can be mixed and diluted with water. They dry to a tough, flexible, waterproof finish.

Addendum Material supplementary to the main content of a book, printed separately at beginning or end of the text.

Additive colours The primary colours of light — red, green and blue — that may be mixed to form all other colours in photographic reproduction.

Advance Money paid to an author or other contributor in advance of publication, chargeable against subsequent ROYALTY payments.

Advance copies, advances Copies of a new publication made up in limited quantity for promotional purposes, before delivery of the main PRINT RUN.

Aerate To use an air stream or manual riffling to separate paper SHEETS to be fed mechanically through a printing machine.

Afterword Information on a work or its author added at the end of the main text. This may not appear until a second or subsequent printing.

Against the grain Folding or marking paper at right angles to the GRAIN **(1)**.

Agate *(US)* Type size of 5½ POINTS.

Agate line *(US)* Measurement of space in newspaper advertising, denoting ¼in depth by one COLUMN width.

Air *(US)* A large amount of white space in a LAYOUT.

Airbrush, airbrushing A mechanical painting tool producing a fine spray of paint or ink, used in illustration, design and photographic retouching.

Albion press Heavy iron, hand-operated printing press, still often used in printing WOODCUTS and LINO CUTS.

Album paper Antique finish paper made from wood PULP, used mainly for the pages of photograph albums.

Albumen plate Lithographic plate with PHOTOSENSITIVE surface coating, originally made from albumen.

Algorithm *(com)* A set of predetermined procedural steps for solving a specific problem.

Aligning numerals see LINING NUMERALS.

Alignment The arrangement of type or other graphic material to level up at one horizontal or vertical line.

All in hand A term referring to a TYPESETTING job when it is in the hands of the compositors.

All up A term referring to a print job when COPY setting is completed.

Alphabet/alphabet length A measure derived from the length in POINTS of the 26 alphabet letters set in LOWER CASE. Thus 39 CHARACTERS **(1)** have a measure of 1½ alphabets.

Alphanumeric set *(typ)* A full set of letters and figures, possibly also including punctuation marks and certain commonly used symbols.

Alterations Changes made to the BODY **(2)** of a text after proofing.

Ampersand The sign (&) used in place of the word 'and'.

Anaglyph A stereoscopic picture made from two superimposed images in complementary colours, viewed by means of spectacles with corresponding colour filters in each lens.

Analog computer A computer using a physical variable, eg voltage, to represent numbers in arithmetical calculations.

Anchoring *(pri)* A method of fixing metal

plates to wooden blocks using screws and solder.

Angle bar The metal bar of a WEB-FED printing press that turns paper between two units of the press.

Angle of view see VIEWPOINT.

Aniline Oily liquid from a nitro-benzene base used in preparing dyes and aniline ink, a volatile, quick drying printing ink.

Animal sized Describes paper which has been hardened or sized with animal glue or gelatin, by passing the finished SHEET through a bath of glue.

Animation A method of film-making that produces movement by rapid projection of a series of sequential still images, usually drawings or cartoons.

Annex (US) A supplement to a technical publication bound with the main BODY (2) of the text.

Annotation (1) A type label added to an illustration. **(2)** Explanatory notes printed in the MARGIN of a text.

Anodized plate A plate used in OFFSET printing, specially treated to harden the surface so it will resist wearing down in the press.

Antihalation backing A protective coat on the non-EMULSION side of a film or plate that prevents light reflecting back into the emulsion.

Antiqua (1) Early TYPEFACE based on 11th- and 12th-century Italian scripts. **(2)** A German term for ROMAN type.

Antiquarian The largest known size of handmade paper, 53 x 31in (1350 x 790mm).

Antique paper Paper with a rough, lightly sized finish used mainly for books, booklets and folders.

Aperture (pho) The opening behind a camera lens that allows light to penetrate to the film. The size of the aperture is variable, governed by the DIAPHRAGM and measured by the F NUMBER.

Aperture card A card MOUNT for the storage of MICROFILM.

Appendix MATTER subordinate to the text of a work and printed after it. An appendix may enlarge on information in the text or substantiate it by means of GRAPHS, statistics etc.

Application software (com) SOFTWARE including basic computer routines and also special user requirements.

Apron (US) Extra white space allowed at the MARGINS of text and illustrations forming a FOLDOUT.

Aquatint An INTAGLIO process that allows reproduction of even or graded tones.

Arabic numerals The numerical symbols 1 2 3 4 5 6 7 8 9 0. See also ROMAN NUMERALS.

Arc light A bright light source used in preparation of plates for PHOTOLITHOGRAPHY. The light is made by an electric current leaping in an arc between two electrodes.

Architectural plan A line drawing showing the ground or floor plan of a building: an elevation drawing shows the proposed designs of vertical faces and a rendering is an illustration of the proposed appearance of the building.

Arithmetic scale A system based on equal measurements eg a chart or GRID with lines spaced equally on the vertical and horizontal levels and indicating fixed value relationships.

Arrowhead (typ) Symbol shaped like an arrowhead used in illustration to direct a LEADER LINE, or as a reference in conjunction with a figure or letter related to CAPTION material.

Art (US) see ARTWORK.

Art lined envelope Envelope with a plain, coloured or patterned lining of extra-fine paper.

Art paper Paper with a hard, smooth surface caused by an even coating of china clay compound on one or both sides.

Artwork MATTER other than text prepared for reproduction such as illustrations, DIAGRAMS and photographs.

As to press Term used in production of gravure printed magazines for proofs showing final position of colour images.

ASA abb American Standards Association. An ASA number appears on film stock to provide a basic quantity from which the length and F NUMBER of an EXPOSURE can be calculated.

Ascender The section of a LOWER CASE letter rising above the x-HEIGHT, eg the upper part of an h or d.

Aspect ratio A term used in COMPUTER GRAPHICS to denote the ratio of width to height in a figure or letter.

Assembled negative Negative of line and HALFTONE COPY used in preparing a printing plate for PHOTOLITHOGRAPHY.

Assembled view In technical drawing, an illustration showing a whole object assembled, often to accompany an EXPLODED VIEW.

Asterisk Sign (*) used to indicate a FOOTNOTE to text or to give special emphasis in line display.

Asynchronous A computer method in which operations commence at varying or irregular intervals, as when the end of one initiates the beginning of another.

Author's alteration/ correction (US/UK) Changes in COPY made by the author after TYPESETTING, but not those made necessary by printer's errors.

Author's proofs GALLEY PROOFS checked and marked by the PRINTER'S READER to be read by the author, who may then make any necessary correction.

Auto indent Instruction entered in a machine for PHOTOCOMPOSITION indicating that text should be automatically indented until the command is cancelled.

Autolithography Printing from an image hand drawn directly on a lithographic stone or plate.

Automated publication (US) Published work of which a COPY is kept on tape, disc or film for future publication with revised MATTER or format.

Automatic dictionary Part of a WORD PROCESSOR or computer that provides an automatic check of spelling for INPUT COPY.

Autopositive
Photographic materials designed to provide a POSITIVE (1) image without a NEGATIVE being required.

Autospacer Mechanism in a TYPESETTING machine designed to include automatic QUADDING.

Auxiliary roll stand A second stand holding a paper roll in a WEB-FED press, allowing continuous printing while the first roll is replaced.

AVA abb Audio Visual Aids. The term refers to teaching and display equipment such as projectors, tape recorders, VIDEO machines etc.

A/W abb ARTWORK.

Axis (pl. axes) Imaginary line defining the centre of an object around which the object rotates or is symmetrical on a flat plane.

Azure Term for the colour of light blue LAID or WOVE PAPERS.

B

Back The part of a book nearest the fold or the edge at which the pages are bound.

Back jacket flap Section of a BOOK JACKET folded inside the back COVER of a HARDBACK book.

Back lining A paper or fabric strip fixed to the back of a book before CASING IN.

Back margin The MARGIN of a page nearest to the SPINE of the book.

Back matter (US) see END MATTER.

Back projection Projection of a TRANSPARENCY on to the back of a translucent screen by bouncing the image off a mirror surface.

Back step collation To COLLATE a book by reference to marks printed on the back fold of each SECTION(1).

Back to back (US) Printing on both sides of a SHEET. See BACK UP.

Back up To print the second side of a SHEET of paper. Backed refers to the sheet when it has been backed up.

Backbone see SPINE.

Background In an illustration or photograph, the part of the image that appears furthest from the viewer, or on which the main

subject is superimposed.

Background art Part of a design such as a pattern or texture forming a background for type and illustrations.

Balance In a layout or design, an arrangement that is visually pleasing, eg an equal relationship between text and illustrations on facing pages.

Balloon A circle enclosing COPY in an illustration; particularly of CARTOONS, the areas containing dialogue. See also BUBBLE.

Bank paper A light, uncoated paper used for making carbon copies.

Banker envelope The most common type of envelope, having a top flap along the longer edge of the rectangle.

Banner A main HEADLINE across the full width of a page.

Bar code A pattern of vertical lines identifying details of a product, such as country of origin, manufacturer and type of product, conforming to the UNIVERSAL PRODUCT CODE. The pattern is read by a computer controlled sensor for stock control purposes.

Barn doors (pho) Flaps fixed to a spotlight or floodlamp to direct the fall of light.

Barrel printer (com) A high speed PRINTOUT mechanism attached to a computer, making information visible in a form legible to the eye.

Baryta paper Paper coated with barium sulphate gelatin. It is used for text impressions on TYPESETTING machines.

Bas relief Three dimensional design in which the image stands in shallow relief from a flat background.

Base Metal or wooden support to which printing plates can be fixed.

Base alignment System of PHOTOCOMPOSITION giving automatic ALIGNMENT of different type sizes from one BASE LINE (1).

Base artwork ARTWORK requiring the addition of other elements, eg HALFTONE positives, before reproduction.

Base film The basic material for contact film in platemaking for PHOTOMECHANICAL reproduction, to which

film positives are stripped.

Base line (1) An imaginary line on which the bases of CAPITALS rest. **(2)** (US) The last line of space on a page containing type MATTER.

Base material Material forming the support for a coating or plating.

Base stock Accumulated material from which different types of papers can be made.

Basic (US) Colloquialism referring to original work, eg a manual or brochure, forming the basis for a revised version.

Basic size A standard size for a particular type of paper, though the SHEET may be cut larger or smaller.

Basic weight (US) The designated weight of a REAM of paper cut to a given standard size.

Bastard (1) (pri) A substandard or abnormal element. **(2)** (pri) A letter foreign to the FOUNT in which it is found. **(3)** A general term meaning a non-standard size eg of type or paper.

Bastard title see HALF TITLE.

Batter Type which is damaged or worn and thus gives a defective IMPRESSION **(2)**.

Bearoff (US) Adjusting spacing in type MATTER to correct JUSTIFICATION and COMPOSITION of the COPY.

Bed The steel table of a printing press on which the FORME is placed for LETTERPRESS printing.

Begin even Instruction to printer to set first line of COPY FULL OUT.

Bellows Folding section of a studio or technical camera, between lens and plate cartridge.

Below the line Advertising term describing costs of promotional items other than the advertisement itself.

Benday prints A series of mechanical tints in the form of celluloid sheets that are used in blockmaking and LITHOGRAPHY to add texture, shading and detail to line drawings.

bf abb BOLD FACE. Instruction to printer to set COPY in bold face.

Bible paper A very thin paper that is also tough and opaque, used mainly in printing Bibles and prayer books.

Biblio A page in the PRELIMS of a book giving details of the PUBLISHER and publishing history of the work.

Bibliography List of publications providing reference material on a particular subject, usually included in the END MATTER of a book.

Bicycling (US) Shipping from one printer to another film or COPY to be used in two or more publications with similar publishing dates.

Billboard Outdoor advertising sign or poster, often large-scale.

Bimetal plate LITHOGRAPHIC plate used in long runs; the printing area is of copper while the non-printing sections are of aluminium or steel.

Binary code Computer coding method in which sets of symbols in data processing are represented by BINARY DIGITS.

Binary digit (com) 1 or 0, the only figures used in BINARY NOTATION.

Binary notation Arithmetic system using combinations of the digits 1 and 0 only to stand for conventional numerical values.

Binder A medium of some liquidity that forms paint when mixed with powder pigment. It is largely the binder that fixes the properties of a particular type of paint.

Binder's board (US) Heavy paperboard covered with cloth, used in binding HARDBACK BOOKS.

Binder's die (US) see BRASS.

Binding edge see SPINE.

Binding methods Methods of securing the leaves of a book, MANUSCRIPT or brochure. Mechanical binding methods include PLASTIC COMB BINDING, RING BINDING and metal clasp attachments. Bookbinding methods include SADDLE-STITCH, SIDE-STITCH, SECTION-SEWN and PERFECT BINDING.

Bit abb BINARY DIGIT, by extension used to refer to a representation of binary digits in any form.

Bit density The number of BITS in a given area or length, eg per inch of magnetic tape.

Black art see BASE ARTWORK.

Black letter Old style of typeface based on broad-nib script, also called Gothic (UK) and Old English (US).

Black out (US) see BLACK PATCH.

Black patch A piece of black (or red) material used to mask the image area on reproduction LINE COPY, leaving a WINDOW (2) in the NEGATIVE for STRIPPING in a HALFTONE.

Black printer (pri) Term for the film printing black in the COLOUR SEPARATION process.

Blackline (US) Text or ARTWORK in black line reproduced by the WHITEPRINT process.

Blad Sample pages of a book produced in booklet form for promotional purposes.

Blanc fixe Barium sulphate, a white filler used with china clay for coating paper.

Blank (US) Thick paper used for posters and advertising display.

Blanket A sheet made of rexine or rubber that covers the impression cylinder of a printing machine. Also, a similar sheet used to cover the FLONG when casting a stereotype.

Blanket cylinder The cylinder of an OFFSET press that transfers the ink image to the paper.

Blanket to blanket press (US) An OFFSET printing press in which paper is fed between two blanket cylinders to print both sides at once.

Bleach out An underdeveloped bromide print used as the basis for a line drawing. The bromide is later bleached away.

Bleed That part of an image that extends beyond the TRIM MARKS on a page. Illustrations that spread to the edge of the paper allowing no MARGINS are described as bled off.

Blind emboss To make an impression without foil or ink, eg on the CASE of a book.

Blind folio Page number counted for reference or identification but not printed on the page itself.

Blind P The CHARACTER P reversed, with the COUNTER solidly filled, used to indicate a new paragraph as **¶**

Blind punching In an automatic LINECASTER, making a perforated tape without running off printed COPY.

Blind stamping (US) see BLIND EMBOSS.

Blinding Poor surface condition on an apparently sound printing plate that causes a substandard image.

Blister card (US) Form of display packaging in which goods are mounted on card and protected by a transparent plastic BUBBLE.

Block (1) (pri) HALFTONE or line illustration engraved or etched on a zinc or copper plate, for use in LETTERPRESS printing. **(2)** A metal stamp used to impress a design on a book COVER. The verb to block means to emboss a book cover. **(3)** (US) (pri) Metal or wood base on which a plate is mounted to TYPE HEIGHT.

Block book A book made by RELIEF PRINTING from page-sized wood blocks, before the advent of movable type.

Block in To sketch in the main areas and reference points of an image as preparation for a drawing or design.

Block letter A SANS SERIF CHARACTER **(1)** cut in a wooden block, that can be used for embossing or printing.

Block printing see RELIEF PRINTING.

Blocking out To mask or paint out sections of ARTWORK or type before reproduction.

Blockmaker A person producing plates for LETTERPRESS printing by the technique of PHOTOENGRAVING.

Blow up (US) To make photographic enlargement of COPY or an image.

Blowback (US) An enlarged print made from MICROFILM, thus 'blown up' 'back' to its original scale or larger.

Blue sensitive (pho) Quality of film that is sensitive to blue or ultra-violet light and may not

Blueline (US) COPY made by the WHITEPRINT process in blue lines on a white background.

Blues, blueprints (pri) Low quality PROOFS for initial checking, printed as white lines on a blue ground. See also OZALID.

Blurb The description of a book or author printed on the jacket or on promotional material.

Body (1) The shank of a type. **(2)** The main portion of a book, excluding PRELIMS or appendices.

Body copy/matter/type (1) Printed MATTER forming the main part of a work, but not including HEADINGS etc. **(2)** *(US)* Body type refers to the actual type used in setting a text.

Body size POINT measurement of a body of type as cast.

Bold, bold face Type with a conspicuously heavy, black appearance. It is based on the same design as medium weight type in the same FOUNT.

Bolts The folded edges of a SHEET or SECTION **(1)** that will be trimmed off.

Bond paper Standard grade of evenly finished paper used for writing and typing. It can also be printed upon.

Book Any work consisting of leaves bound permanently together.

Book block A book that has been FOLDED AND GATHERED and stitched, but not CASED IN.

Book face Old term for a particular TYPEFACE, but now used to mean any type suitable for the text of a book.

Book jacket The printed paper COVER folded around the CASE, in which a book is sold.

Book make up *(US)* The collation and identification of COPY prepared for printing.

Book paper A general classification of papers suitable for book printing.

Book proof IMPOSED PROOFS or PAGE PROOFS put together in book form.

Bookbinding see PERFECT BINDING, SADDLE-STITCH, SIDE-STITCH, SECTION-SEWN.

Booklet A publication larger than a PAMPHLET, but of not more than 24 pages.

Bookplate A printed label, sometimes ornately designed, pasted inside a book to show the owner's name etc.

Border A continuous decorative design or RULE arranged around MATTER on a page.

Bottom out *(US)* To arrange text so there are no unsuitable breaks at the bottom of a page, or so that the page does not end with a WIDOW.

Bounce lighting A method of lighting a subject in studio photography by reflecting light from walls, the ceiling or a suitable reflector.

Bowl The curved part of a type CHARACTER **(1)** that encloses the COUNTER.

Box, box rule An item of type or other graphic MATTER ruled off on all four sides with a heavy RULE or BORDER.

Box feature/story Information in a book presented separately from the running text and illustrations and marked off with a BOX RULE.

Boxhead In a table arranged in COLUMNS**(2)**, the HEADING to each column appearing under the main heading.

bpi *(abb)* BITS per inch. See BIT DENSITY.

Brace *(typ)* A sign used to group lines or phrases, appearing as

}

Bracketed type Type in which the SERIF is joined to the main stem in an unbroken curve.

Brackets see PARENTHESES.

Brass A bookbinder's engraved plate used to block a book COVER.

Brass rules Brass strips of TYPE HEIGHT used to print lines and simple BORDERS.

Break up for colour *(pri)* Instruction to reconstruct a FORME that is to be printed in more than one colour as separate formes for each colour.

Breve A mark indicating pronunciation of a short vowel (ă).

Bristol board Fine board made in various thicknesses and qualities, usually of smooth finish, used for drawing and printing.

Broad fold Method of paper folding in which the GRAIN **(1)** runs along the shorter dimension after folding.

Broadside/broadsheet Old term for a sheet of paper printed on one side only.

Brochure A PAMPHLET or other unbound, short publication with stitched pages.

Broken images *(pri)* Prints produced when a PHOTOMECHANICAL plate is damaged or worn.

Bromide (1) A photographic print on bromide paper. **(2)** A PROOF from PHOTOCOMPOSITION, made on paper rather than on film.

Bronzing Producing a gold or metallic effect by applying powder to a SHEET treated with special printing ink.

Brownprint see VAN-DYKE PRINT.

BS/BSI *(abb)* British Standards Institution. Used as a prefix, BSI indicates that particular standards for a given product have been met.

Bubble Circular enclosure for an enlarged detail in a technical drawing or, more commonly, in cartoons.

Buckram A sized, coarse cloth used in BOOKBINDING.

Buffing The final polishing of a reproduction plate before ETCHING.

Bulk (1) The thickness of the assembled pages of a book, excluding the COVERS. **(2)** The thickness of a SHEET of paper related to its weight.

Bulldog *(US)* Printer's term for the first daily edition of a newspaper.

Bullet *(typ)* A large dot used to precede listed items or to add emphasis to particular parts of a text.

Bundle *(US)* Two REAMS of paper (1000 SHEETS).

Bundling In BOOKBINDING, the tying together of SIGNATURES.

Burn through Exposure of film caused by light penetrating a MASKING **(1)** material.

Burnisher A smooth, curved metal tool used for removing rough spots from printing plates.

Burnout The MASKING of COPY being exposed in a reproduction process, to make space for new insertions.

Burr A rough edge left on a block by a rotating machine.

By-line The name of the author that appears above an article.

Byte *(com)* A group of BINARY DIGITS making up one CHARACTER, letter or FIGURE.

C

© Copyright mark see UNIVERSAL COPYRIGHT CONVENTION.

C type A term for a photographic colour print produced directly from a NEGATIVE. It refers to a method of processing developed by Kodak.

CAD *(abb)* Computer aided design. See COMPUTER GRAPHICS.

Calender A column of metal rollers at the dry end of a papermaking machine through which the paper passes under pressure. This action closes the pores and smooths the surface.

Caliper (1) A measurement of thickness in paper or board expressed as thousandths of an inch (mils) or millionths of a metre (microns). **(2)** The instrument that can measure such a thickness.

Calligraphy The art of fine writing, the term deriving from the Greek words meaning 'beautiful handwriting'.

Cameo (1) *(typ)* A term for TYPEFACES in which the CHARACTERS are reversed to show white on a dark ground. **(2)** *(US)* A brand of dull, coated paper suitable for the printing of HALFTONES or ENGRAVINGS.

Camera ready A term applied to ARTWORK, COPY or PASTE UP that is ready for reproduction.

Camera shake Movement at the point of exposure in use of a hand-held camera that may cause distortion or lack of focus in the image.

Cancel To cut out and replace a wrongly printed LEAF or leaves.

Cancelled numeral *(typ)* A figure crossed through with a diagonal stroke, used in mathematics.

Canvas board A prepared board with simulated canvas texture, suitable for oil or acrylic painting.

Cap line An imaginary horizontal line running across the tops of CAPITALS.

Capital, cap The term for UPPER CASE letters, deriving from the style of inscription at the head, or capital, of a Roman column.

Caps and smalls Type consisting of CAPITALS for initials and SMALL CAPS in place of LOWER CASE letters.

Caption Strictly speaking, the descriptive MATTER printed as a HEADLINE above an illustration, but also generally used to refer to information printed underneath or beside a picture.

Carbon arc lamp A strong light source used in some forms of PHOTOMECHANICAL platemaking.

Carbro A colour printing process using sensitized gelatin matrices carrying the printing colours separately and transferred by IMPRESSION **(2)**.

Card to card printout A method of duplicating an APERTURE CARD.

Card to paper printout A method by which paper copies of a MICROFILM image can be produced from an APERTURE CARD.

Cardboard As distinct from the common type of paperboard, a thick paper made in various colours for display graphics.

Cardinal numbers Numbers as in sequential counting, 1 2 3 etc, as opposed to ordinal numbers which indicate placement, first, second etc.

Caret, caret mark Symbol (⋏) used in preparing COPY and PROOF correcting to indicate an insertion.

Caricature A drawing of a person or thing showing deliberate distortion with comic or satirical intent.

Carriage The part of a printing machine on which the FORME moves back and forth during printing.

Carry forward/over see TAKE OVER.

Carton A box container designed not to be flattened out when not in use.

Cartouche A decorative device used to enclose a title or name in printing.

Cartridge paper A general purpose, rough surfaced paper used for drawing, wrapping, OFFSET printing etc.

Case (1) The stiff COVER of a book, consisting of two boards, a HOLLOW and a binding material. **(2)** *(typ)* A box with separate compartments in which pieces of type are kept. This is the origin of the terms LOWER and UPPER CASE.

Cased/case bound A HARDBACK BOOK, that is, one with stiff outer COVERS.

Casein A substance obtained from curdled milk, used as an adhesive in the manufacture of COATED PAPER and sometimes as a BINDER for paint.

Casing in To insert a book into its CASE and paste it down.

Cassette reader A mechanism in PHOTOCOMPOSITION that 'reads' information stored in a cassette of magnetic tape and transfers the COPY to paper or film.

Cast coated paper Art paper with an exceptionally glossy, enamel finish.

Cast up Printer's calculation of the cost of setting MATTER in type.

Casting-off Making a calculation as to how much space MANUSCRIPT COPY will take up when printed in a given TYPEFACE.

Catchline The temporary HEADING for identification at the top of a GALLEY PROOF.

Cathode ray tube Vacuum tube producing information display electrostatically.

Cel (1) *(abb)* CELLULOSE ACETATE. **(2)** In ANIMATION, a transparent SHEET the proportion of the film frame on which one stage of the sequence is drawn.

Cell (1) *(pri)* A recessed DOT in a PHOTOGRAVURE plate forming part of the image for inking. **(2)** *(US)* see CEL. **(3)** *(US)* A MASK **(1)** used in photographic methods of reproduction.

Cellophane Transparent CELLULOSE ACETATE film that is thin and very flexible.

Cellulose acetate Plastic sheet material, usually transparent or translucent, available clear or coloured and with a shiny or matt finish. It is used as the basis of ARTWORK and OVERLAYS and is the base material of some photographic films.

Centre fold/spread The centre opening of a SECTION (two pages) where one plate may be used to print facing pages with following page numbers. Centre spreads are also called 'naturals'.

Centred TYPE which is placed in the centre of a sheet or type measure.

Centred dot *(US)* A raised dot used as a decimal point between figures.

cf *(abb) confer*, a Latin word meaning 'compare'. cf is used to refer to a FOOTNOTE in text.

Chain lines/marks *(UK/US)* Lines running through LAID paper, caused by the wires of the papermaking machine.

Chain printer A high speed computer printer in which the type is carried on a chain.

Chalking A printing fault caused by ink soaking into the paper leaving pigment deposited on the surface.

Chancery italic A 13th-century style of handwriting on which ITALIC type designs were based.

Change bar A vertical rule in the MARGIN of a revised technical publication indicating a part that varies from the original text.

Chapter drop The level at which text begins underneath a chapter heading.

Character (1) *(typ)* An individual item cast in type, eg a letter, figure, punctuation mark, sign or space. **(2)** *(com)* A set of symbols in data processing which represents a figure, letter etc.

Character assembly An alternative term for TYPESETTING, especially in reproduction methods not using metal type.

Character count The number of CHARACTERS **(1)** in a piece of COPY, or in a line or paragraph.

Character generator *(com)* A system of HARDWARE or SOFTWARE that provides a FOUNT for computer composition.

Charcoal Charred wood used for drawing. Its powdery quality means a FIXATIVE needs to be applied to the drawn line to make it permanent.

Chart A graphic demonstration of information on values and qualities.

Chase A metal frame into which type and

blocks are fitted to make up a page. The type is held in place by FURNITURE and QUOINS.

Chemical pulp Processed wood PULP used in high quality printing papers.

Choke A method of altering the thickness of a letter or solid shape by overexposure in processing.

Chroma The intensity or purity of a colour.

Chromo A printing paper heavily coated on one side.

Chromograph A machine for producing copies of plans, MANUSCRIPTS etc, using ANILINE dye instead of ink.

Chromolin A fast proofing system in which powder is used instead of ink.

Chromolithography Lithographic printing in several colours by traditional techniques.

Chuck The core supporting a paper roll in a WEB-FED printing press.

Chute delivery A particular method of delivering printed material from a press.

Cibachrome Agfa process, a direct method of obtaining photographic colour prints.

Cicero A European unit for measuring the width, or MEASURE, of a line of type and the depth of the page. One Cicero = 4.511mm or 12 DIDOT POINTS. See also PICA.

CIF *abb* Carriage, insurance and freight. A commercial term denoting that a price quote includes delivery.

Circular Advertising MATTER in the form of a single LEAF or folded SHEET.

Circular screen A photographic screen that can be adjusted to prevent MOIRE patterns in colour reproduction.

Circumflex see ACCENT.

Classified ad Newspaper or magazine advertisement without illustration, sold by the line.

Clean proof A printer's PROOF which is free from errors.

Cliché The French term, used also elsewhere in Europe, for a block, stereotype or ELECTROTYPE.

Close up An instruction

to DELETE a space, ie bring CHARACTERS **(1)** together.

Closed h An ITALIC h in which the shorter stroke curves inwards.

Closed loop A computer system in which INPUT controls OUTPUT.

Closed section/ signature In either case, one where BOLTS are uncut.

Club line A short line ending a paragraph, which should not appear at the top of a page in a book.

CMC7 A CHARACTER **(1)** SET used in MICR.

Coated paper A general term for ART, CHROMO and ENAMEL papers or similar groups, in which the surface has a mineral coating applied after the body paper is made. It is also known as surface paper.

Cock up figure/letter see SUPERIOR FIGURE/ LETTER.

Cocked up initial A BOLD FACE CAPITAL that projects above the line of type.

Codet see COLOUR BAR.

Cold composition/type Typewriting or TYPESETTING in which no molten metal is used, such as movable type set by hand, and including methods of PHOTOCOMPOSITION.

Cold pressed A categorization of a type of paper surface. See NOT.

Collate To put the SECTIONS **(1)** or pages of a book in correct order.

Collotype A PHOTOMECHANICAL printing process suitable for fine detail reproductions. Printing is done from a raised gelatin film on glass support and gives CONTINUOUS TONE.

Colophon (1) An emblem identifying a printer or PUBLISHER, appearing usually on the SPINE and TITLE PAGE of a book. **(2)** An inscription placed at the end of a book giving the title, printer's name and location, and date of printing.

Colour *(typ)* The light or heavy appearance of a particular TYPEFACE.

Colour bar/codet A standard set of bars on PROOFS in FOUR-COLOUR PROCESSING, showing the strength and evenness of ink, and the registration of colours.

Colour blind emulsion
Photographic EMULSION
sensitized to blue, violet
or ultraviolet light only.
Colour break The edge
between two areas of
colour in an image.
Colour burnout A
deterioration in the
colour of printing ink
caused by chemical
reactions in mixing or
drying.
Colour chart Chart used
in colour printing to
standardize and select
or match coloured inks
or tints used.
Colour circle Graphic
representaion of the
relationship of PRIMARY
and SECONDARY
COLOURS and successive
colour mixtures and
tonal values.
Colour coder An
instrument capable of
comparing the intensity
of printed colours,
ensuring correct
reproduction.
Colour control bar (1)
The set of small marginal
marks placed on each of
the three NEGATIVES
used in making blocks
for colour printing,
which enable the printer
to superimpose them
when building up a
picture. **(2)** The set of
progressive PROOFS
supplied by the plate-
and blockmaker as a
guide to the printer.
Colour correction The
adjustment of colour
values in reproduction to
obtain a correct image.
Colour filters Thin
SHEETS of coloured
glass, plastic or gelatin
placed over a camera
lens to absorb or allow
through particular
colours in the light
entering the camera.
Colour identification A
mark designating the
colour of each plate
used in reproducing
ARTWORK with two or
more colours.
Colour negative film
Film which provides a
colour image in
NEGATIVE form after
processing.
Colour positives A set of
a screened positive
COLOUR SEPARATIONS.
Colour reproduction A
blanket term for several
reproduction methods in
which the use of
photographic MASKS **(2)**
improve the quality of
colour.
Colour reversal film A
film which provides
colour images in positive
form after processing.

Colour separation
Division of colours of a
CONTINUOUS TONE
multicoloured ORIGINAL
or LINE COPY into basic
portions by a process of
photographic filtration.
The portions are
reproduced by a
separate printing plate
carrying a colour.
Colour separations The
number of images or
pieces (SUBJECTS) to be
separated in the COLOUR
SEPARATION process.
Colour sequence The
accepted order of
LETTERPRESS printing.
Colour temperature A
term describing the
colour composition of a
light source in
photography measured
in degrees Kelvin, a
system based on a
supposed absolute
darkness rising to
incandescence.
Colour transparency A
positive photographic
image produced in
colour on transparent
film.
Colour value The tonal
value of a colour as
compared to a light-to-
dark scale of pure
greys.
Coloured edges The
edges or top of a book
which have been
coloured with a brush-on
fluid.
Column (1) A section of
a page divided
vertically, containing
text or other MATTER. It
is measured by the
horizontal width. **(2)** A
vertical section in
tabulated work.
**Column inch/
centimetre** A measure of
space used to calculate
the cost of display
advertising in a
newspaper or
periodical. The measure
is one COLUMN width by
one inch (or one
centimetre) depth.
Column rule The light-
faced RULE used to
separate COLUMNS in
newspaper.
**Combination line and
halftone** A combined
block or plate used to
reproduce photographs
with superimposed
figures, letters, diagrams
etc.
Command An instruction
given to a computer by
its operator.
Commercial a The type
symbol (@) used to mean
'at'.
Commercial art A term
used to describe
ARTWORK intended for

use in advertising or
promotion, as distinct
from fine art.
Comp (1) *abb*
COMPREHENSIVE.**(2)** *abb*
COMPOSITOR.
Compose To set COPY in
type.
Composing room The
area of a printing works
specifically designated
for TYPESETTING and
MAKE UP **(2)**.
Composite artwork
ARTWORK combining a
number of different
elements.
Composition Type
which has been set in a
form ready for
reproduction by
LETTERPRESS printing or
PHOTOLITHOGRAPHY.
Composition size A
description of any type
up to a size of 14 points,
used mainly in setting
text.
Compositor The person
responsible for setting
type, whether by hand
or machine process.
Comprehensive *(US)* A
LAYOUT of type and
illustrative material
produced to a good, but
not finished standard.
See PRESENTATION
VISUAL.
Computer A device or
machine capable of
processing information
according to a
predetermined
PROGRAM, or set of
instructions.
**Computer
console/terminal** The
section of a computer
allowing for
communication by the
operator, that is a
keyboard for INPUT and
a device for information
display.
Computer graphics The
use of computers to
generate an OUTPUT of
information in graphic
form, eg as a picture,
diagram or printed
CHARACTERS **(1)**.
Computer input devices
Methods of transmitting
instructions, queries and
information to a
computer in a
prescribed form, eg
keyboard, punched
cards, paper tape,
OPTICAL CHARACTER
RECOGNITION. See also
MAGNETIC INK
CHARACTERS.
Computer languages
Coding systems
developed to deal with
specific types of
communication with
computers. COBOL
(Common Business
Oriented Language) was

developed for commercial programs; ALGOL (algorithmic language) and FORTRAN (Formula Translator) were devised for scientific and mathematical PROGRAMS. There are many different languages for use at various levels of computer activity.

Computer output devices Methods by which information is transmitted by a computer in a form recognizable to humans. See also VDU.

Computerized composition/ computer typesetting The use of computers to control various aspects of PHOTOCOMPOSITION such as CHARACTER (2) assembly. The computer can be programmed with details of format, tabulation, rules of punctuation, type sizes, measure etc.

Concertina fold Method of paper folding in which each fold runs in the opposite direction to the one before to form a pleated effect.

Condensed A TYPEFACE with an elongated, narrow appearance.

Contact print, contacts Photographic print or prints made by direct contact with an original POSITIVE (1) or NEGATIVE at same size.

Contact printing frame see VACUUM FRAME.

Contact screen A HALFTONE SCREEN made on a film base which has a graded DOT pattern. It is used in direct contact with a film or plate to obtain a halftone NEGATIVE from a CONTINUOUS TONE ORIGINAL. They provide better definition than the conventional glass screen.

Contents A page of a book listing the articles or chapters in it.

Continuous fold A paper folding system to convert rolls of paper into CONCERTINA FOLDS.

Continuous tone Photographs or coloured ORIGINALS in which the subject contains continuous shades between the lightest and the darkest tones, without being broken up by dots.

Contour lines (1) In drawing, lines describing the silhouette and volume of a form. **(2)** In mapmaking, lines representing different levels in the height of land.

Contrast The degree of separation of tones in a photograph in the range from black to white.

Contre jour A photographic term meaning to take a picture with the camera lens facing towards the light source.

Controlling dimension The width or height of an image taken as the basis for enlargement or reduction.

Converting To produce articles of stationery or packaging that require minimal printing.

Cool colours A relative term often used to describe blue, green and other colours with a blue or green cast.

Copperplate printing An INTAGLIO process used in short run printing, producing a sharp, but very black image.

Copy MATTER to be set in type.

Copyboard (US) see VACUUM FRAME.

Copyfitting see CASTING OFF.

Copyholder A person who reads aloud from ORIGINAL COPY while another checks and marks the PROOF.

Copying machines Machines designed to produce immediate copies from originals. See BLUELINE, DIAZO, PHOTOSTAT, WHITEPRINT, XEROXING.

Copyright see UNIVERSAL COPYRIGHT CONVENTION.

Copywriting A term applied to writing of COPY specifically for use in advertising.

Corner marks The marks on a printed SHEET acting as TRIM MARKS, and also sometimes as REGISTER MARKS.

Corporate identity/ housestyle The elements of design by which a company or other institution establishes a consistent and recognizable identity through communication, promotion and distribution material. See also LETTERHEAD, LOGOTYPE.

Correction overlay A TRANSLUCENT OVERLAY, registered to ARTWORK, on which corrections are made.

Corrigendum, corrigenda A note inserted in a publication after printing to correct an item or items in the text.

Cosmetics A term used in COMPUTER GRAPHICS to describe the general appearance of a computer generated image, eg sharpness, tonal contrast.

Counter The inside area of the TYPEFACE eg the centre of an 'o' or space between the vertical strokes of an 'n'.

Counter-mark A WATERMARK of the papermaker's initials, placed opposite the normal watermark.

Counting keyboard A PHOTOCOMPOSITION keyboard that shows the position of CHARACTERS (1) in a line to indicate the need for an END OF LINE DECISION.

Cover The paper, board, cloth or leather to which the BODY (2) of a book is secured by glue and thread.

Cover papers Papers for the COVERS of books, pamphlets etc.

cpi *abb* CHARACTERS (1) per inch. A measure of the information accommodated in particular computer systems.

cpl *abb* CHARACTERS (1) per line. The measure used by editors and typesetters in preparing and printing COPY.

Crash finish Paper which has a coarse linen-like finish.

Crease see SCORING.

Creasing (1) A linear indentation made by machine in thick paper providing a hinge. **(2)** A printing fault producing deep creases.

Credit/courtesy line A line of text accompanying an illustration giving the name of an organization or individual supplying the picture or ARTWORK.

Crimping (US) see CREASING.

Crop, cropmark The part of a photograph or illustration that is discarded after it has been trimmed.

Cropped A term applied to a book with overtrimmed MARGINS.

Cross front The description of the camera in which the lens can be moved laterally in relation to the film.

Cross-head Subsection, paragraph HEADING or numeral printed in the BODY **(2)** of text, usually marking the first subdivision of a chapter.
Cross line screen see HALFTONE SCREEN.
Cross reference Instruction to the reader to refer to another part of the text for related information.
Cross section Illustrator's view of an object showing it as if cut through to expose the internal workings or characteristics.
Cross stemmed W One in which the central strokes cross rather than meet.
Crow quill A term referring to a very fine pen, derived from the original use of a cut crow's quill.
Crown Standard size of printing paper 15 x 20in (381 x 508mm).
CRT *abb* CATHODE RAY TUBE.
C/T *abb* COLOUR TRANSPARENCY.
Curl Measurement of the height to which the edges of the paper will curl, especially applied to those that must be used in wet or damp processes.
Cursive A running script where the letters are formed without raising the pen.
Cursor *(com)* A moving symbol on a VDU used as a reference point by the operator for arranging COPY on the screen.
Curved plate A plate used in a ROTARY-PRESS that curves around the PLATE CYLINDER.
Curves Templates for designers and draftsmen, made of plastic or metal. French curves combine several curves in one shape while others are produced for specific purposes, to be used in technical drawings.
Cut (1) A shortened version of WOODCUT, used to describe a relief or block print. **(2)** *(US)* A metal relief plate from which an image is printed. **(3)** An instruction to an editor meaning 'cut text to fit'.
Cut dummy Cut PROOFS of illustrations used in sequence as a guide to MAKE UP **(2)** of pages.
Cut edge The three edges of a book which are cut with a GUILLOTINE.

Cut flush A term describing a book with even COVER and pages as the cutting is done after the cover has been attached.
Cutline *(US)* **(1)** A CAPTION to an illustration. **(2)** An instruction to the printer to insert an illustration during MAKE UP**(2).**
Cutout (1) A term referring to a SILHOUETTE HALFTONE where the background dots have been removed. **(2)** *(US)* A shape cut out of paper stock with a steel DIE, eg in the soft COVER of a book to expose COPY on the TITLE PAGE below.
Cyan A shade of blue used in FOUR-COLOUR printing.
Cylinder press A printing press in which the FORME is carried on a FLAT BED under a paper-bearing cylinder for an IMPRESSION **(2)** to be made at the point of contact.
Cyrillic alphabet CHARACTERS **(1)** used in writing or printing Russian.

D

Dagger A type CHARACTER **(1)** used to refer to FOOTNOTES to a text.
Daisy wheel printer A typewriter mechanism common to WORD PROCESSOR systems, with a flat, circular head for printing CHARACTERS **(1)**.
Dampening Necessary process in LITHOGRAPHY of dampening the printing plate to prevent ink spreading.
Dark field illumination A method of checking the quality of HALFTONE DOTS by viewing them in angled light against a dark background.
Dash A punctuation mark (—) usually known as an EM RULE.
Data A term meaning factual information, now particularly applied to information used in computer work.
Data bank The store of information in a computer.
Data carrier The device or medium used in a computer to record DATA.
Data points Symbols used with lines in plotting information on a GRAPH.

Data processing The processing of information via a computer or other mechanical or electronic device.
Database A general computer file of information that can be drawn on or updated by all users having access, but without imposing a limited or specific use of the file.
Dateline Type placed above a newspaper item giving date and place of its origin.
Datum The singular of DATA, though data is now commonly accepted as a singular noun in computer usage.
De luxe edition A smarter edition than the standard one, printed on higher-grade paper, with specially cast type and expensive binding.
Dead matter Leftover MATTER that is not used.
Dead metal In LETTERPRESS ENGRAVING, the areas of a plate that do not print.
Deadline The final date set for completion of a particular job.
Decal A printed transfer image.
Deckle edge The rough uneven edge of handmade paper.
Dedicated A term describing equipment with a unique function that can be used only for that purpose and is not otherwise adaptable.
Deep-etch halftone A HALFTONE plate with unwanted screen dots removed, leaving areas of plain paper on the printed SHEET.
Deep-etching The removal, by ETCHING, of unwanted material on HALFTONE plates to give a white background.
Delete Instruction meaning to take out.
Delineate To accentuate outlines in line ARTWORK by making them heavier.
Demy A standard size of printing paper 17½ x 22½in (440 x 560mm).
Densitometer An electronic precision instrument used to measure the quantitive colours or density in a colour TRANSPARENCY.
Density Of type, the amount and compactness of type set within a given area or page. Of a TRANSPARENCY or printed image, the measure of tonal values.

Depth The thickness of a three-dimensional object measured downwards from its surface.

Depth of field The area in front of or behind the point of focus in a photographic image at which other details remain in acceptable focus.

Descender The part of a LOWER CASE letter that falls below the x-HEIGHT.

Detail paper/layout paper A thin, TRANSLUCENT paper with a hard surface used for LAYOUTS and sketches.

Developer The chemical used to bring up an image on photographic film, paper or plate.

Diacritical mark A mark indicating the particular value or pronunciation of a CHARACTER (1). See ACCENT.

Diaphragm A sectioned, adjustable disc behind a camera lens that can be opened or closed to fix the APERTURE.

Diapositive A photographic TRANSPARENCY in which the image is positive.

Diazo abb Diazonium. A method of reproducing in limited quantities from a transparent or TRANSLUCENT ORIGINAL on paper, cloth or film. The image is exposed on to a light-sensitive coating of diazo salts and dyestuff and the print may be blue, black or another colour.

Didot point The continental unit for type. It measures 0.0148in whereas an English point is 0.013837in.

Die An INTAGLIO engraved stamp used for impressing a design.

Die cutting To cut paper, card or board to a particular design with a metal DIE, for packaging and display work.

Die stamping A form of printing where all the CHARACTERS (1) are in relief.

Dielectric coated paper Paper on which an image is printed through the action of a liquid toner on an electrostatically charged DOT pattern. It is used in computer work.

Differential spacing The spacing of each CHARACTER (1) of type according to its individual width.

Diffusion transfer

process A method of reproduction used in various types of copying machines to transfer an image to paper or a flexible printing plate.

Digital computer A computer that operates on DATA represented in digital form.

Digitize To convert an image into a form that can be processed, stored and electronically reconstructed.

Digitizing pad/tablet (com) An INPUT device that translates freehand drawing into digitized form for computer use.

Dimensions In describing representations of three-dimensional objects, the dimensions used are length, width and height.

DIN abb Deutsche Industrie Norm: a code of standards published in Germany, still used in rating FILM SPEEDS.

Dingbat (US) A general term for ORNAMENTS.

Dinky A term referring to a half roll (WEB) of paper, halved by width not diameter.

Dinky dash see JIM DASH.

Diphthong A term meaning two vowels pronounced as one syllable, also commonly applied to two vowels printed as a LIGATURE.

Diploma paper A fine paper made specially for printing of certificates, official documents etc.

Direct colour separation COLOUR SEPARATION in which a HALFTONE SCREEN is used in the original separation to produce screened NEGATIVES directly.

Direct cost The costs of a project incurred directly from the job in hand, not including the normal overhead costs of a business.

Direct entry photocomposition A computer typesetting system in which INPUT and OUTPUT are combined in one unit.

Direct image master/plate A plate used in LITHOGRAPHY, often made of paper, on which COPY can be typed or drawn directly. It is only suitable for short run printing.

Directional Term such as 'left', 'above', 'top', appearing in a CAPTION to direct the reader to

the relevant picture.

Dirty proof A heavily corrected PROOF.

Dis, diss abb Distribute.

Disc/disk see MAGNETIC DISC.

Display advertisement Advertising MATTER designed to a size or quality to attract immediate attention.

Display board Heavy, dull finish, coated board in various colours.

Display matter/type Larger TYPEFACES designed for HEADINGS etc, usually above 14pt in bookwork.

Display size The size of type used for HEADINGS, advertising MATTER etc. It is always greater than 12 point so clearly distinguishable from BODY TYPE (2).

Distribution rollers The rollers on a printing press that control an even distribution of ink to the roller that contacts the FORME.

Ditto marks Symbols indicating repetition of the MATTER directly above.

Doctor blade A device used in INTAGLIO printing processes to wipe excess ink from the surface of a plate. The blade is made of flexible metal.

Documentary A term used in cinefilm or still photography to describe images concerned with actual events.

Dodging (pho) A method of obtaining greater contrast when printing a photograph by the selective use of MASKING (3).

Dogleg (US) Colloquial term for a LEADER LINE that is angled towards its point of reference.

Dot The smallest basic element of a HALFTONE.

Dot and tickle A colloquial expression for stipple technique in drawing.

Dot area The pattern of a HALFTONE, that is both the DOTS and the spaces in between.

Dot etching A method of reducing the size of HALFTONE DOTS by chemical action in processing, to alter the tonal values of an image.

Dot for dot reproduction A direct method of producing printing film by photographing a previously screened image. A maximum of 10 percent enlargement or reduction can be achieved.

Dot formation The pattern of DOTS in a HALFTONE SCREEN.

Dot gain An aberration occurring in the making of HALFTONE film or plates, when the DOTS become slightly enlarged. A dot gain scale is included in PROOFS to check this occurrence.

Dot loss The devaluation or disappearance of a HALFTONE DOT on a printing plate.

Dot matrix The pattern of DOTS used as the basis of CHARACTER **(1)** formation in the OUTPUT of certain types of computer.

Double burn To use two or more NEGATIVES to expose an image on to a sensitized plate.

Double coated paper Paper with a heavy coating on one or both sides.

Double dagger A symbol used as a reference mark for FOOTNOTES to text.

Double digest fold One of the four basic folds forming a SHEET into a SIGNATURE in WEB OFFSET printing.

Double image The appearance of two impressions of an image on one surface in printing or photography.

Double spread/page spread Two facing pages of a publication.

Down stroke A heavy stroke in a type CHARACTER **(1)**, originally the downward stroke of a pen in CALLIGRAPHY.

Down time Loss of time in a given job due to machine breakdown, etc, or when time is a chargeable factor.

Draft To compose COPY or an illustration in a basic form to be refined, or an item so prepared. A final draft is copy that is ready for printing.

Drafting machine An item of drawing equipment combining the functions of a T SQUARE, STRAIGHTEDGE, SET SQUARE and PROTRACTOR.

Drawdown (1) The evacuation of air from a VACUUM FRAME. **(2)** A smear of ink produced by a smooth blade on paper, used to check quality and tone.

Drawn on Describes a paper book COVER glued to the back of the book.

Driers Substances, usually metallic salts, that can speed ink drying.

Drilling To make holes in paper or binding with a rotating DIE.

Driving out Arranging the spaces in a line of type to fill the line.

Drop The number of lines of text in a COLUMN as allowed on the GRID.

Drop cap (typ) A large initial at the beginning of a text that drops into the lines of type below.

Drop down see CHAPTER DROP.

Drop folios The numbers printed at the bottom of each page.

Drop letter see DROP CAP.

Drop out/dropped out halftone Areas removed from a HALFTONE NEGATIVE, print or plate by MASKING **(2)**.See also HIGHLIGHT HALFTONE and SILHOUETTE HALFTONE.

Drop shadow A shadow behind an image ' designed to bring the image forward.

Drop tone see LINE CONVERSION.

Dropped initial see DROP CAP.

Drum (1) A drum-shaped image carrier used in some machines for PHOTOCOMPOSITION. **(2)** An image carrier or recording device used in electronic scanners.

Drum plotter A COMPUTER OUTPUT DEVICE that marks information on a roll of paper rotating on a drum, by means of a moving writing tool.

Dry ink Powder used in some copying machines to create the image. It is sealed by heat or chemical action.

Dry mounting The use of heat sensitive adhesives.

Dry offset see LETTERSET.

Dry stripping STRIPPING of a film after it has been processed and dried.

Dry transfer lettering CHARACTERS **(1)** transferred to the page by rubbing them off the back of a SHEET.

Dual roll stand A stand supporting two WEBS fed simultaneously through a press to increase production.

Duck foot quotes see GUILLEMETS.

Duct The ink reservoir in a printing machine.

Ductor roller (pri) A roller carrying ink or water between the FOUNTAIN roller and the DISTRIBUTION ROLLER.

Dull finish A matt paper finish. See also ENAMEL PAPER.

Dull seal (pri) A term for paper stock having an adhesive backing.

Dummy The prototype of a proposed book in the correct format, paper and bulk but with blank pages.

Duotone Also called a duplex HALFTONE, an illustration process using two colours. Two NEGATIVES are made from a MONOCHROME ORIGINAL, one for the darker shade with the greater detail, the other for the lighter flat tint.

Dupe abb DUPLICATE.

Duplex board/paper Paper or board of two layers pasted together to give a different colour or surface quality on each side.

Duplex halftone see DUOTONE.

Duplicate A copy of an ORIGINAL that is exact in every way and at exactly the same size.

Dust wrapper/jacket see BOOK JACKET.

Dutch paper Describes any DECKLE-EDGED paper produced in the Netherlands.

Dye based ink Ink obtaining its colour from ANILINE dye.

Dye transfer print A method of making photographic colour prints using gelatin relief matrices. A MATRIX is made for each of the three PRIMARY COLOURS, red, yellow and blue, and soaked in appropriate dye solution. These are then placed in turn on a gelatin COATED PAPER which absorbs dye from each to produce the full image.

Dyeline see DIAZO.

E

E13B A type FOUNT of numerals and signs used in MAGNETIC CHARACTER RECOGNITION.

E & OE abb Errors and Omissions Excepted. A term included in an invoice meaning that any errors in the invoice may be subject to correction.

Ear The advertising space or spaces beside the front-page title-line.

Easel-binder A three-dimensional display stand with ring binding.

Edges The three CUT EDGES of a book.

Editing To prepare a MANUSCRIPT for publication.

Editing terminal A display unit giving a visual check of INPUT in PHOTOCOMPOSITION.

Edition The whole number of copies of a work printed and issued at one time.

Edition bound *(US)* see CASED BOOK.

eg *abb exempli gratia*, a Latin term meaning 'for example'.

Eggshell finish The rough finish found on drawing paper and notepaper as a result of omitting CALENDERING.

Egyptian A group of display types with heavy SLAB SERIFS and little contrast in the thickness of strokes.

Eight sheet A poster size measuring 60 x 80in (153 x 203cm).

Electrostatic processes A copying or printing process using static electricity to deposit POWDER INK on a support to make the image.

Electrotype A duplicate printing FORME made in a galvanic bath by precipitating copper on a MATRIX.

Element (1) In book MAKE UP **(2)**, any item of the FRONT MATTER, BODY **(2)** or END MATTER. **(2)** In advertising, any component of the advertisement, such as COPY or illustration.

Elevation A drawing showing the vertical PROJECTION of an item of equipment or machinery, or of an architectural structure.

Ellipse A regular oval shape corresponding to an oblique view of a circular plane.

Ellipsis A sequence of three dots (. . .) indicating that part of a phrase or sentence has been left out.

Elliptical dot screen A HALFTONE SCREEN with graduated DOT pattern that includes elliptical dots forming middle tones.

Em A unit of linear measurement,12 POINTS or 4.5mm.

Em quad A space in type that is the square of the type size.

Em rule/dash A dash used in punctuating text,

the length of one EM.

Embossing RELIEF PRINTING or stamping in which DIES are used to raise letters above the surface of paper, cloth or leather.

Emulsion The light sensitive coating of a photographic material.

Emulsion down In making a printing plate, the direct contact of film with EMULSION side down on the plate. If the emulsion is uppermost the image formed is slightly haloed due to the thickness of the film.

Emulsion speed see FILM SPEED.

En A measurement half the width of an EM, used in CASTING OFF.

En quad A space in type half the width of an EM QUAD.

En rule/dash A dash (-), approximately half an EM.

Enamel paper see COATED PAPER.

End even Instruction to a typesetter to end a section of COPY with a full line.

End matter Parts of a book that follow the main BODY**(1)** of the text. See APPENDIX, BIBLIOGRPAHY, INDEX, GLOSSARY.

End of line decisions Decisions made by a COMPOSITOR as to JUSTIFICATION of type and WORD BREAKS at the end of a line. In computer TYPESETTING this function may be included in the computer PROGRAM.

End papers The leaves of paper at the front and end of a book which cover the inner sides of the boards, securing the book to its CASE.

Engine sizing A method of sizing paper by the addition of emulsified resin to cleaned paper PULP.

Engraving The design or lettering etched on a plate or block and also the print taken from such a plate.

Erasing/eradicating Methods of removing errors from COPY using a chemical solvent or abrasive material.

Erratum An author's or printer's error discovered after the book has been printed.

Esparto A long rough grass with soft fibres used for paper.

Estimate Calculation of the cost of work on a

printing order.

Et seq *abb et sequens*, a Latin term meaning 'and the following'.

Etching A metal plate treated with acid and with certain parts protected by the application of a GROUND. It is also a print taken from the etched plate.

Even pages Lefthand pages, ie those with even numbers.

Even smalls SMALL CAPITALS used without a larger sized CAPITAL at the beginning of a word.

Even working A printed work divided into a number of SECTIONS of equal size, eg 16, 32, 48 pages.

Exception dictionary A list of WORD BREAKS that are exceptions to the standard guidelines, stored in a computer used in PHOTOCOMPOSITION.

Exotic A traditional term for a TYPEFACE with CHARACTERS **(1)** of a language not based on LATIN letterforms.

Expanded/extended type Type with a flattened rectangular appearance.

Exploded view Drawing of an object showing its component parts separately but arranged in such a way as to indicate their relationships within the object when assembled.

Exposure The amount of light allowed to contact a PHOTOSENSITIVE material. The exposure is the combination of length of contact and intensity of light acting upon the material.

Exposure meter An item of photographic equipment that measures light intensity and is used to calculate EXPOSURES.

Extract Material in a publication quoted from another published work. It is often made distinct from the main text by use of a small TYPEFACE or by indenting the extract.

F

F and G see FOLDED AND GATHERED.

f number/stop The notation for relative APERTURE which is the ratio of the focal length to the diameter of the aperture. The numbers are marked on the device which sets the aperture size.

Face The printing

surface of any type CHARACTER (1). It also refers to the group or FAMILY to which any particular type design belongs, as in TYPEFACE.

Facsimile An exact reproduction or copy.

Fade out blue A light blue used in marking reproduction COPY. The blue is not registered by the camera.

Fadeback see GHOSTING.

Family A group of printing types in series with common characteristics in design, but of different weights such as ITALIC, BOLD, CONDENSED, EXPANDED etc.

Fan fold see CONCERTINA FOLD.

Fashion boards Simple body boards lined with good RAG PAPER on one side, and thin paper on the other to prevent warping.

Fast emulsion/film A PHOTOSENSITIVE material that records an image in a relatively short EXPOSURE. See MATTER.

Fat face A TYPEFACE with extreme contrast in the widths of thin and thick strokes.

Fat matter (pri) Term for COPY with a large proportion of spacing, allowing rapid setting. Dense copy is known as lean MATTER.

Fatty A mask used with INTERNEGATIVES to enlarge COPY slightly. This allows for exact registration of butted elements by lapping one over the other.

Fax abb FACSIMILE. A slang term applied particularly to an image reproduced by electronic scanning techniques.

Feathering The method of biting areas of a plate using drops of acid, controlling their movement with a feather.

Featherweight paper A light, bulky paper preferably with a high ESPARTO content made with little or no CALENDERING.

Feedback In computer operations, a system where OUTPUT returns to INPUT to modify or expand the information. It may act as a system of self-correction.

Feeder Apparatus for feeding and positioning paper SHEETS in printing presses and paper

processing machines.

Feet The base of a piece of type. It is recessed at the centre to form two 'feet' on which it stands.

Feint ruling Thin lines ruled on a SHEET as a writing guide.

Felt finish Paper finish applied in the manufacturing machine by felt that marks the paper roll.

Felt side The top side or printing side of paper. See also WIRE SIDE.

Felting The binding together of FIBRES in the wet PULP.

Ferrotype A photographic print made on thin metal plate.

Fibre A plant cell composed of cellulose used as the basic element of paper-making material.

Figure number The reference number given to an illustration.

Figure title The title given to an illustration, as distinct from a CAPTION describing the picture.

Figures An alternative name for numbers. ARABIC NUMERALS are used more frequently than Roman ones.

Filler An extra figure or piece of COPY in a magazine or newspaper put in to fill space in a page or COLUMN (1).

Fillet An embossed line used as a decorative device on a book COVER.

Filling in/up A fault in printing when ink fills spaces between HALFTONE DOTS or the COUNTERS of type to produce small areas of solid tone.

Film (1) Transparent plastic material, usually CELLULOSE ACETATE. **(2)** Cellulose acetate coated with light-sensitive EMULSION for photographic recording of an image.

Film assembly FILM NEGATIVES or POSITIVES **(1)** assembled in correct positions to make plates for PHOTOLITHOGRAPHY.

Film negative A photographic image on film in which the HIGHLIGHTS and SHADOWS are reversed; also used extensively in REPROGRAPHIC PRINTING.

Film positive (1) A black image on a background of clear or TRANSLUCENT film. **(2)** A POSITIVE image on a film base

made as a contact print from stripped NEGATIVES. It is used as a MASK in INTAGLIO platemaking.

Film sizes Standard measurements for sheet film or numerical codings for roll film corresponding to usual film widths.

Film speed Standard speed ratings are given to all types of photographic film to allow calculation of EXPOSURE. See ASA and DIN.

Filmsetting see PHOTOCOMPOSITION.

Filmstrip A section of roll film from which images may be projected separately as stills.

Filter A gelatin, glass or plastic sheet which may be placed over or in front of a camera lens to alter the colour or quality of light passed through to the film.

Filter factor (pho) An increase in EXPOSURE necessary if a FILTER is used.

Final draft COPY fully prepared for TYPESETTING.

Fine rule A line of hair-line thickness.

Finial letter A CHARACTER **(1)** in certain TYPEFACES devised as the end letter in a word or line, not used elsewhere.

Finish The surface given to paper during manufacture.

Finished artwork see ARTWORK.

Finished rough see PRESENTATION VISUAL.

Finisher An artist or illustrator who inks over or finishes ARTWORK drawn up by another artist.

Firmware A computer PROGRAM that can only be altered by replacing HARDWARE.

First generation A copy of an ORIGINAL made by direct EXPOSURE or photographic reproduction.

Fish eye lens A WIDE-ANGLE LENS that produces a distorted image with a pronounced apparent curve.

Fist The name given to an INDEX mark used in printing, shown as a pointing hand.

Fit The ALIGNMENT and registration of individual images within a page.

Fit up halftones A term

in LETTERPRESS printing describing separately made HALFTONE plates placed together on a MOUNT.

Fix, fixer Colloquial term for a chemical used in photographic processing to make an image permanent. See HYPO.

Fixative A clear varnish solution that, sprayed over ARTWORK or a drawing, dries to a protective coating without altering surface qualities.

Fixed word spacing A method of TYPESETTING employing a standard size for spaces between words, leaving lines UNJUSTIFIED.

Flag see NAMEPLATE

Flange An edging on a HALFTONE plate used in LETTERPRESS printing. It is below type height and allows space for securing the plate to a MOUNT.

Flare (1) Non-image-forming light caused by reflection and scattering so that the quality of a photographic image is degraded. **(2)** Reflected light in PHOTOMECH – ANICAL reproduction that distorts or obscures the true image.

Flash exposure A second exposure in HALFTONE processing that reinforces the DOTS in dark areas. These would otherwise run together and print solid.

Flat An opaque based material with cut-out WINDOWS, in which are inserted NEGATIVES of COPY to be printed by PHOTOLITHOGRAPHY. The flat is then used as a composite image in preparing the printing plate.

Flat bed cylinder press This press has the printing FORME on a plane surface, as opposed to a curved printing surface. The forme is placed and moved to and fro under the cylinder.

Flat bed plotter A COMPUTER OUTPUT DEVICE using a WRITING HEAD to draw on paper or film laid over a flat support.

Flat copy A PHOTOMECHANICAL image without a wide range of tonal values, such as LINE COPY.

Flat plan (1) A diagrammatic plan of the pages of a book used to establish the distribution of colour, chapter lengths etc. **(2)** A diagram or chart showing the sequence of events involved in a process or activity.

Flat tint halftone A HALFTONE printed over a background of flat colour.

Flexography A method of LETTERPRESS printing from rubber or flexible plates.

Flimsy Semi-transparent BOND PAPER used for planning by the layout department.

Flippy, flippy floppy *(com)* A FLOPPY DISC usable on both sides.

Floating accent *(typ)* An ACCENT mark set on a separate piece of type from that of the CHARACTER **(1)** it affects.

Flocking A decorative, slightly three-dimensional effect obtained in printing by blowing fibres over an adhesive ink base.

Flong The sheet of papier-mâché used to make a MOULD from a FORME for casting a STEREOTYPE PLATE.

Flop A PHOTOMECHANICAL image that has been deliberately or accidentally REVERSED LEFT TO RIGHT.

Floppy disc *(com)* MAGNETIC DISC made of flexible plastic.

Flow line A line indicating the relationship of parts in an object when they are drawn separately, eg as an EXPLODED VIEW.

Flowchart (1) A schematic diagram showing the sequence of a process or related series of events. **(2)** See FLATPLAN. The plan of a book shown as a sequential drawing of the proposed design and LAYOUT of pages.

Flowers Type ORNAMENTS used to embellish printed MATTER, for example, chapter HEADINGS, TITLE PAGES etc.

Fluorescent ink Ink used in poster and display work that has bright and luminous colour due to phosphorous content, natural or synthetic.

Flush cover The COVER of a book cut to the same dimensions as the pages inside it.

Flush left, right COPY aligned at left or right MARGINS. See RANGE.

Flush mount In LETTERPRESS printing, the mounting of a plate and type, or two plates, in close fit, requiring removal of the FLANGE.

Flush paragraphs Paragraphs in which the first word is not indented but set flush with the vertical line of the text. See also FULL OUT.

Fly fold A folding method producing four pages from a SHEET.

Fly leaf Another term for END PAPERS, the part which is not stuck down.

Flyer A cheaply produced BROADSHEET or CIRCULAR for promotion purposes.

Flying paster An automatic mechanism on a WEB-FED press for running in a new web without interruption to the printing process.

FOB *abb* Free on board. A commercial term denoting that a price quoted does not include delivery charge.

Focal length A property of a camera lens indicating its focusing ability. It is a measurement between lens and film when the image of a distant object is in sharp FOCUS in the camera.

Focus A point at which light rays converge. In photography, light rays are bent by the camera lens to converge on the film in such a way as to produce a sharp, clearly defined but much reduced image of the subject.

Fog A grey blur obliterating part or all of a photographic image on film or paper, caused by uncontrolled EXPOSURE of the material to light.

Foil An extremely thin, flexible metal sheet applied as decoration to a blocked or embossed design.

Fold to paper A method of folding a SECTION **(1)** after printing by aligning the edges of the SHEET.

Fold to print A method of folding a SECTION **(1)** after printing by reference to page numbers or other matter printed on the SHEET.

Folded and gathered sheets/F and Gs COPY which is collated but not trimmed and sent to the PUBLISHER for approval of printing before binding begins.

Folding methods see

CONCERTINA FOLD, FRENCH FOLD, GATE FOLD, PARALLEL FOLD, and RIGHT-ANGLE FOLD.

Foldout An extension to the LEAF of a book, making it wider than the standard page width so it must be folded back onto the page.

Foliation In book publishing, the practice of numbering leaves, that is alternate pages, rather than each page.

Folio (1) The book size formed when a SHEET is folded making the pages half the size of the sheet. **(2)** A LEAF of paper numbered only on the front. **(3)** A page number and the RUNNING HEADLINE of a page.

Follow copy Instruction to the COMPOSITOR to follow the spelling and punctuation of a MANUSCRIPT, even if unorthodox, in preference to the HOUSE STYLE.

Follow on see RUN ON.

Font A corruption of FOUNT.

Foolscap Standard size of printing paper 13½ x 17in (343 x 432mm).

Foot (1) The MARGIN at the bottom of a page or the bottom edge of a book. **(2)** The undersurface of a piece of type.

Foot margin The MARGIN at the bottom of the page in a publication.

Footnotes Short explanatory notes, printed at the foot of the page or at the end of a book.

Fore edge, foredge The outer edge of a book parallel to the back.

Foredge margin The outer side MARGIN of a page in a publication.

Foreshorten In illustration, to depict the apparent distortion of perspective in a receding form or plane.

Foreword Introductory remarks to a work or about the author.

Format The general appearance or style of a book.

Formatting To PROGRAM standard commands for a computer used in PHOTOCOMPOSITION, corresponding to directions in the type MARK UP.

Forme, form Type matter and blocks assembled into pages and locked up in a

CHASE ready for LETTERPRESS printing.

Forty eight sheet A standard poster size measuring 120 x 480in (305 x 1220cm).

Forwarding The binding of a book after sewing and before CASING IN.

Foundry proof A PROOF from a FORME prepared for stereotyping or electrotyping.

Fount A complete supply of a TYPEFACE.

Fountain A reservoir for ink supply in a printing press. The term is also used for a similar mechanism that supplies a solution for dampening the rollers of an OFFSET press.

Four-colour process A method of printing in full colour by COLOUR SEPARATION, producing four plates for printing in CYAN, yellow, MAGENTA and black.

Foxed The term is applied to book pages discoloured by damp which has affected impurities in the paper.

Frame (*US*) see BOX RULE.

Free line fall see RAGGED RIGHT and UNJUSTIFIED.

French curves see CURVES.

French fold A term used to describe a SHEET of paper that has been printed on one side only and then folded twice to form an uncut four-page section.

French folio Thin, smooth, sized paper.

Fresnel lens A lens used to concentrate the beam of a photographic spotlight.

Friction feed A paper feeding mechanism in a printing or copying machine using rubber rollers.

Fringe A halo seen to surround HALFTONE DOTS in the early stages of processing.

Front jacket flap The part of a BOOK JACKET that folds inside the front COVER of a book.

Front lay edge see LAY EDGES.

Front matter (*US*) see PRELIMS.

Front projection A method of superimposing images in a photograph by projecting one image on to a two-way mirror placed between camera and subject.

Frontispiece An illustration facing the

TITLE PAGE of a book.

Fugitive colours Colours or inks which are not permanent and change or fade when exposed to light.

Full binding A BOOK-BINDING made completely of leather.

Full faced type (*US*) see TITLING.

Full measure The width of a line of type as measured in PICAS.

Full out An instruction to the printer to set type with lines starting at the MARGIN, that is not indented.

Full point A full stop.

Full shadow A heavy outline to a letter or line of type.

Full space The horizontal space between two lines of type.

Full word wrap In PHOTOCOMPOSITION, the transfer of a full word to the following line to avoid a WORD BREAK.

Furnish The ingredients used in paper manufacture.

G

g/m²/gsm, grams per square metre A unit of measurement for paper used in printing.

Galley Long, shallow, metal tray used by COMPOSITORS to hold type after it has been set.

Galley proof PROOFS taken from the GALLEY before COPY is divided into pages.

Gang up (1) To print a SHEET of paper with several different jobs, to be divided appropriately. **(2)** To place a group of ORIGINALS of the same proportions together for camera work or scanning.

Gang shooting In PHOTOLITHOGRAPHY, to make one NEGATIVE containing several pages of COPY for transfer to a printing plate. The pages are arranged to form a sequence that can be folded into page order.

Gatefold A paper fold in which both sides are folded across the middle of the SHEET in overlapping layers.

Gathering Placing the SECTIONS of a book in the correct order for binding.

Gelatin process A duplication method using gelatin as the medium for transferring a carbon image as in GRAVURE printing.

Generation One stage of a process of reproduction.

Ghosting (1) To decrease the tonal values of the surrounding parts of an image to make the main object stand out more clearly. This can be done by photographic processing or by AIRBRUSHING. **(2)** In technical illustration, to depict parts of an image that would not normally be visible, eg parts of an engine covered by its casing.

gigo, GIGO *abb* Garbage In — Garbage Out. A principle in computer programming that poor quality INPUT produces equally poor OUTPUT.

Gilt edges/top The three edges, or top of a book, which are covered with gold leaf and rubbed down, preventing the absorption of dust.

Glassine A TRANSLUCENT, grease resistant paper used for wrappings and in stationery.

Gloss ink A printing ink consisting of a synthetic resin base and drying oils. These inks dry quickly, without penetration, and are suitable for use on COATED PAPERS.

Glossary A list giving definitions of terms related to a particular subject.

Glossy print A photographic print with a glossy surface.

Glued back only Reference to a paper COVER which is glued to the back of a book only, leaving the sides loose.

Glued or pasted down to ends A paper COVER glued at back, with each side also glued or pasted to the first and last leaves of the book.

Glyphic A TYPEFACE originating from carved rather than scripted letters.

Gold blocking The stamping of a design on a book COVER using gold leaf and a heated DIE or block.

Golden section A division supposed to give harmonious proportions. If a line is divided unequally the relationship of the two sections should be the same as that of the larger section to the whole. It is in practice a ratio of about 8:13.

Goldenrod An opaque, orange paper ruled with a GRID used in preparing FLATS for PHOTOLITHOGRAPHY.

Golfball A colloquial term for the printing head of a typewriter in the form of a faceted ball, originally a feature of IBM machines.

Gothic see BLACKLETTER.

Gouache Opaque watercolour for which the pigments are mixed with white lead, bone ash or chalk.

Gradation The smooth transition from one tone or colour to another, or the range of values between black and white.

Grain (1) In paper, the pattern of fibres in a manufactured SHEET. **(2)** *(pho)* The density of tiny silver crystals in a photographic EMULSION.

Grain direction The direction the FIBRES lie in a SHEET of paper.

Graining The process by which a LITHOGRAPHIC plate is given a moisture-retaining surface. Abrasive powder and either glass or steel marbles are used. Mechanical agitation produces the required surface.

Grammage see g/m^2

Graph/chart A representation of the relationships of values and quantities drawn up from vertical and horizontal axes by the plotting of reference points and lines.

Graphic (1) *(typ)* A TYPEFACE originating from drawn rather than scripted letter forms. **(2)** A general term meaning related to written or drawn symbols.

Graphic design Design based on or involving two dimensional processes, eg ILLUSTRATION, TYPOGRAPHY, PHOTOGRAPHY and PRINTING METHODS.

Graphic/graphical display terminal An electronic display unit used in PHOTOCOMPOSITION or COMPUTER GRAPHICS.

Graphics tablet A device for plotting co-ordinates used in giving information to a computer, using a flat board and an electro-magnetic pen.

Graphoscope A magnifier used for close viewing of photographs or ENGRAVINGS.

Graticule A linear GRID placed over an image giving reference to points on the image, eg lines of latitude and longitude on a map.

Gravure An INTAGLIO printing process. See PHOTOGRAVURE.

Grey scale A tonal scale included in a TRANSPARENCY enabling the printer to check reproduction of tones.

Grid A measuring guide used by designers to help ensure consistency. The grid shows type widths, picture areas, trim sizes etc.

Grid drawing A method of copying an image on an altered scale by drawing a grid over it and plotting key points on a correspondingly larger or smaller grid.

Gripper edge The edge which is caught by the GRIPPERS as a SHEET of paper is fed into a CYLINDER PRESS.

Gripper margin An extra MARGIN on a SHEET where it is gripped on the press, later trimmed away.

Grippers On job presses, these are the iron fingers attached to the PLATEN to keep the SHEET in place and take it off the type after the IMPRESSION **(2)**. On CYLINDER PRESSES, they are the short curved metal fingers attached to an operating rod which grip the sheet and carry it round the impression.

Ground A thin coating made from pitch, gum-mastic, asphaltum and beeswax which protects the non-image-bearing parts of an ETCHING plate from the action of the acid.

Groundwood A cheap wood PULP, such as that used to make NEWSPRINT.

Guards Narrow strips of linen or paper to which the inner MARGINS of single plates are pasted before sewing them with the SECTIONS of a book.

Guides see GRIPPERS.

Guillemets Quotation marks used in French and some German publications (« »).

Guillotine A machine for cutting a large number

of SHEETS of paper accurately.

Gum arabic A liquid used in platemaking processes. It dries to form a protective finish.

Gutter A term used in imposition for the space made up of FOREDGES of pages plus the trim. Commonly, the channel down the centre of a page is incorrectly described as the gutter.

Gutter bleed An image allowed to extend unbroken across the central MARGINS of a DOUBLE SPREAD.

H

H & J, H/J *abb* HYPHENATION and JUSTIFICATION. See also END OF LINE DECISIONS.

Hairline rule The thinnest RULE that it is possible to print.

Hairlines The very fine strokes of a TYPEFACE.

Hairspace Mainly used for letter spacing, the very narrow space between type.

Halation The spreading of lights around the HIGHLIGHTS of an image.

Half-bound A book with its back and corners bound in one material, the sides in another.

Half sheet work The construction of FORMES so that each SHEET will be printed with two whole SECTIONS, half a sheet folding to one section.

Half-title The title of a book as printed on the LEAF preceding the TITLE PAGE.

Half up ARTWORK completed at one and a half times the size at which it will be reproduced.

Halftone Process by which CONTINUOUS TONE is simulated by a pattern of dots of varying size. A halftone block is a zinc or copper printing plate prepared by this process.

Halftone blow up The enlargement of a HALFTONE NEGATIVE to coarsen the screened DOT pattern.

Halftone screen A sheet of glass or film bearing a network of lines ruled at right angles. The screen is used to translate the subject of a HALFTONE illustration into DOTS.

Hand press A printing press in which the plate is inked and the paper is fed and removed by hand.

Hanging indent A setting where the first line of each paragraph is set FULL OUT to the COLUMN measure and the remaining lines indented 1 EM.

Hanging punctuation Punctuation marks allowed to fall outside the MEASURE of a piece of text.

Hard copy (1) A copy on paper of MATTER prepared for printing, used for revision or checking. **(2)** A computer printout for checking INPUT to the machine.

Hard disc see MAGNETIC DISC.

Hard dot A HALFTONE DOT in the second or third stage of processing, with good density and sharpness.

Hard size Paper which contains the maximum amount of SIZE.

Hardback book/hardcover book *(UK/US)* A CASED book with a stiff board COVER.

Hardware A term for equipment. It generally applies to the physical apparatus in a computer.

Head The MARGIN at the top of a page.

Head bolt The thickening of a fully folded SHEET before it is trimmed.

Head to foot arrangement The placement of COPY on either side of a SHEET to align the top of the first page with the bottom of the page overleaf.

Headband A cotton or silk cord sewn to the top of the back of a book.

Heading The title introducing a chapter or subdivision of printed MATTER. It is set in a style or size of type that distinguishes between heading and text, and between main and subsidiary headings.

Headless paragraph A paragraph set apart from other text but without a separate HEADING.

Headline The title of a book as printed at the top of every page of text.

Headpiece A decorative device added to a HEADING.

Heat set inks Ink designed to dry particularly quickly when the printed MATTER is passed through a drier.

Heavy *(typ)* An alternative term for BOLD.

Hectography A duplication process based on the use of gelatin plates.

Height The vertical dimension of an image.

Hickie, hickey A spot with a blank halo appearing in printing due to a speck of dust or hard substance adhering to the printing plate or BLANKET.

Hieroglyph An element of language recorded in the form of a PICTOGRAM or symbol rather than as a written word.

High gloss ink A viscous ink that does not soak into paper and dries to a glossy surface.

High key A photographic image exposed or processed to produce light tones overall.

Highlight The lightest tones of a photograph or illustration.

Highlight halftone A HALFTONE plate in which DOTS appearing in HIGHLIGHT areas are etched out. See DROP OUT HALFTONE.

Holding line *(US)* see KEYLINE.

Hollow The strip of brown paper placed in the centre of a CASE to stiffen the SPINE.

Hologram/holograph (1) An image with three dimensional illusionism created by the action of lasers. **(2)** In publishing, the term holograph refers to a MANUSCRIPT hand-written by the author.

Honing A technique of removing image areas from a printing plate by mechanical means.

Hooking A method of attaching a single LEAF to a SECTION **(1)** by means of a GUARD.

Horizontal dimension The width of an image, sometimes controlling reduction or enlargement in printing.

Hot metal General term for composing machines casting single pieces of type from molten metal.

Hot press lettering A method of laying down CHARACTERS **(1)** in metal foil on board, using type under heat and pressure.

Hot-pressed Paper glazed by heated metal plates.

House corrections PROOFS or script altered by the PUBLISHER or printer, as distinct from the author.

House organ A publication produced by a company for information to its own employees or customers.

House style (1) The style of spelling, punctuation and spacing used in a printing or publishing house to ensure consistent treatment of COPY during TYPESETTING. **(2)** CORPORATE IDENTITY

H/T *abb* HALFTONE.

Hue The distinguishing property of a pure colour, not including any white or black.

Hygroscope A device for measuring how much humidity is picked up from the air by paper.

Hyphenation The use of a hyphen (-) to divide one word between syllables or to create a compound form from two or more words.

Hypo *abb* Hyposulphate. A term applied to the FIXER used in photographic processing, though the solution used is in fact sodium thiosulphate.

I

ibid *abb ibidem*, a Latin term meaning 'in the same place' used in notes to a publication to repeat a reference.

Ideal format A size of photographic NEGATIVE measuring 60 x 70mm.

idem A Latin term meaning 'the same', used as a reference in FOOTNOTES.

Idiot tape see UNJUSTIFIED TAPE.

ie *abb id est*, a Latin term meaning 'that is'.

Illustration (1) A drawing, painting, diagram or photograph reproduced in a publication to explain or supplement the text. **(2)** A term used to distinguish a drawn image from one that is photographed.

Image The SUBJECT to be reproduced as an illustration on a printing press.

Image area The amount of space given to a particular image in design and printing, assumed to be square or rectangular even if the image is not.

Image carrier In PHOTOCOMPOSITION, that part of the system that stores the INPUT. See also MAGNETIC DISC,

DRUM.

Imitation cloth/leather A BOOKBINDING material, usually of paper, made to simulate the appearance of leather or cloth.

Imperfection A book which has been incorrectly bound.

Imperial A size of printing and drawing paper 22 x 30in (56 x 76mm).

Impose/imposition To arrange pages of type in a FORME so that when the SHEET is folded the text will read continuously.

Imposed proof The PROOF from a FORME.

Impression (1) All copies of a book printed at one time from the same type of plates. **(2)** The pressure applied to a frame of type by the cylinder or PLATEN.

Impression cylinder The cylinder of a ROTARY PRESS carrying paper into contact with the inked plate or BLANKET CYLINDER.

Imprimature A Latin term meaning 'let it be printed'. It used to be a statement to show that permission to print a work had been given by the appropriate authority.

Imprint The printer's imprint is the name of the printer and the place of printing. It is required by law if the paper or book is meant to be published. The PUBLISHER's imprint is the name of the publisher with place and date of publication.

Imprint page The page following the TITLE PAGE of a book, carrying details of printing, COPYRIGHT etc. See also BIBLIO.

In camera process Photographic process in which the print is developed inside the camera. See POLAROID.

In house A process or service carried out within a company, not bought in from an individual or organization.

In pro *abb* In proportion. A term used to direct the enlargement or reduction of an original image.

Increment see LINE INCREMENT.

Indentation Any setting short of the COLUMN measure.

Index The section of a publication giving alphabetical listing of

subjects, proper names etc mentioned in the book, with page references.

Index board Coloured board made by machine, used for INDEX GUIDES.

Index guide The markers of a filing system designed to give ready access to items divided alphabetically or by subject. See STEP, TAB and THUMB INDEX.

Index letter CAPITAL used to key a reference between an illustration and the CAPTION or text.

India paper A very thin but strong opaque paper, made from rags and used for printing Bibles and dictionaries.

Indirect letterpress see LETTERSET.

Inferior figure/letter A small figure or letter printed at the foot of ordinary letters and cast partly below the base line, for example in chemical formulae, such as H_2O.

Initial A large CAPITAL often found at the beginning of a chapter. It is usually dropped to a depth of two or three lines below the first line.

Initial caps Instruction to the printer to set the first letter of a word or phrase as a CAPITAL.

Ink drier A chemical agent added to ink to speed drying and prevent smudging.

Ink duct The FOUNTAIN supplying ink to a printing press.

Ink jet printer A printing device attached to a computer, that uses high speed ink jets to form an image.

Ink squash A spread of ink outside the required details of an image, occurring during printing.

Inked art ARTWORK drawn up first in pencil for checking and then completed in ink.

Inkers The rollers on a printing press which apply ink to the type and block surfaces.

Inking roller A printing machine roller that carries ink from the FOUNTAIN to the plate or FORME.

Inline lettering TYPEFACE with a white line inside the shape, following the outline of the letter.

Inner forme The FORME that includes the pages of a CENTRE SPREAD.

Input The information given to a computer for processing.

Insert An instruction to the printer to include extra COPY.

Inset A SHEET or part of a sheet placed inside another which is not part of the book's normal PAGINATION.

Intaglio A printing image below the surface of the plate.

Intensification Chemical methods of improving the DENSITY of a NEGATIVE.

Interface A jargon word meaning the point of interaction between a machine and its operator or between two technical systems.

Interlaying Placing SHEETS of paper between a printing plate and its block or MOUNT.

Interleaved (1) A book with blank leaves between the printed pages for handwritten notes. **(2)** A book with thin tissue inserted to protect the illustrations. **(3)** A plate with a thin LEAF bearing a descriptive CAPTION pasted to its inner MARGIN.

Interlinear spacing The method of establishing space between lines of type in PHOTOCOMPOSITION.

Interlock An effect produced by joining together type CHARACTERS **(1)** in PHOTOCOMPOSITION. See also LIGATURE.

Intermediate A transparent or TRANSLUCENT COPY of an ORIGINAL from which other copies can be made.

International paper sizes A range of standard paper sizes adopted by the ISO. The papers are designated A, B and C series and are available in proportionate sizes, divided in ratio to the largest SHEET.

Internegative A photographic NEGATIVE forming the intermediate stage in making a print from a FLAT ORIGINAL.

Interrogating typewriter A device connected to the central processing system of a computer that can receive OUTPUT from or insert DATA into a program stored in the computer's memory.

Introduction The opening SECTION **(2)** of a book written either by the author as part of the text or by another person commenting on the purpose and content of the author's work.

Inverted commas A pair of commas printed above the BASELINE of type ('') used to open or close a quotation.

i/o *abb* INPUT/OUTPUT.

iph *abb* IMPRESSIONS **(2)** per hour.

Iris see DIAPHRAGM.

ISBN *abb* International Standard Book Number. A reference number given to every published work, identifying area of origin, PUBLISHER, title and check control, encoded in a ten-digit number. A new ISBN is given to each new EDITION of a book.

ISO *abb* International Standards Organization. A Switzerland-based organization which has been responsible for standardizing many elements common to design, photography and publishing.

Italic Type with sloping letters. Indicated in a MANUSCRIPT by a single underline.

Ivory board A smoothly finished white board used for ARTWORK and display printing.

J

Jacket The paper wrapper in which a book is sold.

Jaw folder A paper folder attached to a WEB-FED printing press, that cuts and folds a SIGNATURE.

Jim-dash A short RULE dividing items in a newspaper.

Job press A hand-fed, small scale printing press.

Jobbing work Small everyday printing such as display cards, letter-headings etc as distinct from bookwork.

Jogging To vibrate paper stock to bring the edges into line before trimming. A jogger may be attached to a printing press or form a separate unit.

Joint The flexible part of a CASE between the boarded side and the SPINE.

Jump In a publication, printed MATTER carried over to continue on a succeeding page.

Justification Spacing of words and letters so that each line of text finishes at the same point.

K

Keep down Instruction used in newspaper printing to keep text in LOWER CASE type.

Keep in An instruction to a COMPOSITOR to keep spaces narrow between words.

Keep out The opposite of KEEP IN, to use wide spaces between words.

Keep standing To keep plates ready for possible REPRINTS.

Keep up Instruction to keep text in UPPER CASE type.

Kern, kerning The part of a letter which overhangs the next.

Key The block or plate containing the main outlines of the design. It acts as a guide for the position and registration of the other colours.

Key letters/numbers (1) References used to key in COPY to a LAYOUT. **(2)** Numbers forming references between a technical drawing and description of parts in the CAPTION.

Key plate see BLACK PRINTER.

Keyboarding A term referring to the first procedure in PHOTOCOMPOSITION, that of typing in COPY to be recorded in the machine for setting.

Keyline An outline drawing in ARTWORK that shows the size and position of an illustration or HALFTONE image.

Keyword index In computer systems for information retrieval, the use of a significant word from the title of a document as an index word in the computer's memory store.

Kicker Newspaper or magazine term for a line of type appearing above or below the title of a feature.

Kill An instruction to distribute type or DELETE COPY.

Kiss impression An IMPRESSION **(2)** in which ink is put on paper by the lightest possible surface contact and not impressed into it. This technique is necessary when printing on COATED PAPERS.

Klischograph A German electronic PHOTOENGRAVING machine which produces a plastic, zinc, copper or magnesium HALFTONE plate.

Knocking up The adjustment on one or two edges of SHEETS so that they can be cut squarely.

Kraft paper Strong brown paper made from sulphate PULP. It is often used for packing books.

KWIC/KWOC *abb* Keyword in Context/Keyword Out of Context. It applies to the content in relation to title of words in a KEYWORD INDEX.

L

Lacuna A gap or space in a text where COPY has been lost or damaged.

Laid paper Paper showing the wire marks of the mould or DANDY ROLL used in manufacture.

Laminate To protect paper or card and give it a glossy surface by applying a transparent plastic coating through heat or pressure.

Landscape/horizontal format *(UK/US)* An image in which the width is noticeably greater than the height.

Lap The slight overlapping of two printed colours to ensure there is no fault in the REGISTRATION. See also FATTY.

Large face The larger version of type cast in two different sizes on one BODY **(1)**.

Latent image A photographically recorded image that can be made apparent by chemical processing.

Lateral reversal The TRANSPOSING of an image from left to right, as in a mirror reflection. See also FLOP.

Latin A term for TYPEFACES derived from letter forms common to western European countries, especially those with heavy, wedge-shaped SERIFS.

Latitude *(pho)* The range of EXPOSURES that all produce an acceptable image on a given type of film.

Lay down A term for placing.

Lay edges The two edges of a SHEET which are placed FLUSH with the side and front lay gauges or marks on a printing machine to ensure that the sheet will be removed properly by

the GRIPPERS, and have uniform MARGINS when printed.

Layout An outline or sketch which gives the general appearance of the printed page, indicating the relationship between text and illustration.

Lays see GRIPPERS.

LCD *abb* Liquid crystal display. The kind of electronic display device commonly seen in pocket calculators.

Lead (1) Spaces less than type height which are used to space out HEADINGS and text. **(2)** The main story in a newspaper or the opening story.

Leaded Type which is set with LEADS **(1)** between the lines.

Leader A group of dots, usually three (. . .).

Leader line/rule A line on an image keyed into ANNOTATION.

Leaf (1) Refers to newly formed SHEETS of paper before they are dried and finished. **(2)** Each of the folios which result when a sheet of paper is folded. Each side of a leaf is called a page.

Leaf edge The opposite edge to the GRIPPER edge.

Legend The descriptive MATTER printed below an illustration, more often called CAPTION.

Lens flare The diffusion of light tending to occur in a camera lens if the light source is very strong.

Letraset Proprietary name for DRY TRANSFER LETTERING on a plastic sheet that is rubbed down on paper or board in preparing ARTWORK, ANNOTATION **(1)** etc.

Letterhead The HEADING on a piece of stationery, usually the name, address and telephone number of a business or individual, and the LOGOTYPE, if one exists.

Letterpress A printing process. The image is raised and inked to produce an impression. It also refers to the text of a book, including line illustrations but excluding plates.

Letterset A term deriving from LETTERPRESS and OFFSET, describing a method of offset printing from a relief plate.

Letterspacing The insertion of space

between the letters of a word to improve the appearance of a line of type.

lhp *abb* Lefthand page.

Library binding BOOK-BINDING strong enough to endure continual handling.

Library of Congress number A reference number given to the American edition of a book and recorded at the Library of Congress. This is common practice but not required by law.

Library shot/pic A picture or illustration taken from an existing source, not specially commissioned.

Lift The number of SHEETS of paper that can be cut all together or handled in a single operation.

Lifted matter Type MATTER already set which is taken out of one job to be used in another.

Lifting see PICKING.

Ligature Tied letters in type, such as fi.

Light face The opposite of BOLD FACE.

Light-fast ink Ink that is not susceptible to fading colour when exposed to light over a period.

Light pen A device used with a VDU to retrieve information from a computer, using a drawn symbol rather than keyboard instructions.

Light table/box A table or box with a TRANSLUCENT glass screen top illuminated from below, used for viewing or working with any photographically produced material, eg TRANSPARENCY STRIPPING, RETOUCHING.

Limp binding A form of binding using a flexible COVER eg paper, cloth or leather, and no board stiffener.

Line and halftone An illustration process in which line and halftone NEGATIVES are combined, printed onto a plate and etched as a unit.

Line block A printing plate made of zinc or copper consisting of solid areas and lines. It is reproduced directly from a line drawing without tones. It is mounted on a wooden block to type height.

Line board A smoothly finished support suitable for line illustrations and ARTWORK.

Line conversion A photographic process of converting HALFTONE or CONTINUOUS TONE COPY into line images. Middle tones are eliminated to increase contrast.

Line copy COPY consisting of black line or solid masses on white, with no intermediate tones.

Line endless tape see UNJUSTIFIED TAPE.

Line feed The measure, expressed in POINTS, of the movement of paper or film from one line to the next in PHOTOCOMPOSITION.

Line gauge The printer's RULE. It is calibrated in PICAS and is 72 picas long (11.952 in).

Line increment The smallest allowable increase in the basic measure between lines in TYPESETTING.

Line interval The distance between the BASE LINES of following lines of type. Where metal type is used, the BODY SIZE dictates the interval.

Line original An original image prepared for line reproduction.

Line printer A printing device attached to a computer that prints one line at a time at very high speed.

Line up When two lines of type, or a line of type and a block, touch the same imaginary horizontal line.

Line weight The relative thickness of RULES or lines used in illustration.

Linecaster This is the generic term for all keyboard-operated slug-casting composing machines, LINOTYPE or Intertype.

Linen tester A magnifying glass designed for checking the detail of a HALFTONE DOT pattern.

Lining figures/numerals A set of numerals aligned at top and bottom.

Lining up/lineup table *(UK/US)* A table used in preparing and checking the ALIGNMENT of PASTE UP, FLATS etc. It has an illuminated top with a gridded surface and movable scales.

Linocut A RELIEF PRINTING surface of linoleum on which the background to the design is cut away with a knife, gouge or engraving tool.

Linotype The first keyboard-operated composing machine to employ the principle of the circulating MATRIX and cast type in solid lines or slugs. It was invented by the German/American engineer Ottmar Mergenthaler and first used in 1886.

Linting The adhesion of loose scraps from the surface of paper to the BLANKET CYLINDER in OFFSET printing. See also PICKING.

Lith film A film used in preparing PLATES in PHOTOCHEMICAL reproduction. It omits middle tones and increases contrasts.

Lithography Printing from a dampened, flat surface using greasy ink, based on the principle of the mutual repulsion of oil and water.

Live matter A FORME awaiting printing, stereotyping or electrotyping.

Loading The addition of a substance such as china clay in papermaking, to give better opacity and finish.

LOC see LIBRARY OF CONGRESS NUMBER.

loc cit *abb loco citato*, a Latin term for 'in the place named', used as a reference in FOOTNOTES.

Logarithmic scale A measurement scale of variable ratios used in making GRAPHS or charts.

Logic mode A method of automatic programming used in PHOTOCOMPOSITION that can be overriden by the keyboard operator if necessary.

Logo *abb* LOGOTYPE.

Logotype A word or several letters cast as one unit.

Long-bodied type Type larger than normal such as 10 point or 12 point.

Long descenders The DESCENDERS of a TYPEFACE that are extended compared to the usual design of the face.

Long ink Ink mixed to a consistency of flow that can be drawn out in a thread without breaking.

Long letters Type CHARACTERS **(1)** that extend right across the shank.

Long page A page with type extended by one or two lines to avoid an inconvenient break.

Long S The S used in old forms of printed English, resembling an F.

Look-/see-through *(US/UK)* The visibility of an image through paper when seen against the light.

Loose leaf A BINDING METHOD that allows the easy removal of individual leaves.

Low key A photographic image given dark tones overall by the lighting or processing methods applied.

Lower case The small letters in a FOUNT of type.

lpm *abb* Lines per minute. The rate of printing of a COMPUTER OUTPUT DEVICE.

M

Machine composition Methods of TYPESETTING involving the use of keyboard operated machines.

Machine direction The path of paper through a papermaking machine that dictates the GRAIN **(1)** of the paper.

Machine glazed paper Machine finished paper with a high gloss surface on one side.

Machine-made paper The continuous WEB of paper made on cylinder machines.

Machine proof A PROOF taken when corrections marked on the GALLEY PROOF and PAGE PROOF have been made and the FORME is on the printing machine. This is the last opportunity for correcting mistakes before the final printing.

Machine readable DATA used in computers encoded in a form recognizable to the computer.

Machine sheet A general term for any printed SHEET coming off the press.

Macron A symbol denoting pronunciation of a long vowel, printed as a horizontal line above the letter.

Macrophotography The photographing of small objects by means of a special lens or lens adaptor.

Magazine A storage device such as that which holds the FOUNT in a HOT-METAL composing machine.

Magenta The name of the shade of red established as one of the standard four-colour LETTERPRESS printing inks.

Magnetic disc The storage device of a computer in the form of a soft or rigid disc with a magnetic coating that records information.

Magnetic ink characters *(com)* CHARACTERS **(1)** printed in magnetizable ink which are readable both by humans and by appropriately equipped machines.

Main exposure The first exposure in the processing of a HALFTONE image.

Majuscules An alternative term for CAPITALS.

Make-up (1) The SHEET indicating the placing of the various items on a page. **(2)** The actual assembling of the page.

Making A term referring to one whole batch of MACHINE-MADE PAPER.

Making ready In printing,the surface on which the paper or plate rests has to be built up in places to give an overall evenness of impression. This is called making ready, the build-up backing is known as make ready.

Manilla A tough, buff coloured paper used in the manufacture of stationery.

Manuscript Refers to the written or typed work which an author submits for publication.

Marbling Decorative paper used for binding books, and sometimes the book EDGES. It is done by dipping the SHEET in a bath of colours floating on a surface of gum. The colours do not mix but can be combined into patterns with the use of a comb, and transfer readily to the paper surface.

Marching display A display unit used in PHOTOCOMPOSITION allowing the operator to check the most recent INPUT up to about 40 CHARACTERS **(1)**.

Margins The blank areas on a printed page which surround the MATTER.

Marked proof The PROOF, usually on GALLEYS, supplied to the author for correction. It contains the corrections and queries made by the

printer's READER.

Mark up To mark up is to specify every detail needed for the COMPOSITOR to set the COPY. The mark up is copy with instructions written on it.

Mask (1) A material used to block out part of an image in photography, illustration or LAYOUT. **(2)** A photographic image modified in tone or colour.

Masking (1) Applying a protective layer to an illustration to cover an area while other parts are painted or AIRBRUSHED. **(2)** Blocking out part of an image with opaque material to prevent reproduction or to allow for alteration in COPY. **(3)** A technical method of adjusting values of colour and tone in PHOTOMECHANICAL reproduction.

Master cylinder The cylinder of a printing press that transfers ink from reservoir to plate.

Master plate The plate containing the image for OFFSET printing.

Master proof A printer's PROOF read and marked with corrections and queries.

Masthead Details about a PUBLISHER printed in the editorial or contents page of a newspaper or periodical.

Mat *abb* MATRIX.

Mathematical signs Type symbols corresponding to mathematical concepts and processes, eg +, = etc.

Matrix (1) The brass DIES used in HOT METAL composition. **(2)** The impression in papier-mâché taken from a page of type for stereotyping and the stereotyper's FLONG after moulding.

Matt art A clay-coated printing paper with a dull finish.

Matter Either MANUSCRIPT or COPY to be printed, or type that is composed.

Mean line The imagined line showing the top limit of x-HEIGHT.

Measure The width of a setting, usually measured in PICA EMS.

Mechanical *(US)* A term for CAMERA READY COPY or ARTWORK.

Mechanical binding BINDING METHOD

securing leaves through punched or drilled holes by means of a metal or plastic device, for permanent or LOOSE LEAF binding.

Mechanical pulp Untreated paper pulp used as the basis of NEWSPRINT and low quality papers.

Mechanical tints Tints consisting of DOT or line patterns that can be laid down on ARTWORK before or during reproduction processing.

Medallion An illustration printed on paper, pasted to the front of the CASE of a book.

Media Plural term used in referring to information sources, eg radio, television, publishing etc.

Medium (1) A standard size of printing paper 18 x 23in (455 x 585mm). **(2)** The liquid, usually linseed oil, in which the pigment of a printing ink is dispersed. **(3)** An alternative name for BENDAY tint. **(4)** The weight of TYPEFACE midway between light and bold.

Memory Systems such as those in computers that collect and store information.

Merge A method of combining tapes used in PHOTOCOMPOSITION to add in corrections to an original tape.

Metallic ink A printing ink which produces an effect of gold, silver, copper or bronze.

Mezzotint INTAGLIO printing process producing a range of tones.

mf/mtf *abb* More follows/more to follow, marked on COPY being prepared for TYPESETTING.

MF *abb* MACHINE FINISHED PAPER.

MG *abb* MACHINE GLAZED PAPER.

MICR *abb* MAGNETIC INK CHARACTER recognition.

Microfiche A SHEET containing a collective of MICROFORM images, arranged on a GRID pattern.

Microfilm The sensitized vehicle for recording of MICROFORMS.

Microform An image reproduced photographically on an extremely small scale. It may be positive or negative, transparent or opaque. Microforms are generally used to store published information without bulk and can be read through equipment specially designed to enlarge the images to a legible form.

Microimage see MICROFORM.

Microphotography The technique of reducing an ORIGINAL to a MICROFORM.

Middle space In hand-set type, a standard word space measuring one quarter of an EM.

Mill brand The TRADE MARK and brand name of the manufacturer.

Mill ream A bulk quantity of handmade or MOULDMADE PAPER (472 SHEETS).

Millboards Strong grey or black boards of good quality used for the COVERS of a book.

Miniscules An alternative term for LOWER CASE letters.

Minus leading/linespacing see NEGATIVE LINESPACING.

Mixing The combination of TYPEFACE designs and sizes contained in a single PHOTO MATRIX.

Mock up The rough visualization of a publication or packaging design showing size, colour, type etc.

Modern face A TYPEFACE with vertical stress, strong stroke contrast and unbracketed fine SERIFS.

Moiré A printing fault where HALFTONES appear as a mechanical pattern of DOTS.

Monochrome An image made up of varying tones but in only one colour.

Monogram A design formed from the INITIALS of a name.

Monograph A publication dealing with a single person or subject.

Monophoto The trade name of the PHOTOCOMPOSITION system produced by the manufacturers of MONOTYPE.

Monotype (1) The trade name for composing machines which cast single types. **(2)** The process of making a painting on glass or metal and then taking an IMPRESSION **(2)** on paper. Only one impression can be taken.

Montage Assembling portions of several drawings or photographs to form a single ORIGINAL.

Mordant An adhesive for fixing gold leaf. It is also any fluid used to etch lines on a printing plate.

Morocco Tanned goat-skin which is finished by glazing or polishing and used in BOOKBINDING.

Mottling An uneven IMPRESSION **(2)**, especially in flat areas. It is usually caused by too much pressure or unsuitable paper or ink.

Mould A flat impressed SHEET made by beating or pressing a FLONG onto a type, for casting a stereo.

Mouldmade paper A manufactured, imitation handmade paper.

Mount The base used to support a printing plate and bring it type high.

Mounting and flapping A method of presentation for ARTWORK, involving mounting the work on board and protecting the surface with a hinged SHEET of ACETATE or tissue.

Mounting board A heavy board used for mounting photographs or ARTWORK.

Movable type The principle of an old fashioned method of TYPESETTING in which single pieces of type were used rather than slugs.

MS, MSS abb MANUSCRIPT(S).

Mull Coarse variety of muslin which forms the first lining of a CASE-BOUND book. Also known as scrim.

Multiple exposure In photography, stages of the same subject or separate images superimposed to form one image in EXPOSURE or PROCESSING.

Multiple flats FLATS used in printing successive pages where it is required that some elements of the design are matched from page to page.

Multi-ring binder BINDING METHOD using a number of closely spaced rings to secure leaves.

Multisheet drawing ARTWORK requiring more than one drawing to make up the whole image.

Munsell colour system A system of colour measurement and notation which defines all colours in terms of hue, value and CHROMA.

Mutton, mutt The term for an EM QUAD.

N

Nameplate The bold or elaborate printing of the title of a newspaper, as it usually appears at the top of the front page.

Naturals see CENTRE FOLD.

Neck line The amount of white or leading under a RUNNING HEAD.

Needle printer A COMPUTER OUTPUT DEVICE printing CHARACTERS **(1)** based on a DOT MATRIX.

Negative Photographic film that has been exposed and processed to fix a reverse tone or colour image from which POSITIVE **(1)** prints can be made.

Negative line feed see REVERSE LINE FEED.

Negative line spacing In PHOTOCOMPOSITION, a LINE INTERVAL smaller than the POINT size of the type.

Newsprint The paper used for printing newspapers, characteristically absorbent because it is unsized.

Newton rings Patterns occurring when there is interference in the path of light at the contact of two lenses or a convex lens and a plane surface.

Next reading/text matter An instruction to place advertisement COPY next to editorial copy in a publication.

Nickel facing A deposit applied to blocks, usually stereos, which gives a harder and longer-lasting surface.

Nipping Pressing a book after sewing but before FORWARDING. This flattens the BOLTS and expels air from between the SHEETS.

Nomenclature (US) see ANNOTATION **(1).**

Non-counting keyboard A keyboard used in PHOTOCOMPOSITION that does not provide the operator with details for making END OF LINE DECISIONS.

Non-impact printing PRINTOUTS produced without a plate or cylinder, eg by a WRITING HEAD.

Non-lining figures/numerals A set of numerals designed with DESCENDERS, therefore not of standard height and ALIGNMENT as are LINING FIGURES.

Nonpareil The name for an old type size (approximately equal to 6 POINTS). It is still used as an alternative term to indicate spacing.

Not A finish in high quality RAG PAPERS, which is midway between ROUGH and HOT-PRESSED.

np *abb* New paragraph. A mark used in editing and PROOF correction.

O

Oblique stroke see SOLIDUS.

OCR *abb* OPTICAL CHARACTER RECOGNITION.

Octavo A SHEET of paper folded in half three times, to make eighths or sixteen pages. It also refers to a standard BROADSIDE divided into eight parts.

Off-line Work done in relation to a computer process but not as direct use of the computer.

Offprint A REPRINT of an article or other part of a publication, produced as a separate item.

Offset lithography A method of lithography by which the image is not printed direct from the plate but 'offset' first onto a rubber covered cylinder, the BLANKET, which performs the printing operation.

Offside The part of the CASE which comes at the end of the book.

Old face/old style *(US)* Type characterized by diagonal stress and sloped, bracketed SERIFS.

On-line Interconnected functions in computer work under the direct control of a central computer.

One and a half up ARTWORK prepared at one and a half times the size at which it will be printed.

One third reduction The amount of reduction (66%) involved in printing an image prepared at ONE AND A HALF UP.

Onion skin A thin, TRANSLUCENT paper with a glazed finish used for carbon copies and OVERLAYS.

Opacity The term used

to describe non-transparency in printing papers.

Opaline A semi-opaque paper, fine and with a highly glazed finish.

Opaquing To paint out unwanted areas in a NEGATIVE with opaque solution before processing the image.

op cit *abb opere citato*, a Latin term meaning 'in the work quoted', used as a FOOTNOTE reference.

Optical alignment An arrangement of CHARACTERS (1) allowing a degree of projection on the left-hand MARGIN so the main strokes of the letters are aligned.

Optical centre A point within a rectangle slightly higher than the actual geometric centre, at which an object or image appears to be centrally placed.

Optical character recognition (OCR) Device for the electronic scanning of COPY and its coversion into photoset MATTER without keyboard operation.

Optical/optically even spacing The adjustment of letterspaces between CHARACTERS (1) to give an even appearance to a line of type.

Optical type fount A FOUNT used in OPTICAL CHARACTER RECOGNITION.

Order *(US)* The relative importance of HEADINGS in a text, determining the style in which they are set.

Original *(pri)* Any MATTER or image intended for reproduction.

Ornament *(pri)* Decorative elements used with type MATTER, such as FLOWERS, BORDERS etc.

Orphan A single word that stands at the top of a page when COPY has been set.

Orthochromatic Refers to photographic materials sensitive to green and yellow as well as blue light.

Out of register see REGISTER.

Outer forme The FORME containing MATTER, for the outer pages of a folded SECTION.

Outline letters TYPEFACES in which the letters are formed of outlines rather than solid strokes.

Overexposure A fault in platemaking caused when the light source is too close to the VACUUM FRAME.

Overhang cover A book COVER that projects past the trimmed edges of the leaves.

Overhead projector A machine for projecting images drawn on a transparent ACETATE slide or roll, by passing the image through an overhead lens and turning it through 90° on to a flat surface.

Overlay (1) A transparent SHEET used in the preparation of multicolour ARTWORK. **(2)** A TRANSLUCENT SHEET covering a piece of ORIGINAL ARTWORK, on which instructions may be written.

Overmatter MATTER set which does not come within the appropriate space.

Overprint Printing over an already printed area.

Overs, overruns Paper issued beyond the bare requirements to allow for make ready, SPOILS etc. It also refers to the quantity produced above the ordered number.

Oversize A description of COPY made at a larger size than that intended in reproduction.

Ozalid A trade name referring to a method of copying PAGE PROOFS by the DIAZO process.

P

Packager A company offering a service or commodity as a complete unit or package.

Packing To place paper under a PLATE or BLANKET in printing to ensure firm contact of surfaces to produce an even quality of print.

Page One side of a LEAF.

Page frame A page printed with details, such as a FIGURE NUMBER, page number or RUNNING HEAD, leaving space for an illustration to be inserted.

Page make up (1) See MAKE UP. **(2)** In PHOTOCOMPOSITION, a display showing COPY as it will appear on a page.

Page printer A COMPUTER OUTPUT DEVICE capable of printing a complete page at high speed. See also LINE PRINTER.

Page proofs PROOFS of

type which have been PAGINATED . It refers to the secondary stage in proofing, after GALLEY PROOFS and before MACHINE PROOFS.

Pages to view The number of pages visible on one side of a SHEET that has been printed on both sides.

Pagination The term given to numbering the pages of a book.

Pallet (1) A wooden storage device on which SHEETS of paper are stacked. **(2)** The brass finishing tool used for impressing straight lines on COVERS. **(3)** A small hand-tool in which letters are placed and heated to stamp the COVER of a book.

Pamphlet A short publication presented unbound and in a soft COVER.

Panchromatic Photographic material which is sensitive to all visible colours and to ultraviolet light.

Pantograph An instrument for copying a design. The COPY can be the same size, reduced or enlarged.

Pantone matching system A registered trade name for a system of colour matching in designer's materials such as inks, papers, marker pens.

Paper plate A photosensitized plate used in OFFSET printing for short RUNS, on which MATTER can be typed or drawn directly.

Paper to paper see FOLD TO PAPER.

Paperback A book with a soft outer COVER made of paper.

Paragraph mark A type CHARACTER **(1)** resembling a reversed P, used to denote the start of a paragraph if text is not indented. See BLIND P.

Parallax (pho) The difference in an image as seen through the camera viewfinder and as recorded on film. There is a slight discrepancy most noticeable in TWIN LENS REFLEX cameras.

Parallel A type CHARACTER **(1)** in the form of a double vertical bar, used as a reference mark for FOOTNOTES.

Parallel fold A SHEET **(1)** folded in half widthways and then in half again, the second fold parallel to the first.

Parchment Goat or sheepskin, scraped and dressed with lime and pumice and used for writing on.

Parentheses/brackets A punctuation mark or ORNAMENT, which appears as ( ).

Paring In hand-binding, paring is thinning and chamfering the edges of leather to give a neat turn-in over the boards.

Pass The full operational cycle of a machine used in printing or PHOTOCOMPOSITION.

Paste-up A LAYOUT of a number of pages used to plan the positioning of illustrations, CAPTIONS and text.

Pastel Drawing material in the form of sticks made from PIGMENT bound in glue and allowed to harden.

Pasting in/on see TIPPED ON.

Patent A licence granted to a person registering a new invention, object or process, that protects the inventor's rights.

PE abb Printer's error. A PROOF CORRECTION MARK showing where an error is the fault of the TYPESETTER, not from editor's or author's COPY.

Peculiars Type CHARACTERS **(1)** for non-standard accent-bearing letters used when setting certain foreign languages.

Percentage reduction/enlargement The indication of sizing for reproduction of an image.

Perfect binding A binding method in which the leaves of a book are trimmed at the back and glued, but not sewn.

Perfecting see BACK-UP.

Perfecting press, perfector A press which prints both sides of the paper at a single PASS. All LETTERPRESS rotaries and WEB-OFFSET machines are perfectors.

Perforate (1) Print perforation is to make broken slotted rules so that MATTER can be torn off. **(2)** Pin-hole perforation is to punch holes eg in postage stamps.

Period A punctuation mark, the full stop.

Perspective Systems of drawing objects in three-dimensional representation on the basis of a fixed point, or points, of view.

Phonogram A symbol designed as the written equivalent of a spoken sound: **thær** (there)

Photo matrix The storage device holding FOUNTS for use in PHOTOCOMPOSITION. It may be in the form of a disc, a disc segment, a film strip or a drum.

Photocomposition The production of DISPLAY LINE and text by photographic means on film or paper. Photocomposing machines assemble lines of letters from various forms of PHOTO MATRIX.

Photocopy A COPY produced immediately from an ORIGINAL by one of several methods involving photographic techniques.

Photodirect The description of a method of producing plates for PHOTOLITHOGRAPHY from ORIGINAL ARTWORK without an INTERNEGATIVE being made.

Photoengraving A PHOTOMECHANICAL method of producing etched line or HALFTONE plates.

Photogelatin process see COLLOTYPE.

Photogram An image made by the direct action of light on sensitized paper.

Photograph A representational image formed by the action of light on a sensitized material.

Photogravure The process of printing from a PHOTOMECHANICALLY prepared surface, which holds the ink in recessed cells.

Photoheadliner A machine designed to arrange display type and produce an image by photographic methods.

Photolithography A method of lithographic printing in which the image is transferred to the plate photographically and printed on a lithographic printing machine. This is sometimes known as OFFSET.

Photomechanical (1) Methods of making printing PLATES that involve photographic techniques. **(2)** The assembly of type or illustrations for transfer to a printing plate.

Photomechanical transfer A mechanical method of quickly producing photoprints from flat ORIGINALS for use in PASTE UP, PRESENTATION VISUALS etc.

Photomicrography A technique of photographing minute objects using a combination of camera and microscope.

Photomontage The use of images from different photographs combined to produce a new, composite image.

Photo-opaque A general term for opaque solutions used to paint out parts of process NEGATIVES.

Photopolymer plates Sensitized plastic plates on which NEGATIVES can be printed down; a RELIEF PRINTING surface is formed by a chemical WASH-OUT. PHOTOCOMPOSED pages can thus be converted into LETTERPRESS printing surfaces, either by printing direct from the photopolymer plate or moulding from it to make STEREOTYPE PLATES.

Photoprint (1) In PHOTOCOMPOSITION, a PROOF of type MATTER of suitable quality for reproduction. **(2)** A print of an image produced photographically.

Photosensitive A material treated chemically to become light-sensitive.

Photostat A FACSIMILE COPY of a document — typed, written, printed or drawn.

Photostatic printing see XEROGRAPHY.

Phototypesetting see PHOTOCOMPOSITION.

Pi characters (US) see SPECIAL SORTS.

Pica The old name for 12 POINTS, the unit of measurement used in setting.

Picking Lifting of small scraps of the paper surface in printing, caused by tacky ink or poor quality paper.

Pictogram/pictograph A sign in the form of a picture showing a simplified image of the object symbolized.

Pie, pi Type which has been accidentally mixed.

Pigment Finely ground solid matter forming the colouring agent of paints and printing inks.

Pin register A method of securing OVERLAYS to keep them in REGISTER.

Pinhole An unexposed speck on a photographic NEGATIVE, sometimes caused by dust on a lens or film.

Planographic Methods of printing from a flat surface, as in LITHOGRAPHY.

Plastic comb/coil binding Mechanical BINDING METHOD using a plastic SPINE with ringed teeth to secure leaves.

Plastic film Materials used for lamination and packaging, such as CELLOPHANE, varying in properties such as thickness and flexibility.

Plate (1) An electro or stereo or set-up type. **(2)** A sheet of metal bearing a design, from which an IMPRESSION **(2)** is printed. **(3)** A full page book illustration, printed separately from the text often on different paper. **(4)** A photographic plate; a whole plate measures 8½ x 6½in (212 x 162mm),a half plate measures 6½ x 4in (162 x 187mm).

Plate cylinder On a printing press, the cylinder that supports the inked plate.

Platen press A printing press in which a flat plate, or platen, is lowered and pressed against a horizontal FORME.

Plot To mark the main reference points on a GRID or GRAPH.

Plugging A condition in platemaking when COPY is marked or damaged and DOT areas have filled in.

Ply A measurement of the thickness of board stock, deriving from the number of layers in the composition of a SHEET.

PMS abb PANTONE MATCHING SYSTEM.

PMT abb PHOTOMECHANICAL TRANSFER.

Pocket envelope An envelope with the flap opening on the shorter of its dimensions.

Point Standard unit of type size. In the British-American system it is 0.01383in, or 72 to the inch. The Continental (DIDOT) point is calculated differently.

Point of sale The term for display equipment and advertising matter placed in a sales area close to the commodity it describes.

Polarizing filter A FILTER used in photography which eliminates reflections from water and glass and which will also adjust colour balance.

Polaroid A trade name of photographic materials capable of self development. The term also covers equipment used with such materials.

Portrait An upright image or page.

Positive (1) An image made photographically on paper or film, usually derived from a NEGATIVE. **(2)** A photographic colour TRANSPARENCY or film with a positive image, used in platemaking.

Poster A large-scale display or advertising sign on card or heavy paper.

Posterization A method of separating the tones of a CONTINUOUS TONE ORIGINAL, making one NEGATIVE for each grade of flat tone. The series of negatives is then reassembled to form a composite print.

Postlims see END MATTER.

Pothook The sharply curved terminal of a CHARACTER **(1)**, particularly notable in ITALIC TYPEFACES, as:

h

p, pp abb page, pages.

Powderless etching A process which gives a faithful reproduction, greater depth between the fine lines and a smooth, even SHOULDER. The plates print well, and are ideal for subsequent electro or stereotyping.

Preface An author's statement in the PRELIMS of a book.

Prelims, preliminary matter The pages preceding the BODY **(2)** of a book. They usually consist of HALF TITLE, title, PREFACE and CONTENTS.

Pre-make-ready The checking and preparation of printing plates or FORMES before they are made ready on the press.

Preprint (1) Any MATTER printed separately and pasted to CAMERA READY COPY or ARTWORK. **(2)** A SHEET, or sheets, printed in advance of a publication to form a loose INSERT in bound copies.

Presentation visual Material prepared as a sample of the proposed appearance of a printed work. Also called a FINISHED ROUGH, it may consist of drawings, typeset COPY, photographically produced prints, or a combination of such elements.

Press proof The last PROOF to be read before giving authorization for printing.

Press run In the printing of a publication, the total number of copies produced in one printing.

Primary colours Pure colours from which all other colours can be mixed. In SUBTRACTIVE COLOUR MIXING, used in printing, they are MAGENTA, CYAN and yellow. The primary colours of light, or ADDITIVE COLOURS, are red, blue and green.

Print origination In printing, all preparatory work completed prior to proofing.

Print run The number of copies required from a printer and the process of printing the copies.

Print to paper An instruction to print a quantity according to the supply of paper available without fixing the number of copies required.

Printer The FILM (or plate) of a single colour produced in the COLOUR SEPARATION PROCESS.

Printer's ornament see ORNAMENT.

Printer's reader see READER.

Printing down frame see VACUUM FRAME.

Printing processes The main classes of printing processes are INTAGLIO, PLANOGRAPHIC, RELIEF, STENCIL. All these rely on the contact of surfaces under pressure.

Printmaking A term referring to printing processes used in making fine art print editions.

Printout (1) *(com)* A general term for the record of information made by a printing device attached to a computer. **(2)** An enlarged COPY made from a MICROFORM.

Process camera A camera designed for process work in PHOTOMECHANICAL reproduction techniques.

Process colours see CYAN, MAGENTA, yellow.

Process engraving The name given to several PHOTOMECHANICAL methods of producing relief blocks or plates for printing illustrations.

Process inks Printer's inks in the PROCESS COLOURS.

Process white An opaque white GOUACHE for correction and MASKING (2) of ARTWORK intended for reproduction.

Program The set of instructions given to a computer that determines its methods of processing information.

Progressive proofs The PROOFS taken in colour printing as a guide to shade and registration. Each colour is shown separately and also imposed on the preceding colour.

Projection The representation of a three-dimensional object or a line or figure from a given VIEWPOINT or by graphic conventions. The main types of projections are axonometric, conical, cylindrical, isometric, orthographic, parallel and PERSPECTIVE.

Promotion Presentation and advertising intended to encourage the production and marketing of a product.

Proof An IMPRESSION (2) obtained from an inked plate, stone, screen, block or type in order to check the progress and accuracy of the work. It is also called PULL.

Proof correction marks A standard set of signs and symbols commonly understood by all those involved in preparing COPY for publication.

Proof reader A person who reads PROOFS to correct and revise COPY where necessary.

Proofing press A press, sometimes hand-operated, usually smaller than that used in the full PRINT RUN, on which COPY is proofed.

Proportional dividers Designer's equipment used in drawing where enlargement or reduction of an image is required, and for converting measurements, eg IMPERIAL to metric.

Proportional scale Designer's equipment used in SCALING UP or DOWN ARTWORK or photographs.

Proportional spacing A method of spacing CHARACTERS (1) in COLD COMPOSITION, to accommodate the different widths of the letters and figures.

Protractor A circular or semi-circular drawing instrument used to measure angles.

Proud A description of type MATTER that is designed to stand in isolation from the general text of a page.

Prove An alternative term for proofing.

Publisher The company or individual responsible for the distribution and marketing of published works.

Publisher's ream A bulk quantity of paper (516 SHEETS).

Pull see PROOF.

Pull out see FOLD OUT.

Pull out section Pages of a periodical that can be detached all together and kept as a separate entity.

Pulling see PICKING.

Pulp The basic material used in papermaking, broken down chemically or mechanically.

Punch register A device used in close REGISTER work, requiring holes punched in COPY, film or plate so they can be assembled on register pins.

Put down/up An instruction to the printer to change CHARACTERS (1) to LOWER CASE (down) or CAPS (up).

Put to bed The state of printing plates or FORMES when they are secured to the press ready to print.

Q

QA *(US)* abb Query author, used as a mark on COPY being edited.

QED *abb Quod erat demonstrandum,* a Latin term meaning 'a thing which has been proved'.

qv *abb Quod vide,* a Latin term meaning 'which see', used to accompany a cross-referenced term.

Quad Four times the normal paper size — 35 x 45in (890 x 143mm).

Quadding Filling out a line of type by extending spaces with EN or EM QUADS.

Quarter-bound A case-bound book using a stronger material for the back than for the sides.

Quarto A piece of paper folded in half twice, making quarters or eight pages.

Quire 24 or 25 SHEETS of paper or 1/20th of a REAM.

Quires, quire stock The SHEETS of a book which are printed but not folded.

Quotes, quote marks The use of INVERTED COMMAS or apostrophes before and after a word or phrase to indicate that it is a quotation.

R

ⓇThe symbol denoting a REGISTERED DESIGN.

R&D *abb* Research and development.

RA paper sizes The designation of untrimmed paper sizes in the series of INTERNATIONAL PAPER SIZES.

RIP *abb* Rest in proportion. Instruction in SIZING UP ARTWORK or photographs where the other dimensions or images are to be reduced or enlarged in proportion to a given dimension.

R-type A direct process of producing photographic colour prints, developed by Kodak. R19 is the production of a print from ARTWORK, R14 from a TRANSPARENCY.

Rag paper High quality writing paper made from rag PULP.

Ragged left/right Typeset COPY in which the lines of type are not aligned at left/right. See UNJUSTIFIED.

Ram *abb* Random access memory. A computer storage device from which DATA is available on demand.

Raised capital see COCKED UP INITIAL.

Raised point/dot *(typ)* A point printed at half the height of CAPITALS rather than on the BASE LINE.

Ranged left/right A form of setting in which lines of unequal length form a vertical either on the lefthand side of the COLUMN **(1)** or on the right.

Ranging figures see LINING FIGURES.

Raw tape see UNJUSTIFIED TAPE.

Reader A person who reads and corrects the printer's PROOFS against the ORIGINAL MANUSCRIPT.

Reader screen A display device for the enlargement of MICROFORMS.

Real time processing Computer processing which controls an activity and keeps pace with the actual time in which the activity occurs.

Ream 500 SHEETS of paper.

Rear projection see BACK PROJECTION.

Reciprocity law failure *(pho)* An exception to mathematical law in photographic processing. A short EXPOSURE under a bright light source does not give the same density of image as a long exposure in a dim light, ie halving the light intensity is not matched by doubling the length of the exposure.

Recto The righthand side of a book.

Reducer A chemical which acts upon a photographic image to reduce its density.

Reel fed see WEB FED.

Reference marks Type symbols used in text to refer to FOOTNOTES. See ASTERISK, DAGGER, DOUBLE DAGGER, PARALLEL, PARAGRAPH MARK.

References Publications or documents referred to in a published work, with details listed in FOOTNOTES or the END MATTER of the work. See BIBLIOGRAPHY and APPENDIX.

Reflection copy *(US)* COPY/ARTWORK which is reproduced by photographic means, using light reflected from its surface.

Register The correct ALIGNMENT of pages with the MARGINS in order. It is also the correct positioning of one colour on another in colour printing.

Register marks In colour printing, the crosses, triangles and other devices used to position the paper correctly.

Register ribbon The ribbon fastened at the back of a book for a book-marker.

Registered design A design officially registered by a PATENT office, to give some protection against plagiarism.

Relief printing Printing methods in which the image is obtained from a raised surface. See FLEXOGRAPHY, LETTERPRESS, LINO CUT, WOODCUT, WOOD ENGRAVING.

Relief stamping see DIE STAMPING.

Remainders Books sold at less than the usual published price. This may be a method of stock clearance or the books may be produced specifically for quick sale.

Remote access *(com)* Access to a central computer system from a distant terminal, linked by telecommunication equipment.

Reportage *(pho)* A style of photo-journalism conveying information through graphic images.

Reprint The second or subsequent printing of a publication.

Reproduction copy see CAMERA READY.

Reproduction proof/repro High quality PROOFS on art paper, which can be used as ARTWORK.

Reprographic printing Techniques of copying or duplicating printed material.

Resin coated paper Paper for photographic printing in which the sensitized surface is strengthened with a layer of polyethylene.

Resolution The efficiency of a PHOTOMECHANICAL or COMPUTER GRAPHICS system in reproducing fine detail.

Resolving power The capacity of a photographic lens or EMULSION to record fineness of detail.

Rest in proportion/pro see RIP.

Retainer fee A fee paid to a designer or consultant by a client to retain his/her availability, not a fee for work carried out.

Reticulation The clustering of molecules in a film EMULSION, causing a disruptive linear pattern on a sensitized surface. This may occur through temperature changes affecting the emulsion during PROCESSING.

Retouching Methods of altering the image in ARTWORK or photography, to make corrections, improve or change the character of the image.

Retree A term referring to a batch of paper that is of substandard quality.

Retroussage The term given to flicking a soft rag lightly over a wiped INTAGLIO PLATE, to draw out the ink slightly and give a softer line.

Reversal film (1) Colour film producing a positive image. **(2)** A contact film reproducing the tonal values of an ORIGINAL image.

Reverse b to w *abb* Reverse black to white. An instruction to the printer to reverse the tones of an image.

Reverse field VDU A visual display unit that can show images either as dark on light or light on dark.

Reverse indent see HANGING INDENT.

Reverse l to r *abb* Reverse left to right. An instruction to the printer to reverse an image laterally. See FLOP.

Reverse leading/line feed In PHOTOCOMPOSITION, the device for returning to a line already set on film or paper to add in COPY.

Reverse out see SAVE OUT.

Reverse P see BLIND P, PARAGRAPH MARK.

Reverse reading COPY that reads backwards, as it may appear on a LETTERPRESS printing surface. It is the opposite of RIGHT READING.

Revise A PROOF which incorporates corrections or revisions marked on an earlier proof.

Rider roller Printing press cylinder that rotates under the force of another cylinder.

Right-angle/chopper fold *(UK/US)* The standard method of folding a SECTION **(1)**. A SHEET is folded in half, than halved again at right angles to the first fold.

Right reading COPY that reads as normal, eg text reading from left to right.

Ring binder A mechanical binding device in which leaves are secured through punched holes by means of metal rings.

Rivers The streaks of

white spacing produced when spaces in consecutive lines of type coincide.

Roll stand A stand supporting the WEB of a WEB-FED printing press.

Roll-up A check of the first IMPRESSIONS **(2)** taken while a printing plate is being inked.

ROM *abb* Read only memory *(com)* The MEMORY store in a computer that contains its predetermined PROGRAM.

Roman Ordinary vertical type as distinct from ITALIC.

Roman numerals A system of numerical notation based on the symbols I (one), V (five), X (10), L (50), C (100), D (500) and M (1000), used in combinations to represent any figure.

ROP (1) *abb* RUN OF PRESS. **(2)** *abb* RUN OF PAPER. See PRINT TO PAPER.

Rotary press A REEL or WEB-FED newspaper press which uses a cylindrical printing surface. The papers are delivered folded and counted, ready to be dispatched.

Rotogravure INTAGLIO printing performed on a ROTARY PRESS.

Rough A sketch showing a proposed design.

Rough draft An initial stage of a MANUSCRIPT or text, that will be subsequently edited or rewritten.

Roulette An engraving tool with a freely-running toothed wheel which makes a series of small indentations on the plate.

Round and back Refers to a concave appearance at the FOREDGE of a book and a convex back with a projecting SHOULDER.

Router A machine which uses a rotating cutter to remove the superfluous parts of a wood or metal HALFTONE block.

Royal A size of printing paper 20 x 25in (508 x 635mm).

Royalty Money paid to an author or contributor from the sales of a published work.

Rub-ons *(US)* A colloquial term for DRY TRANSFER LETTERING.

Rules Metal strips, of type height, in various widths and lengths, used for printing lines. It is also a term for lines generally.

Ruling pen A drawing instrument with two tapering metal fingers between which ink or paint is held.

Run The number of impressions taken from a FORME at one time.

Run-in heading A HEADING leading into text starting in the same line, as distinct from a heading placed above text.

Run-of-paper (1) See PRINT TO PAPER. **(2)** The position of advertising matter in a newspaper or periodical which gives no display advantages.

Run of press Colour printing included as a standard feature of printing for newspapers, journals or trade publications.

Run on Instruction to printer that the text is continuous and no new paragraph is to be made.

Run ragged see RAGGED RIGHT.

Run through work The printing of even parallel lines across a SHEET, using a machine designed for the purpose.

Runaround Text set to fit around an illustration smaller than page or COLUMN width.

Runners Numbers, placed in the MARGIN of a text to form references for identifying particular lines.

Running head The line of type which repeats a chapter HEADING etc at the top of a page.

Running text A BODY of text which runs over from one page to another even when there are breaks for illustrations and diagrams.

S

Saddleback book A book with INSET leaves, secured by stitching.

Saddle-stitch/wire A method of stitching brochures:they are opened over a saddle-shaped support and stitched through the back.

Sans serif A TYPEFACE without SERIFS and usually without stroke contrast.

Satin finish A smoothly finished paper with a sheen to the surface.

Save out Also called reverse out, to reproduce text, lettering or line illustration as a white image on a solid or

HALFTONE ground, by PHOTOMECHANICAL techniques.

sc, s caps *abb* SMALL CAPS.

Scale drawing An illustration, such as a map or TECHNICAL DRAWING, which represents an object and its parts in correct proportion to the actual size.

Scaling, scaling up To determine the degree of enlargement or reduction necessary to reproduce an original image within a given area of a design. The scaling may be represented as a percentage of the image area or in figures proportionate to the dimensions of the original, using a diagonal bisection of the image to govern the increased or reduced measurements.

Scamp A rough sketch showing the basic idea for an advertisement or design.

Scanner A device used in PHOTOMECHANICAL reproduction to identify electronically the density of colours in an image for COLOUR SEPARATION.

Scatter proofs PROOFS for checking the quality of illustrations in PHOTOMECHANICAL reproduction. To reduce proofing costs, as many images as possible are proofed altogether, with no reference to correct positions in a LAYOUT.

Schematic A drawing or diagram showing the components and procedures of a particular activity or system.

Score To make a crease in paper or card so that it will not be damaged by folding.

Scotch print A material for proofing which can be used to transfer an image from LETTERPRESS to FILM.

Scraperboard/ scratchboard (*UK/US*) A prepared board with a gesso surface. First it is inked and then scraped or scratched with a point or blade to give the effect of a white line engraving.

Scratch comma (*typ*) A comma in the form of a short, oblique line.

Screen see HALFTONE SCREEN.

Screen angle The position of a HALFTONE SCREEN as arranged in converting images to HALFTONE when two or more must be overprinted to avoid MOIRE.

Screen clash A disruptive pattern in an image produced when two or more HALFTONE SCREENS have been positioned at incorrect angles.

Screen printing Printing method in which ink is forced through the fine mesh of a fabric or metal screen. The image is formed by a stencil made photographically on the screen or a cut stencil that adheres to the screen fabric.

Screen ruling The grid on a CONTACT or HALFTONE SCREEN.

Screen tester A device for identifying the screen size used in a printed HALFTONE image.

Scribing A method of altering or correcting an image on film or metal plate by scratching the surface.

Script A TYPEFACE designed to imitate handwriting.

Scumming A condition when the non-printing areas of a PHOTOMECHANICAL PLATE attract ink and transfer it to paper.

Second cover The page area on the inside of the front COVER of a publication.

Secondary colours Colours obtained when two PRIMARY COLOURS are mixed.

Section (1) A SHEET folded to create four or more book pages. See also SIGNATURE. **(2)** (*US*) A division of a publication, either smaller than a chapter or consisting of more than one chapter.

Section mark A type CHARACTER **(1)** used as a reference mark, or to identify the beginning of a new SECTION **(2)**.

Section sewn book A book in which SECTIONS **(1)** are sewn together with thread after GATHERING.

Sectionalizing To make divisions in a technical publication allowing numerical identification of text MATTER and illustrations.

See through see LOOK/SEE THROUGH.

Self cover A book with a COVER of the same paper stock and printed at the same time as the leaves.

Self ends ENDPAPERS formed from a LEAF from the first SECTION **(1)** at the front, and the last section at the back of a book.

Self quadder A mechanism of LINOTYPE machines providing automatic QUADDING.

Sensitive material A material with the surface chemically treated to make it receptive to light.

Sensitometry The science for measuring the properties of PHOTOSENSITIVE materials.

Separate see OFFPRINT.

Separation see COLOUR SEPARATION.

Separation artwork ARTWORK in which a separate layer is created for each colour to be printed, usually by means of TRANSLUCENT OVERLAYS.

Sepia toning A method of changing black-and-white photographic prints to sepia (brown) tones with chemical bleach and dye.

Serif The small terminal stroke at the end of the main stroke of a letter.

Serigraphy An alternative term for SILKSCREEN PROCESS.

Set (1) The width of a type BODY**(1)**. **(2)** It is used as an instruction as in 'set to 12 PICAS' or as a description, ie 'handset'. **(3)** It has a special sense to describe the proportions of the EM of a size of type.

Set and hold An instruction to the printer to set MATTER in readiness for future use.

Set close Describes type set with the minimum of space between the words and no extra space between sentences.

Set off (1) The accidental transference of an image from one SHEET to the back of the next impression. **(2)** In LITHOGRAPHY, it refers to an impression taken from a KEY outline of a design which is powdered with a non-greasy dye while the ink is damp, then placed on the stone or plate and passed through the press.

Set solid Refers to type set without leading (line spaces).

Set square A flat piece of metal or plastic in the form of a right-angled triangle, used as a drawing aid.

Sewn book Any book, the SECTIONS (1) of which have been sewn together with thread.

Sexto, 6to A SHEET trimmed or folded to one sixth its basic size.

Shaded letter *(typ)* **(1)** Letterforms, such as OUTLINE LETTERS, given a three-dimensional appearance by heavy shadows beside the main strokes. **(2)** Letterforms filled with hatched lines rather than solid tone.

Shadow The darkest tones of an image, the opposite of HIGHLIGHT.

Sharpness A property of a photographic image relating to its degree of clarity or FOCUS.

Sheet A single piece of paper.

Sheet fed A printing machine into which SHEETS are fed singly.

Sheet proof see IMPOSED PROOF.

Sheet stock A mass of printed SHEETS held ready for binding.

Sheet work The SECTIONS (1) of a book printed by backing up a SHEET with a different FORME from the front.

Sheeter A device that cuts SHEETS from a WEB in a WEB-FEB printing press.

Sheetwise Printing the pages of a SECTION (1) by printing first one side, then the other of a SHEET.

Shelf life The period during which PHOTOSENSITIVE materials remain in prime condition.

Shelfback see SPINE.

Short and see AMPERSAND.

Short ink Printing ink with a heavy texture that does not flow easily.

Short page A page with text shorter than usual length, adjusted to improve the LAYOUT or accommodate a break.

Shoulder The projection down each side of a book's SPINE, obtained by ROUNDING AND BACKING.

Shoulder notes The marginal notes at the top outer corners of a paragraph.

Show through The fault in which a printed impression on one side of the paper is visible on

the other side through the paper.

Shrink wrapping Thin, transparent plastic film used in packaging. It is sealed tight around an object by heat action.

Shutter The mechanism of a camera that allows light to pass through from lens to film.

Side heading A subheading set FLUSH LEFT in the text.

Side notes Notes in the FOREDGE MARGIN or occasionally in the GUTTER, outside the normal type area.

Side-stab/stitch A method of securing the SECTIONS (1) of a book, with wires passed through close to the BACK.

Signature The letter at the TAIL of the first page of each SECTION (1) in a book, running in alphabetical order, which serves as a guide to the binder in GATHERING.

Silhouette A drawing of an object showing simply the outline filled with solid tone or colour.

Silhouette halftone A HALFTONE image in which background tones have been reduced or eliminated to emphasize the outline of an object.

Silkscreen printing SCREEN PRINTING using a screen made of silk, the traditional method often still used in printing fine art editions.

Single-colour press A printing press that has the facility to print only one colour at a time, requiring separate runs for prints of more than one colour.

Single lens reflex A rollfilm camera in which the image seen in the viewfinder and that recorded on the film are transmitted through the same lens.

Single printing Printing a SHEET on both sides by the WORK AND TUMBLE or WORK AND TURN methods.

Sinkage *(US)* see CHAPTER DROP.

Sixteen mo, 16mo A SHEET folded or trimmed to one sixteenth its basic size.

Sixteen sheet A standard poster size measuring 120 x 80in (3050 x 2030mm).

Size A gelatinous solution used to coat paper, to glaze or seal the surface and render

the paper less porous. Size may be based on glue, CASEIN, starch or a similar substance.

Size/sizing up see SCALING UP.

Slab serifs SQUARE SERIFS of almost the same thickness as the uprights, used in most 'EGYPTIAN' TYPEFACES.

Slash see SOLIDUS.

Slip The broad strip of paper on which a GALLEY PROOF is printed.

Slip case An open sided CASE to hold one or more books, with their SPINES showing.

Slip page A GALLEY PROOF containing MATTER for one page.

Slip proof see GALLEY PROOF.

Slip sheeting *(US)* see INTERLEAVED.

Slit A cut made on the printing press by a rotary knife between IMPRESSION CYLINDER and delivery.

Sloped roman A TYPEFACE commonly termed ITALIC but actually a sloping version of ROMAN type.

Slur This results from movement between type and paper during IMPRESSION (2).

Small capitals Capital letters which are smaller than the standard and usually aligned with the ordinary line of type. They are indicated by a double underlining in MANUSCRIPT.

Small face The smaller version of a TYPEFACE cast in two sizes on one BODY (1).

Soft A description of photographic paper that produces an image with low tonal contrast.

Soft copy (1) In PHOTOCOMPOSITION, the COPY displayed to the keyboard operator on a viewing screen. **(2)** *(US)* Typed copy used for checking a text before CAMERA READY copy is produced.

Soft cover A book COVER which is neither a CASE nor a SELF COVER. See also PAPERBACK.

Soft dot A HALFTONE DOT with a soft EMULSION, and thus softer edges, which makes ETCHING correction easier.

Soft focus A photographic effect in which the image is slightly diffused to soften the lines and edges of a shape without distorting the true FOCUS . There are different ways of achieving the effect, such as with a specially made filter or shooting through a glass plate smeared with petroleum jelly.

Software A term used for computer PROGRAMS and general items. It also refers to paper and magnetic tape.

Solarization A method of creating photographic prints which are part positive and negative, by exposing the PHOTOSENSITIVE material to light during processing of a negative or print.

Solidus Type CHARACTER (**1**) in the form of an oblique stroke (/).

Solus position The position of an advertisement on a page where there is no other advertising MATTER.

Sort One individual piece of type.

Space A non-printing graded unit for spacing out a line of type.

Spaceband In mechanical methods of TYPESETTING, a wedge-shaped piece used to vary the space between words.

Special sort Type CHARACTERS (**1**) not normally included in a FOUNT ie fractions, musical symbols etc.

Specification, spec A description of the components, characteristics and procedures of a particular job, product or activity.

Specimen page A PROOF or specially made up page assembled as an example of a proposed style of design.

Spectral sensitivity The relative sensitivity of a photographic material to different wavelengths of light.

SPH *abb* SHEETS per hour.

Spine The centre of the CASE of a book which runs down the BACK when it is cased in.

Spiral binder A spiral wire holding the leaves of a book together.

Spirit duplicating A method of printing up to 100 copies from a master image typed or drawn directly on a SHEET backed with ANILINE dye. COPY paper damped with a spirit solvent is placed in

direct contact with the master sheet to transfer the dye image.

Splayed M A term for the CHARACTER M when the outer strokes are sloped.

Split boards Boards used for LIBRARY BINDING. A thick and thin board are pasted together, leaving a split about 1½in (37.5mm) wide for inserting END PAPERS and tapes.

Split dash/rule A line used in type decoration that is broken at the centre by a BULLET, STAR or other type ORNAMENT. The line itself is thick at the centre and tapers towards the ends.

Split duct/fountain A FOUNTAIN supplying inks of more than one colour to a printing press for simultaneous printing on one SHEET.

Spoils, spoilage Badly printed SHEETS which are discarded before delivery of a job.

Spotting RETOUCHING of photographic prints to cover tiny spots and blemishes affecting the image.

Spraygun A painting tool that emits a fine spray of liquid medium, paint or ink, similar in effect to an AIRBRUSH but a larger and less delicate instrument.

Spread see DOUBLE SPREAD.

Sprinkled eges The edges or top of a book speckled with splashes of coloured fluid.

Square The portion of the inside of a CASE which projects beyond the CUT EDGES of a book.

Square back book A binding which is collated and sewn, but not ROUNDED AND BACKED.

Square serif see SLAB SERIF.

Squared up halftone A HALFTONE image confined to a rectangular shape.

SRA paper sizes The designation of untrimmed paper for bled work in the series of INTERNATIONAL PAPER SIZES.

S/S *abb* Same size. An instruction to the printer to reproduce an image at the same size as the ORIGINAL.

Standard aspect ratio see ASPECT RATIO.

Standing type/ matter/forme Type MATTER composed

by any method, that is held for reprinting if required.

Star A TYPOGRAPHICAL ORNAMENT.

Starburst filter *(pho)* An attachment for a camera lens that diffuses light from a strong, concentrated source to transmit a 'starburst' effect to the film.

Stat *abb* PHOTOSTAT.

Status lines In PHOTOCOMPOSITION, the first lines input by the keyboard operator showing the identification and specifications of the job.

Stem The most distinctive vertical stroke, or that closest to vertical, in a type CHARACTER(**1**).

Stencil duplication A simple method for printing a relatively small number of copies using a paper stencil cut on a typewriter or with a scribe.

Step and repeat A PHOTOMECHANICAL method of using negative or positive images to produce a multiple or repeated image.

Step index An INDEX GUIDE in a book or file in which steps are cut down the FOREDGES of the pages to provide a reference guide to the contents.

Stereotype plate A duplicate LETTERPRESS plate made by casting from a MOULD.

Stet A Latin word meaning 'let it stand'. It is used in PROOF correcting to cancel a previously marked correction.

Stiff leaves END PAPERS attached by glue to the full width of the first and last leaves of a book.

Stipple A mechnical method of obtaining a background which could not be achieved by hand in the ORIGINAL. These areas are indicated by blue shading on the ORIGINAL.

Stock (1) The metal part of a printing roller, covered with COMPOSITION. **(2)** The printer's term for paper etc to be used for printing.

Stop bath A solution used in the processing of photographic materials to stop development before the image is placed in the FIXER.

Stop out A chemical treatment for printing

plates that removes any unwanted COPY or marks.

Straight matter *(US)* A BODY **(2)** of text without breaks for HEADINGS, diagrams etc.

Straightedge A drawing aid in the form of a steel or transparent plastic rule with long, straight edges, one usually bevelled.

Strap A subheading that appears above the main HEADLINE of a newspaper or magazine story.

Strawboard A thick board manufactured from straw PULP, sometimes used to make the CASE of a book.

Stress The apparent direction of a letterform, given emphasis by the heaviest part of a curved stroke.

Strike on composition see DIRECT IMPRESSION.

Strike through The effect of printing ink soaking right through a SHEET.

Stripping Assembling two or more images to produce a composite or multiple image for PHOTOMECHANICAL reproduction.

Stripping up as one Assembling two or more images to combine them into a single image for PHOTOMECHANICAL reproduction.

Stylus (1) A precision stylo-tipped drawing instrument used in many aspects of design. **(2)** An instrument for drawing on stencils used in STENCIL DUPLICATION. **(3)** The device that controls printing of an image in COMPUTER GRAPHICS. **(4)** A sharp, fine point used for direct engraving on metal plate.

Subhead The HEADING for the division of a chapter.

Subject Term for any image which is to be reproduced or originated.

Subscript see INFERIOR FIGURE/LETTER.

Subtractive colour mixing The reproduction of colours by overprinting PRIMARY COLOURS in different relative densities, thus gradually subtracting the reflection of light from the white of the paper.

Subsidiaries see END MATTER.

Suction feed Mechanical

paper feeding device using air suction to pass paper into a press or machine.

Summary Text MATTER printed before the main BODY **(2)** of a text in a long or highly technical publication. It gives an abbreviated description of the purpose, CONTENTS and conclusions of the work.

Supercalendered paper Smooth-surfaced paper produced by rolling it between metal CALENDERS or rollers.

Superior figure/letter Small figures or letters set above normal CHARACTERS **(1)** as in $12^2 = 24$.

Superscript see SUPERIOR FIGURE/LETTER.

Supplement Material added to a publication separately or included in a REPRINT that supplies added detail to the text.

Surprinting (1) *(US)* see OVERPRINT. **(2)** *(US)* The addition of line ARTWORK to a plate already bearing a HALFTONE image.

Swash characters OLD FACE ITALIC types with CALLIGRAPHIC flourishes.

Swatch A colour specimen.

Swell Extra bulking at the back of a book caused by the way the SECTIONS **(1)** have been sewn together.

Swelled dash/rule A RULE which prints as a thick line in the centre, tapering at both ends.

Symbol A letter, figure or drawn sign that represents or identifies an object, process or activity.

Symmetrical An object or image that, cut in half by an imaginary dividing line, appears the same on either side of the line.

Synopsis A condensed version of the thesis and CONTENTS of a book, giving a clear breakdown of the likely or actual progression of the text.

T

T square A drawing aid in the form of a STRAIGHTEDGE with a cross bar at one end that can be aligned to the edge of a drawing board when ruling parallel lines.

Tabbing (1) A colloquial term for TABULATING. **(2)** The procedure of

making a TAB INDEX.

Tab index An INDEX GUIDE similar to a STEP INDEX, except that the reference guides project from the pages of the book instead of being cut into them.

Tablet see DIGITIZING PAD.

Tabloid A page half the size of a BROADSHEET.

Tabular work Type MATTER set in COLUMNS **(1)**.

Tabulate, tabulating To arrange COPY such as text or figures in the form of a columnar table, according to fixed measures.

Tack The adhesive quality of a medium, eg printing ink, and of adhesives and adhesive tape.

Tail The bottom edge of a book.

Tail margin The MARGIN at the bottom of a page, also called FOOT MARGIN.

Tail piece A design at the end of a SECTION **(2)**, CHAPTER or book.

Take back An instruction to the printer, marked on a PROOF, to take back CHARACTERS **(1)** , words or lines to the preceding line, COLUMN **(1)** or page.

Take in An instruction to the printer, marked on a PROOF or MANUSCRIPT, to include extra COPY supplied.

Take over An instruction to the printer, marked on a PROOF, to carry CHARACTERS **(1)** , words or lines forward to the following line, COLUMN **(1)** or page.

Tape perforator The machine in mechanical composition systems, such as LINOTYPE and INTERTYPE, that encodes keyboarded information on tape, which is then used to control the TYPESETTING.

Tear sheet An image, feature or advertisement torn from a periodical and filed as reference material.

Technical illustration A specialist branch of GRAPHIC DESIGN dealing with illustrations of all types depicting technical machines, systems and processes.

Telecopier The trade name of a system that transmits graphic images via a normal telephone system.

Telephoto lens A camera lens designed to

focus on distant objects since it gives a larger image than standard types of lenses.

Teleprinter A printing device similar to a typewriter, which prints out information communicated by a computer or TELEX link.

Teletypesetter, TTS The trade name of a particular type of TAPE PERFORATOR.

Telex An international telegraph system in which subscribers are provided with a TELEPRINTER to receive or transmit information via public telecommunication lines.

Template Shape or SHEET with cutout forms and designs, used as a drawing aid.

Text The written or printed MATTER forming the main BODY (1) of a publication.

Text type/matter Any TYPEFACE of a suitable size for printing text, usually up to 14 point.

Thermocopy A COPY produced by the action of heat, rather than light as in a PHOTOCOPY.

Thermography The process in which freshly printed SHEETS are dusted with resinous powder which forms a raised surface when fused with heat.

Thick The description of a word space used in hand-set type, measuring one third of an EM.

Thin A word space as above measuring one fifth of an EM.

Third dimension printing Methods of producing a three-dimensional illusion in printed MATTER, eg by laminating a printed surface with a special type of clear plastic.

Thirty two mo, 32mo A SHEET cut or folded to one thirty-second of its basic size.

Thirty two sheet A poster size measuring 120 x 160in (3040 x 4060mm).

Threadless binding see PERFECT BINDING.

Throughput A unit of time measured as the period elapsing between start and finish of a particular job.

Throw out see FOLD OUT.

Thumb index An INDEX GUIDE consisting of rounded sections cut in the FOREDGES of a book.

Tied letter see LIGATURE.

Tight A term referring to an image that characteristically is usually small and detailed, with clear definition and very little white space in its design.

Time exposure (pho) A relatively long EXPOSURE intended to capture movement or obtain definition of a dimly lit subject.

Tint (1) The effect of the admixture of white to a solid colour. **(2)** Also, the effect achieved by breaking up colour into a percentage using dots which allow white paper to show through.

Tip in/on An illustration printed on a single page and inserted separately in a book, by pasting one edge.

Tissues (US) see LAYOUTS.

Title page The right-hand page at the front of a book which bears the title, the names of author and PUBLISHER, the place of publication and other relevant information.

Title sheet/section The first printed SHEET or SECTION (1) of a publication.

Title verso, T/V The page opposite the TITLE PAGE of a book.

Titling A HEADLINE type, always in CAPITALS.

Tonal value The relative densities of tones in an image. See also COLOUR VALUE.

Tone line process A method of producing line art from a CONTINUOUS TONE ORIGINAL by combining a negative and positive film image.

Tone separation see POSTERIZATION.

Tooling A method of impressing decorations and lettering on the COVERS of books by hand, using brass letters, PALLETS, rolls and DIES.

Tooth The surface quality of paper that enables it to hold a painting, drawing or printing medium.

Tracing materials TRANSLUCENT forms of paper, cloth and ACETATE used as the basis of ARTWORK for direct reproduction.

Trade books Books produced by PUBLISHERS for general retail sale.

Trade mark A word or

symbol identifying a product or service and linking it to the manufacturer or supplier.

Tranny abb TRANSPARENCY.

Transfer A film or ACETATE SHEET bearing an image for transfer to a printing PLATE.

Transfer lettering Preprinted lettering or other images stored on a transparent sheet of CELLULOSE ACETATE. Dry lettering is transferred to paper or art board by burnishing the shape from the front of the sheet. Wet transfers are applied using water.

Transitional Type forms which are neither OLD FACE nor MODERN, but include Fournier and Baskerville.

Translucent The description of materials that transmit light but are not fully transparent, that is, an image cannot be seen clearly through the material.

Transparency A photographically developed image on transparent film. The term usually refers to a positive image in colour, though it is also applicable to any image on a transparent base.

Transpose To correct the wrong order of CHARACTERS (1), words, lines or images on a MANUSCRIPT or PROOF.

Triangle (US) An alternative term for SET SQUARE.

Trim marks Marks incorporated in a printed SHEET to indicate where paper STOCK (2) is to be trimmed or cut to required size.

trs abb TRANSPOSE.

Tungsten film Photographic colour film intended for use in artificial light created by tungsten bulbs.

Turn up A piece of type inserted upside down in composition to show where a specific CHARACTER (1) is temporarily unavailable.

Turnaround (1) The length of time elapsing between the start and finish of a particular job. **(2)** (com) A document containing computer OUTPUT that is used in clerical activity separate from the computer and returned to the computer file as updated or corrected INPUT.

Turned commas see INVERTED COMMAS.

Turned over cover The COVER of a book with FLAPS turned inside at the FOREDGE.

Twelve mo, 12mo A SHEET folded or cut to one twelfth its basic size.

Twice up ARTWORK or COPY prepared at twice the size at which it will be reproduced.

Twin lens reflex A roll-film camera with two separate lenses, one serving the viewfinder and the other transmitting the image to the film.

Twin-wire paper A machine manufactured paper with a smooth finish on both sides.

Two revolution press A printing press with a cylinder rotating twice for each IMPRESSION (1) without interruption for inking of the plate or FORME.

Two up, three up Printing method in which more than one image, or a multiple of the same image, is printed on one side of a SHEET by one process.

Type, typeface The raised image of a CHARACTER (1) cast on a rectangular piece of metal used in LETTERPRESS printing.

Type area The area of a page designed to contain text MATTER and illustrations forming the BODY (2) of the work.

Type family A term covering all the variations and sizes of a basic TYPEFACE design. See BOLD FACE, CONDENSED, EXPANDED, LIGHT FACE.

Type mark up Instructions marked on COPY to be printed giving the COMPOSITOR details of POINT size, TYPEFACE etc.

Type page (US) see TYPE AREA.

Type scale/gauge A rule marked with a scale of type measurements, POINTS, EMS, PICAS etc, used by designers and COMPOSITORS.

Type series Manufacturer's identification of type families and sizes by designation of a series number.

Type specimen sheet A sample SHEET showing the forms of letters, figures, punctuation marks, signs etc available in a given

TYPEFACE, often including an example of the type as set.

Type to type see FOLD TO PRINT.

Typescript A typed MANUSCRIPT.

Typesetting Methods of assembling TYPE for printing, by hand, machine or photographic techniques.

Typewriter A machine for writing producing the resemblance to printed COPY, but usually with fixed TYPEFACE, size and spacing. Some typewriters are equipped with proportional spacing accommodating different letter widths; in GOLFBALL typewriters the writing head can be changed to alter the typeface.

Typo (US) abb Typographic error. A term referring to an error in typewritten or typeset COPY. See also LITERAL.

Typographer One whose occupation is TYPOGRAPHY.

Typography The art, general design and appearance of printed MATTER using type.

U

Ultraviolet Lightwaves beyond the visible portion of violet waves in the electromagnetic spectrum, which can be absorbed by some PHOTOSENSITIVE materials.

Uncoated book paper Paper used in printing books, catalogues etc, in a range of finishes including ANTIQUE (rough) and SUPERCALENDERED (smooth).

Undercutting Faulty ETCHING of a block which results in weakening the metal of the block.

Underlay Colour, tone or pattern effect laid in underneath ARTWORK or a photograph or illustration.

Underscore/underline A RULE printed beneath a word or portion of text.

Unit system A system of machine composition in which CHARACTER (1) widths conform to unit measurements associated with the set.

Universal Copyright Convention An international assembly that in 1952 agreed

protection for the originator of a text, photograph, illustration etc to prevent use of material without permission or acknowledgement. The work must carry the copyright mark ©, the name of the individual or organization holding copyright and the date of publication.

Universal Product Code An agreed coding system for product identification.

Unjustified Lines of type which are centred or which align only at one MARGIN and are not adjusted in spacing to fill out the full measure of the line.

Unjustified tape Tape produced in PHOTOCOMPOSITION when text MATTER is to be set UNJUSTIFIED, ie END OF LINE DECISIONS are not made by the keyboard operator.

Unsewn binding see PERFECT BINDING.

Upper case The CAPITAL letters in a FOUNT of TYPEFACE.

Uprating film To calculate the EXPOSURE of a film based on a higher ASA number than is standard for the film. The underexposure is compensated for during PROCESSING.

Upstroke (typ) The finer stroke in a type CHARACTER (1), originally the downward stroke of a pen in CALLIGRAPHY.

uc/lc abb UPPER CASE/LOWER CASE.

UV abb ULTRAVIOLET.

V

Vacuum forming A method of shaping plastic sheet by heating it until it softens and forcing it down over a relief MOULD by creating a vacuum beneath the mould.

Vacuum frame A frame for making positive or negative process images by direct contact with an ORIGINAL. The frame is illuminated and creation of a vacuum ensures stable contact between surfaces.

Value see TONAL VALUE, COLOUR VALUE.

Vandyke print A print of PHOTOCOPY producing the image as a dark brown print, either negative or positive.

Varnish A transparent solution mixed with ink

or printed over ink to produce a glossy surface finish.

VDU/VT *abb* Visual display unit/visual display terminal. A device for displaying information forming the INPUT or OUTPUT of a computer operated system.

Vellum The treated skin of a calf, kid or lamb, used as a writing surface.

Velox A print of COPY from a CONTINUOUS TONE ORIGINAL that has been pre-screened as a HALFTONE image and may be used in PASTE UP or CAMERA-READY COPY.

Verso The lefthand page of a book.

Vertical dimension The measurement of an image from top to bottom.

Vertical page *(US)* A page in which COPY is RIGHT READING when the page is held in a vertical position.

vide A Latin term meaning 'see', used as a reference in FOOTNOTES.

Video *abb* Videotape recording. Literally television but more commonly refers to a method of recording visual images on tape with sound, with facility for viewing the recording as it is being made. The image monitor is a television set.

View camera A camera in which the image to be photographed is viewed on a ground glass screen behind the film plane at the back of the camera.

Viewpoint The direction from which an illustrator represents a particular object to provide the best analytical or aesthetic study.

Vignette A small illustration or decoration without a BORDER.

Vignetted halftone A HALFTONE image in which tones gradually BLEED out into the background.

Visual A mock up of the proposed appearance of a design or LAYOUT presented as a rough drawing, or if more highly finished, as a PRESENTATION VISUAL.

Visualizer A device for producing immediate prints from an ORIGINAL in enlargement or reduction.

viz *abb videlicet*, a Latin term meaning 'namely' used when citing a reference in FOOTNOTES.

W

Walk off The deterioration of the image on a printing plate, occuring during printing.

Wallet envelope An envelope with a rectangular FLAP.

Wallet fold see GATEFOLD.

Washout The rinsing, cleaning and drying of NEGATIVES, film, plates etc during processing.

Wash-up Clean ink from the printing press.

Watercolour printing Printing process using water-based inks and relatively porous paper so that colours are absorbed and can be mixed by overlapping the layers printed.

Watermark A distinctive design incorporated in paper during manufacture.

Web A continuous roll of paper.

Web-fed A printing press supplied with paper from a WEB, rather than in separate SHEETS.

Web-set An OFFSET press working from a WEB or reel of paper.

Weight The degree of boldness of a TYPEFACE.

Wet on wet Colour printing in which the first colour of ink is still wet when the subsequent colours are printed.

Wet stripping The stripping away of a film base when the image has been processed but while the film is still wet.

wf *abb* Wrong fount, a mark used in PROOF correction where a CHARACTER (l) of the wrong TYPEFACE has been printed.

White line A space between lines of type equivalent to the spacing between lines of type plus the height of an additional line.

Whiteprint A reproduction method producing copies at the same size as the ORIGINAL by direct contact, the image being formed by a light-sensitive dye. The original for this process must be on transparent or TRANSLUCENT material.

Wide-angle lens A camera lens giving an unusually wide angle of view without distortion. See also FISH EYE LENS.

Widow A single word standing as the last line of a paragraph in typeset COPY.

Wild copy COPY printed separately to be pasted up as part of a chart or diagram, or as ANNOTATION to an illustration.

Window (1) *(typ)* see RIVER. **(2)** An opening cut in a FLAT for insertion of a negative image.

Wire photo A telegraphic method of transmitting a pictorial image.

Wire side The side of paper which has been carried on the wire mesh of a manufacturing machine and is lightly marked by the wire.

Wire stitch/stab One of a line of wire staples passed through the back of a printed SECTION used as a METHOD of binding.

Wood engraving RELIEF PRINTING method similar to WOODCUT, but using the end GRAIN (l) of a wood block and finer tools, to produce a more delicate image.

Woodcut A RELIEF PRINTING method using the side GRAIN (l) of a wood block. Areas not intended to print are cut away below the surface of the block leaving a raised image that can be inked.

Woodfree/freesheet *(UK/US)* Paper made from chemical PULP, containing no wood fibre.

Word break A division of a word at the end of a line of type to fit the line measure and avoid excessive space between words in the line.

Word processor Equipment usually interfaced with a computer, so that INPUT COPY can be stored and automatically printed out at high speed, so the stored information can be quickly corrected or revised.

Word spacing The adjustment of space between words in COPY being set, using fixed or variable space widths according to the method of composition.

Work and tumble To print one side of a SHEET and turn it from front to back to print the second side, keeping the same ALIGNMENT of the side edges on the press.

Work and turn When MATTER for both sides of a SHEET is set in one FORME. After one side of the sheet has been printed it is turned over end for end and backed up from the same forme.

Work and twist To print the same FORME twice on the same side of a SHEET, turning the sheet through 90° between printings.

Work up A type space displaced upwards in LETTERPRESS printing.

Working A single operation performed by a printing machine, eg embossing, inking.

Wove paper This is made on a roll of closely-woven, finely-textured wire, and leaves no marks on the paper surface.

Wrap around plate A curved printing plate that wraps around the cylinder of a ROTARY PRESS.

Wrap around press A LETTERPRESS printing machine using a WRAP AROUND PLATE.

Wrap round/ wraparound A printed SECTION **(1)** of 4 or 8 pages folded round a full sized section when work is GATHERED.

Wrappering cover A paper COVER glued to the SPINE of a publication.

Writing head The stylus device that produces the image on paper in COMPUTER GRAPHICS.

Wrong reading see REVERSE READING.

X

x-height The height of letters with neither ASCENDERS or DESCENDERS eg x.

Xerography A photocopying process in which the image is formed by an electrostatic charge that allows adhesion of powder ink. The ink is sealed by heat processing.

Y

Yapp binding A BOOK-BINDING method in which a limp COVER is applied which projects over the edges of the book's leaves.

Z

Zig zag book A book made up of a continuous strip of paper folded in a CONCERTINA FOLD. If secured at the BACK, printing is only applied to one side of the SHEET. If printed both sides the book must be left unstitched and opened out from either side.

Zinco, zincograph A zinc PLATE used in LETTERPRESS line printing.

Zip-a-tone Mechnical tints printed off CELLOPHANE and used in the preparation of ORIGINAL ARTWORK.

Foreign language accents

Albanian
â ç ë

Czech
á č ď é ě í ň ó ř š ť ú ů ý ž

Danish
å æ ø

Dutch
æ é è ê ë ó ò ô ij

Esperanto
ĉ ĝ ĵ ŝ ŭ (h)

Estonian
ä ö õ š ü ž

Finnish
ä å ö

Flemish
ë ó ij

French
à â ç é è ê î ï ô œ ù û ü

Friesian
ä ê û

German
ä ö ü ß

Hungarian
á é í ó ö ő ú ü ű

Icelandic
á æ ð é í ó ö œ þ ú ý

Italian
à é è í ì î ó ò ú ù

Latvian
ā č ē ǧ ī ķ ļ ņ ō ŗ š ū ž

Lithuanian
ą č é ę š ū ų ž

Norwegian
å æ ø

Polish
ą ć ę ł ń ó ś ź ż

Portuguese
á à â ã ç é è ê í ì ó ò ô õ ú ù

Romauntsch
ö ü

Rumanian
à â ǎ è ì î ş ţ ù

Scottish Gaelic
à é è ì ó ò ù

Serbo-Croatian
č ć đ š ž

Slovak
á ä č ď é í í ľ ň ó ô ŕ š ť ú ý ž

Slovenian
č š ž

Spanish
á é í ñ ó ú ü

Swedish
å ä ö

Turkish
â ç ğ ı î ö ş ü û İ

Welsh
ä â ê ë î ï ö ô ŵ ÿ ŷ

Initial Teaching Alphabet (ITA)

This alphabet has been designed so that each sound is represented by a single character, and it is used to teach people to read. Capital letters are the same as lower case.

æ	ale	e	egg	m	man	p	pig	u	up
ɑ	father	f	fat	n	net	r	run	v	van
a	at	g	gun	ŋ	sing	s	sad	w	wet
au	author	h	hat	œ	toe	ʃh	ship	wh	why
b	bat	ie	tie	o	on	ʒ	vision	y	yell
c	cat	i	ink	ω	book	t	tap	ꙅ	is
ch	chop	j	joy	ⲱ	food	th	thin	z	fez
d	dog	k	kit	ou	out	th	them		
ɛɛ	peel	l	lip	oi	oil	ue	due		

Greek alphabet

Αα	Alpha	Ηη	Eta	Νν	Nu	Ττ	Tau
Ββ	Beta	Θθ	Theta	Ξξ	Xi or Si	Υυ	Upsilon
Γγ	Gamma	Ιι	Iota	Οο	Omicron	Φφ	Phi
Δδ	Delta	Κκ	Kappa	Ππ	Pi	Χχ	Chi
Εε	Epsilon	Λλ	Lambda	Ρρ	Rho	Ψψ	Psi
Ζζ	Zeta	Μμ	Mu	Σσς	Sigma	Ωω	Omega

Greek and Roman numerals

Arabic	Roman	Greek	Arabic	Roman	Greek
1	I	α	20	XX	κ
2	II	β	30	XXX	λ
3	III	γ	40	XL	μ
4	IV	δ	50	L	ν
5	V	ϵ	60	LX	ξ
6	VI	f	70	LXX	o
7	VII	ζ	80	LXXX	π
8	VIII	η	90	XC	φ
9	IX	ϑ	100	C	ρ
10	X	ι	200	CC	σ
11	XI	$\iota\alpha$	300	CCC	τ
12	XII	$\iota\beta$	400	CD or CCCC	υ
13	XII	$\iota\gamma$	500	D	ϕ
14	XIV	$\iota\delta$	600	DC	χ
15	XV	$\iota\epsilon$	700	DCC	ψ
16	XVI	ιf	800	DCCC	ω
17	XVII	$\iota\zeta$	900	CM	
18	XVIII	$\iota\eta$	1000	M	
19	XIX	$\iota\theta$	2000	MM	

Mathematical symbols

Parenthesis	(	Sign of proportion	$::$	Equal to	$=$
Bracket	[	Divided by, solidus	$/$	Is not equal to	$\neq$
Brace	{	Modulus, used thus	$\lvert$ $\lvert x \rvert$	Approximately equal to	$\approx$
Angle bracket, colloquially 'Bra'	$\langle$	Parallel to	$\parallel$	Approximately equal to	$\doteqdot$
Angle bracket, colloquially 'Ker'	$\rangle$	Congruent to	$\equiv$	Approximately equal to	$\triangleq$
Open bracket	$\llbracket$	Equal or parallel	$\#$	Approximately equal to	$\simeq$
Factorial sign	!	Between	$\varnothing$	Difference between	$\sim$
Decimal point	·	Infinity	∞	1 Is not equivalent to / 2 Is not asymptotic to	$\not\sim$
Prime	′	Varies as, proportional to	$\propto$		
Double prime	″	Radical sign	$\sqrt{}$	Is approximately asymptotic to	$\sim$
Triple prime	‴	Plus	$+$		
Quadruple prime	⁗	Minus	$-$	Less than	$<$
Degree	°	Multiply	$\times$	Greater than	$>$
Because or since	$\because$	Divide	$\div$	Not less than	$\not<$
Therefore, hence	$\therefore$	Plus or minus	$\pm$	Not greater than	$\not>$
Sign of proportion	$:$				

Equivalent to or greater than	$\gtrsim$	Less than or equal to	$\leqq$	Is implied by	$\subset$
Equivalent to or less than	$\lesssim$	Less than or equal to	$\leqslant$	Contained as sub-set within	$\subseteq$
Much less than	$\ll$	Not less than nor equal to	$\nleqq$	Contains as sub-set	$\supseteq$
Much greater than	$\gg$	Not greater than nor equal to	$\ngeqq$	There exists	$\exists$
Not much less than	$\lll$	Equiangular geometry	$\measuredangle$	Gamma function	Γ
Not much greater than	$\ggg$	Approaches or tends to the limit	$\rightarrow$	Partial differentiation	∂
Less than or greater than	$\lessgtr$	Mutually implies	$\leftrightarrow$	Digamma function	F
Greater than or less than	$\gtrless$	Implies	$\supset$	Integral	$\int$
				Contour integral	$\oint$

Reference marks

The following marks are available on most founts, and if more than six are required they should be doubled-up — two asterisks, two daggers, etc.

Asterisk	*	Dagger	†	Double dagger	‡
Section mark	§	Paragraph mark	¶	Parallel	‖

Paper weight, substance and volume

Paper weight
Paper weight is expressed in kilogrammes per 1000 sheets (or per 100 boards). This can be calculated by using the following formula:

$$\frac{g/m^2 \times \text{width (cm)} \times \text{Length (cm)}}{1000} = \text{kg per 1000 sheets}$$

Paper substance
Substance is expressed in grammes per square metre (g/m^2), which replaces pounds per ream (in the UK).

Paper volume
The volume of paper is the bulk produced in millimetres for 200 pages or $100 g/m^2$. The following table gives the bulk (in millimetres) produced by standard thicknesses of paper:

	g/m^2	No. of pages							
		64	96	128	160	192	200	224	256
Volume 16 (22 Basis)	70	3.6	5.4	7.2	8.9	10.7	11.2	12.5	14.3
	80	4.1	6.2	8.2	10.3	12.3	12.8	14.3	16.4
	90	4.6	6.9	9.2	11.5	13.8	14.4	16.1	18.4
	100	5.1	7.7	10.3	12.8	15.3	16.0	17.9	20.5
Volume 18 (24¾ Basis)	70	4.0	6.0	8.1	10.1	12.1	12.6	14.1	16.1
	80	4.6	6.9	9.2	11.5	13.8	14.4	16.1	18.4
	90	5.2	7.8	10.4	13.0	15.6	16.2	18.2	20.7
	100	5.8	8.6	11.5	14.4	17.3	18.0	20.2	23.0
Volume 21 (29 Basis)	70	4.7	7.1	9.4	11.8	14.1	14.7	16.5	18.8
	80	5.4	8.1	10.8	13.5	16.1	16.8	18.8	21.5
	90	6.1	9.1	12.1	15.1	18.2	18.9	21.2	24.2
Volume 23 (32 Basis)	70	5.2	7.7	10.3	12.9	15.5	16.1	18.0	20.6
	90	6.6	9.9	13.2	16.6	19.9 ·	20.7	23.2	26.5

Paper usage formulae

To calculate the number of sheets of paper required to print a book (excluding covers):

$$\frac{\text{Number of copies to be printed} \times \text{Number of pages in book}}{\text{Number of pages printing on both sides of sheet}} = \text{Number of sheets required}$$

To calculate the number of copies obtainable from a given quantity of paper:

$$\frac{\text{Number of sheets} \times \text{Number of pages printing on both sides of sheet}}{\text{Number of pages in book}} = \text{Number of copies}$$

ISO C series envelopes

	mm	inches
CO	917 x 1297	36.00 x 51.20
C1	648 x 917	25.60 x 36.00
C2	458 x 648	18.00 x 25.60
C3	324 x 458	12.80 x 18.00
C4	229 x 324	9.00 x 12.80
C5	162 x 229	6.40 x 9.00
C6	114 x 162	4.50 x 6.40
C7	81 x 114	3.20 x 4.50
DL	110 x 220	4.33 x 8.66
C7/6	81 x 162	3.19 x 6.38

Metric prefixes

		Symbol			
mega	means a million times	M	centi	means a hundred part of	c
kilo	means a thousand times	k	milli	means a thousandth part of	m
hecto	means a hundred times	h			
deca	means ten times	da	micro	means a millionth part of	μ
deci	means a tenth part of	d			

Metric setting style

millimetre	mm	degrees Kelvin	°K	vapour density	v.d.
centimetre	cm	alternating current	a.c.	kilometres per hour	km
gramme	g	atomic weight	at.wt.		h^{-1} or
metre	m	molecular weight	mol. wt.		km/h
kilogramme	kg	freezing point	f.p.	square metre	m^2
second	s	melting point	m.p.	square centimetre	cm^2
hour	h	ultraviolet	u.v.	gramme per square	
degrees centigrade	°C	vapour pressure	v.p.	metre	g/m^2

Optical character recognition (OCR)

This typeface is accepted by electronic scanners as a means of inputting matter into a computer without having to key it in manually.

Conversion factors

To convert	To	Multiply by
Inches	Centimetres	2.54
Centimetres	Inches	0.3937
Feet	Centimetres	30.4800613
Centimetres	Feet	0.0328
Yards	Metres	0.914
Metres	Yards	1.094
Miles	Metres	1609.3
Metres	Miles	0.000621
Square inches	Square centimetres	6.45162581
Square centimetres	Square inches	0.155
Square feet	Square metres	0.093
Square metres	Square feet	10.764
Square yards	Square metres	0.836
Square metres	Square yards	1.196
Cubic inches	Cubic centimetres	16.39
Cubic centimetres	Cubic inches	0.061
Cubic feet	Litres	28.3
Litres	Cubic feet	0.0353
Cubic feet	Gallons (imperial)	6.24
Gallons (imperial)	Cubic feet	0.1602
Cubic feet	Gallons (US)	5.1959
Gallons (US)	Cubic feet	0.1924
Gallons (imperial)	Gallons (US)	1.20095
Gallons (US)	Gallons (imperial)	0.83267
Gallons (imperial)	Litres	4.546
Litres	Gallons (imperial)	0.22
Gallons (US)	Litres	3.785306
Litres	Gallons (US)	0.264179
Cubic feet	Cubic metre	0.028317
Cubic metre	Cubic feet	35.31467
Cubic yards	Cubic metres	0.7645549
Cubic metres	Cubic yards	1.307951
Acres	Hectares	0.404686
Hectares	Acres	2.471054
Square miles	Square kilometres	2.58999
Square kilometres	Square miles	0.3861022
Pounds (avoirdupois)	Kilogrammes	0.4536
Kilogrammes	Pounds (avoirdupois)	2.2046
Ounces (avoirdupois)	Grammes	28.35
Grammes	Ounces (avoirdupois)	0.0352
Grains	Grammes	0.065
Grammes	Grains	15.432
Hundredweight (short)	Kilogrammes	45.359237
Kilogrammes	Hundredweight (short)	0.02204623
British fl.oz	US fl.oz	0.961
Us fl.oz	British fl.oz	1.04058
Us fl.oz	ml	29.57270
ml	US fl.oz	0.033815
British fl.oz	ml	30.7728
ml	British fl.oz	0.0325
Hundredweight (long)	Kilogrammes	50.8
Kilogrammes	Hundredweight (long)	0.01968
Tons	Kilogrammes	1016.0
Kilogrammes	Tons	0.000984

To convert	To	Multiply by
Hundredweight (long)	Pounds (avoirdupois)	112.0
Pounds (avoirdupois)	Hundredweight (long)	0.00893
Hundredweight (short)	Pounds (avoirdupois)	100.0
Pounds (avoirdupois)	Hundredweight (short)	0.01
Pounds (avoirdupois)	Tons (long)	2240.0
Tons (long)	Pounds (avoirdupois)	0.000446
Pounds (avoirdupois)	Tons (short)	2000.0
Tons (short)	Pounds (avoirdupois)	0.0005
Tons (metric)	Tons (short)	1.102
Tons (short)	Tons (metric)	0.90718
Lb/ inch^2	Gm/cm^2	70.307
Gm/cm^2	Lb/inch^2	0.014223
Lb/inch^2	Kg/cm^2	0.070307
Kg/cm^2	Lb/inch^2	14.223533
Lb/feet^2	Kg/m^2	4.883
Kg/m^2	Lb/feet^2	0.205
Horsepower	Force de cheval	1.014
Force de cheval	Horsepower	0.9861
Horsepower	Watts	746.0
Watts	Horsepower	0.00134
Watts	Kg m/sec	0.1
Kg m/sec	Watts	10.0

1 US lb = 1 British lb   1 US yd = 1 British yd
(avoirdupois)

To convert Fahrenheit to centigrade:

Deduct 32, multiply by 5, divide by 9

To convert Centigrade to Fahrenheit:

Multiply by 9, divide by 5, add 32

Mathematical formulae

To find the circumference of a circle:

Multiply its diameter by	3.1416
Or divide its diameter by	0.3183

To find the diameter of a circle:

Multiply its circumference by	0.3183
Or divide its circumference by	3.1416

To find the radius of a circle:

Multiply its circumference by	0.1592
Or divide its circumference by	6.2832

ISO A series (untrimmed)

The 'A' series system of sizing paper was first adopted in Germany in 1922, where it is still referred to as 'DIN A'. The sizes were calculated in such a way that each size is made by dividing the size immediately above into two equal parts. The sizes are all the same geometrically, as they are made using the same diagonal. The basic size (AO) is one square metre in area. It is important to remember that the 'A' series sizes refer to the *trimmed* sheet.

The untrimmed sizes are known as 'RA'. About 26 countries have now officially adopted the 'A' system, and it is likely that this system will gradually replace the wide range of paper sizes still used in Great Britain and the USA. 'B' sizes are used when intermediate sizes are required between any two adjacent 'A' sizes.

Unlike the metricated 'A' series of paper sizes, the British and American systems refer to the untrimmed size. In

	inches	mm			
A0	33.11 x 46.81	841 x 1189	**A6**	4.13 x 5.83	105 x 148
A1	23.39 x 33.11	594 x 841	**A7**	2.91 x 4.13	74 x 105
A2	16.54 x 23.39	420 x 594	**A8**	2.05 x 2.91	52 x 74
A3	11.69 x 16.54	297 x 420	**A9**	1.46 x 2.05	37 x 52
A4	8.27 x 11.69	210 x 297	**A10**	1.02 x 1.46	26 x 37
A5	5.83 x 8.27	148 x 210			

	inches	mm			
RA0	33.86 x 48.03	860 x 1220	**SRA0**	38.58 x 50.39	980 x 1280
RA1	25.02 x 33.86	610 x 860	**SRA1**	25.20 x 35.43	640 x 900
RA2	16.93 x 24.02	430 x 610	**SRA2**	17.72 x 25.20	450 x 640

ISO B series (untrimmed)

	inches	mm			
B0	39.37 x 55.67	1000 x 1414	**B6**	4.92 x 6.93	125 x 176
B1	27.83 x 39.37	707 x 1000	**B7**	3.46 x 4.92	88 x 125
B2	19.68 x 27.83	500 x 707	**B8**	2.44 x 3.46	62 x 88
B3	13.90 x 19.68	353 x 500	**B9**	1.73 x 2.44	44 x 62
B4	9.84 x 13.90	250 x 353	**B10**	1.22 x 1.73	31 x 44
B5	6.93 x 9.84	176 x 250			

British paper sizes (untrimmed)

Sizes of Printing Papers

Foolscap	17	x	13½	432	x	343
Double Foolscap	27	x	17	686	x	432
Crown	20	x	15	508	x	381
Double Crown	30	x	20	762	x	508
Quad Crown	40	x	30	1016	x	762
Double Quad Crown	60	x	40	1524	x	1016
Post	19¼	x	15½	489	x	394
Double Post	31½	x	19½	800	x	495
Double Large Post	33	x	21	838	x	533
Sheet and ½ Post	23½	x	19½	597	x	495
Demy	22½	x	17½	572	x	445
Double Demy	35	x	22½	889	x	572
Quad Demy	45	x	35	1143	x	889
Music Demy	20	x	15½	508	x	394
Medium	23	x	18	584	x	457
Royal	25	x	20	635	x	508
Super Royal	27½	x	20½	699	x	521
Elephant	28	x	23	711	x	584
Imperial	30	x	22	762	x	559

Sizes of Bound Books

Demy 16mo	5⅝	x	4⅜	143	x	111
Demy 18mo	5¾	x	3¾	146	x	95
Foolscap Octavo (8vo)	6¾	x	4¼	171	x	108
Crown 8vo	7½	x	5	191	x	127
Large Crown 8vo	8	x	5¼	203	x	133
Demy 8vo	8¾	x	5⅝	222	x	143
Medium 8vo	9½	x	6	241	x	152
Royal 8vo	10	x	6¼	254	x	159
Super Royal 8vo	10¼	x	6⅞	260	x	175
Imperial 8vo	11	x	7½	279	x	191
Foolscap Quarto (4to)	8½	x	6¾	216	x	171

Britain sizes are usually referred to by name, but as this can lead to confusion, both the name and the size should be given in any specification.

	inches		mm	
Crown 4to	10	x	7½	254 x 191
Demy 4to	10¼	x	8¾	260 x 222
Royal 4to	12½	x	10	318 x 254
Imperial 4to	15	x	11	381 x 279
Crown Folio	15	x	10	381 x 254
Demy Folio	17½	x	11¼	445 x 286
Royal Folio	20	x	12½	508 x 318
Music	14	x	10¼	356 x 260

American paper sizes (untrimmed)

inches	mm	Bible	Bond/writing	Book (coated and uncoated)	Cover (coated and uncoated)	Gravure	Ledger	Newsprint	Offset (coated and uncoated)	Onionskin and manifold	Opaque circular	Text	Wedding
16 x 21	406.2 x 533.4					●							
17 x 22	431.8 x 558.8		●			●			●	●			●
17 x 28	431.8 x 711.2		●			●			●	●			
19 x 24	482.6 x 609.6		●			●							
20 x 26	508.0 x 660.4			●	●								
21 x 32	533.4 x 812.8						●	●					
22 x 24	558.8 x 609.6		●										
22 x 34	558.8 x 863.6					●	●		●		●		●
22½ x 35	571.5 x 889.0			●				●					
23 x 35	584.2 x 889.0				●								
24 x 36	609.6 x 914.4			●			●						
24 x 38	609.6 x 965.2		●			●		●					
25 x 38	635.0 x 965.2	●		●		●	●	●	●			●	
26 x 34	660.4 x 863.6							●					
26 x 40	660.4 x 1016.0			●	●						●		
26 x 48	660.4 x 1219.2			●									
28 x 34	711.2 x 863.6			●		●		●					
28 x 42	711.2 x 1066.8	●	●	●		●	●	●					
28 x 44	711.2 x 1117.6			●									
32 x 44	812.8 x 1117.6	●		●		●			●				
34 x 44	863.6 x 1117.6		●					●					
35 x 45	889.0 x 1143.0	●		●		●			●		●	●	
35 x 46	889.0 x 1168.4				●								
36 x 48	914.4 x 1219.2			●				●	●				
38 x 50	965.2 x 1270.0	●		●	●			●	●		●		
38 x 52	965.2 x 1320.8							●					
41 x 54	1041.4 x 1371.6			●				●					
44 x 64	1117.6 x 1625.6							●					

Offset litho printing — problem identifier

Problem	Causes
Blinding Image prints very weakly despite looking strong on the plate.	**1** Excess gum on the plate may be preventing the image from accepting ink. **2** The ink rollers may be glazed, thus preventing ink from reaching the plate.
Broken images Parts of the image are not printing or there are fingerprints on the plate.	**1** Tape or opaquing solution may be obscuring part of the image on the film. **2** The vacuum frame glass may be dirty. **3** The plate may be underexposed, causing the image to break up after a few impressions.
Dot gain Colours appear stronger on printing.	**1** Halftone dots on the film may have become larger during exposure or development of the film or plate or on contact duplication of the film. **2** Excess ink on the plate.
Halation Copy appears enlarged at the edges; shadows on the type or the dot spreads.	**1** Overexposure of the plate exaggerating poor stripping. **2** Poor plate contact during exposure.
Hickies Small areas of unwanted solid colour surrounded by a halo.	Specks of dirt on the plate or blanket cylinder.
Picking Fibres of paper lifting, leaving white specks.	**1** Poorly sized paper. **2** Ink too sticky. **3** Suction caused by the blanket cylinder.
Plugging Dirty printed image, with dots filling in.	**1** Fresh developer contaminated by old developer on the plate sponge. **2** Flecks of dried developer or gum on the plate.
Scumming Ink printing on the non-image areas.	**1** Improper sensitization of the plate. **2** Dirty dampening rollers.
Slur Image appears to have 'skidded'.	Movement of paper or plate on the press.

Index